FIVE ARTS

FOR
NANCIBEL AND SEBASTIAN

National Gallery *Photograph by Mansell*

MASACCIO. MADONNA AND CHILD

Frontispiece]

FIVE ARTS

ARCHITECTURE, SCULPTURE, PAINTING, MUSIC, POETRY

BY

F. E. HALLIDAY

WITH TWENTY-THREE ILLUSTRATIONS

GERALD DUCKWORTH & CO. LTD.
3 HENRIETTA STREET LONDON W.C.2

FIRST PUBLISHED JUNE 1946
REPRINTED NOVEMBER 1946, OCTOBER 1955

N 70
H 18

PRINTED IN GREAT BRITAIN BY
LOWE AND BRYDONE (PRINTERS) LIMITED, LONDON, N.W.10

CONTENTS

LIST OF ILLUSTRATIONS

ACKNOWLEDGEMENTS

I AM grateful to the following authors, publishers, and others, for their permission to quote poems and extracts from copyright work:

Mr. Clive Bell and Messrs. Chatto and Windus (*Art*); Messrs. Macmillan and Co. Ltd. (*The Poetics* of Aristotle, translated by S. H. Butcher); Messrs. Jonathan Cape Ltd. (*The Notebooks* of Samuel Butler); Messrs. Macmillan and Co. Ltd. (*Through the Looking-Glass* by Lewis Carroll); Messrs Macmillan and Co. Ltd. (*The Republic* of Plato, translated by J. L. Davies and D. J. Vaughan); Messrs Methuen and Co. Ltd. (*The Greek View of Life* by G. Lowes Dickinson); Mr. T. S. Eliot and Messrs. Faber and Faber Ltd. (*Murder in the Cathedral, Collected Poems*, and *Selected Essays*); Mr. E. M. Forster and Messrs. Edward Arnold and Co. (*Howards End* and *A Passage to India*); Mrs. P. Diamand, the executor of Roger Fry, and Messrs. Chatto and Windus (*Vision and Design*); Messrs. William Heinemann Ltd. (*Notes on Painting* by Gauguin); Messrs. John Lane, The Bodley Head Ltd. (*Art* by Eric Gill); Sir Herbert Grierson and Messrs. Chatto and Windus (*The Background of English Literature*); the Trustees of the Hardy Estate and Messrs. Macmillan and Co. Ltd. (*The Woodlanders* and *The Return of the Native*); Mr. Ernest Hemingway and Messrs. Jonathan Cape Ltd. (*A Farewell to Arms*); Mr. A. P. Herbert and Messrs. Methuen and Co. Ltd. (*What a Word!*); the Poet's family and the Oxford University Press (*Poems* of Gerard Manley Hopkins); the Society of Authors as the Literary Representative of the Trustees of the Estate of A. E. Housman (*A Shropshire Lad* and *Last Poems*); the Society of Authors and the Cambridge University Press (*The Name and Nature of Poetry*); Messrs. Faber and Faber (*Finnegans Wake* by James Joyce); Mr. C. Day Lewis and Messrs. Basil Blackwell (*A Hope for Poetry*); Mr. C. Day Lewis and Messrs. Jonathan Cape Ltd. (*The Georgics of Virgil*); Mr. C. Day Lewis and the Hogarth Press (*A Time to Dance*); Mr. L. W. Lockhart and Messrs. Kegan Paul, Trench, Trübner and Co. Ltd. (*The Basic Traveller*); Mr. David Lo (*Part of a letter to the New Statesman*); Mr. E.

McCurdy and Messrs Gerald Duckworth and Co. Ltd. (*The Notebooks of Leonardo da Vinci*); the family of Mr. Aylmer Maude and the Oxford University Press (Tolstoy, *What is Art?*); Mr. Scott Moncrieff and Messrs. Chatto and Windus (translation of *Du Coté de chez Swann* by Proust); Mr. Henry Moore and Penguin Books Ltd. (*Art in England*); the Society of Antiquaries of London and Messrs. Longmans Green and Co. Ltd. (*The Story of the Glittering Plain* and *Love is Enough* by William Morris); Messrs. Longmans Green and Co. Ltd. (*Idea of a University* by Cardinal Newman); Mr. Eric Newton and Penguin Books Ltd. (*European Painting and Sculpture*); Messrs. Chatto and Windus (*Miners* and *Preface to Poems* by Wilfred Owen); the representative of Walter Pater and Messrs. Macmillan and Co. Ltd. (*Gaston de Latour, The Renaissance, Appreciations*); the Cambridge University Press (*On the Art of Writing* by Sir Arthur Quiller-Couch); the Clarendon Press (*Six Essays on Johnson* by Sir Walter Raleigh); Mr. Herbert Read and Messrs G. Bell and Sons Ltd. (*English Prose Style*); Mr. Herbert Read and Messrs. Faber and Faber Ltd. (*Surrealism* and *Art Now*); Messrs. Allen and Unwin Ltd. (Freud's *Introductory Lectures on Psycho-Analysis*, translated by Joan Riviere); Messrs. Allen and Unwin Ltd., the original publishers of Ruskin's works (*The Nature of Gothic, Stones of Venice, The Seven Lamps of Architecture*); Messrs. Macmillan and Co. Ltd. (*Manual of English Prosody* by George Saintsbury); Professor W. Sargent and Messrs. Charles Scribner's Sons Ltd. (*The Enjoyment and Use of Color*); Messrs Chatto and Windus (*The Art of Writing* by R. L. Stevenson); Messrs. William Heinemann Ltd. (*Personal Reminiscences of Henry Irving* by Bram Stoker); Mr. Adrian Stokes and Messrs. Faber and Faber Ltd. (*Colour and Form*); Messrs Chatto and Windus (*Queen Victoria* by Lytton Strachey); Messrs William Heinemann Ltd. (Swinburne's *Poetical Works*); Messrs. Constable and Co. Ltd. (*Letters* of Van Gogh); Messrs. William Heinemann Ltd. (*The Gentle Art of Making Enemies* by J. M. Whistler); Mr. C. Williams-Ellis and Messrs. Jonathan Cape Ltd. (*The Pleasures of Architecture*); Mr. Leonard Woolf and the Hogarth Press (*To the Lighthouse* and *Death of the Moth* by Virginia Woolf); Mrs. W. B. Yeats and Messrs. Macmillan and Co. Ltd. (*Collected Poems* of W. B. Yeats).

If there are any faults or omissions I apologize, and would be glad to be informed of them so that mistakes may be corrected.

In a book that attempts to cover so wide a field it is inevitable that the author should owe much to the work of others. My indebtedness to the works of Roger Fry and of Mr. Clive Bell is sufficiently obvious in the chapters on the visual arts; but in addition I acknowledge with gratitude my indebtedness in the historical summaries to the works of Mr. W. J. Turner and the late Mr. P. A. Scholes (Music), and of Professor C. H. Reilly and Sir Banister Fletcher (Architecture). A few of the quotations have been taken from Mr. Martin Armstrong's anthology, *The Major Pleasures of Life*. If this book does no more than encourage readers to turn to the works of these writers it will have served an important part of its purpose.

Finally I would thank Mr. Paul Bloomfield for reading the script, for his encouragement and advice; and Mr. George Milsted for his unfailing sympathy and help.

O, reason not the need: our basest beggars
Are in the poorest things superfluous:
Allow not nature more than nature needs,
Man's life's as cheap as beast's.

King Lear.

PREFACE

THIS book is ultimately an attempt to approach poetry by way of the other arts to one or more of which the reader may be more responsive; for after all the arts are fundamentally the same, the expression of the artist's aesthetic experience. In any event it seems probable that none of them can adequately be studied in isolation save by a few who are sensitive to all the elements that go to make a work of art; that for instance an appreciation of the more obvious formal qualities of visual art may lead to the recognition of similar qualities in poetry and music, while an appreciation of the temporal rhythms of poetry and music may make more apparent the spatial rhythms of the visual arts. Though the main object is to relate poetry to the other arts the method has the advantage that it may arouse an interest in architecture, sculpture, painting, and music for their own sakes.

The subject is so important because not only the practice but also the appreciation of any form of art is a spiritual and a creative activity, and there is a real danger that if man's creative instinct is not actively encouraged, his spiritual, that is his emotional, development will be arrested at the adolescent stage, and that if it is frustrated it will be perverted and his emotional energy driven to find compensation in destruction. It is suggested, therefore, that an appreciation of art is every bit as important as a knowledge of civics in the making of good citizens, not only because the good citizen will not tolerate an ugly environment, but because in creation man finds his greatest happiness.

The main thesis advanced is that a work of art must be judged without prejudice as a thing in itself, by its appearance or sound, and not by what it represents. Thus, though pleasure may be derived from other elements in a work of art, the more prominent and insistent they are the more likely are they to distract attention from its essential quality: the artist's expression of his experience, considered as a thing with an independent existence. It is not suggested that this is the correct approach for young and adolescent children, who should read mainly for the sake of the story, and imitate for the sheer joy of imitation. But those who are approaching or have reached maturity should realize how little a fine painting has in common with a photograph, and how much more than a story is the meaning of poetry.

The quotations at the end of each chapter form an integral part of the book, for they have been carefully chosen in the hope that they will stimulate thought and encourage criticism; at least they should show how from the time of Plato these problems have occupied men's thoughts.

It is scarcely necessary to add that the book makes no pretence to finality, and that any over-confidence is apparent rather than real, for it would be tedious to qualify every statement and to introduce every assumption with an apology. There can of course be no final definition of beauty or of poetry, no authoritative ruling as to the pleasure that may be derived from a work of art; and aesthetics makes sense only if it is a means to an end, the discovery by the individual of what beauty, poetry, and aesthetic pleasure mean for him.

PART ONE

CHAPTER I

THE AESTHETIC SENSE

THE word beauty is, with some justification perhaps, regarded with suspicion. It is one of those words that have inevitably accumulated a multitude of associations, and because of its powerful emotional content has been so exploited by unscrupulous and uncritical writers that it is threatened with exhaustion and the loss of its power to evoke anything but a humourless haze of high-seriousness, accompanied by a feeling of depression. But that this is not true of all contexts is proved by the astonishing freshness of the word as used by Shakespeare, particularly in his *Sonnets* and early plays.

Beauty is also indefinable, save as a quality that affects the aesthetic sense and excites the aesthetic emotion, in much the same way that the quality of humour appeals to our sense of humour and rouses the corresponding emotion of laughter. One difficulty is, of course, that there is no objective standard of beauty; it is entirely a personal affair. Given a little mathematical ability, we should all arrive at much the same conclusion as to the number of cubic feet of air in a room; that is an objective fact, and not a matter of opinion. But we shall not all agree as to the amount of beauty to be seen in a landscape or a picture. Some may see much, some little, others none at all. This is a matter of opinion.

It is important to distinguish the aesthetic emotion from the other emotions. A tune, for example, may evoke pleasant memories, and for that reason be called beautiful. But is it beautiful because it has this powerful emotional charge, or does the tune possess the quality of beauty apart from its memorable effects? Is beauty simply a quality producing a high concentration of pleasurable emotion, or is it something independent, or semi-independent, of the other emotions? We rarely look at or listen to a thing with unmixed feelings, so that it is easy to confuse indiscriminate feelings of pleasure with aesthetic emotion.

It should be possible to reject at once the idea that beauty is a quality producing a certain intensity of pleasurable emotion; for

13

this would mean that desire or pride, or any pleasurable sensation, however undesirable, provided the concentration were right, would be an aesthetic reaction. This is obviously nonsense; but if we are to say that beauty evokes pleasurable and at the same time socially desirable emotions, we are faced with the difficulty of an arbitrary selection and rejection of emotional stimuli.

It seems more reasonable to assume that there is an aesthetic sense affected by some quality other than those which affect the other senses, and that aesthetic emotion is excited by this quality; that, for example, the pleasure derived from the story in a narrative poem or from the recognition of a likeness in a portrait has little, perhaps nothing, to do with the emotion excited by its beauty, which is dependent primarily on the way in which the story is written or the portrait painted. That the pleasure derived from the story or the recognition may contribute to the aesthetic effect is not denied, for the very good reason that it is impossible to prove or disprove it; but that it is not essential is suggested by the fact that the aesthetic emotion may be moved by something devoid of representation or literary content; by a piece of music, a porcelain bowl, or by a line of poetry where the meaning is negligible, as in

The stretched metre of an antique song.

If this is so, is the emotion aroused by natural beauty the same as that aroused by a work of art? In the highest sense, a work of art is the expression of an emotional experience in some medium —stone, bronze, paint, words, or musical tones—in such a way that it may be transferred to other people. But this emotional experience must be something more than an intense feeling of, say, love or sorrow; it is the experience of the emotion within the emotion, the rarer experience of the beauty within joy or sorrow. Thus in *King Lear* the beauty is distilled from the sorrow, and the reader or spectator of the play experiences the aesthetic emotion of the author. In the same way a painting of a landscape is, or should be, an expression of the beauty inherent in and abstracted from the object. In other words, the emotion experienced by the artist is aesthetic, whether derived directly from some visible or audible phenomenon, or indirectly from an emotion aroused by it. The mere reproduction of an ordinary emotion or a scene is not enough—that is the way of sentiment; the expression must be such that the original aesthetic emotion is transferred to the spectator or listener. It is probable that most people are in-

Photograph by Anderson

S. Vitale, Ravenna

BYZANTINE MOSAIC (6TH CENT.).   THE EMPRESS THEODORA

GAUGUIN.   NEVERMORE

capable of isolating this aesthetic element from the confusion of other emotions, which is what the artist does, whether consciously or unconsciously, when creating his work of art; it is exceedingly difficult to recognize even in a work of art where the artist has done it for us; but in so far as this can be done the emotion aroused by natural beauty may be the same as that excited by a work of art.

Obviously this indefinable quality of beauty takes many forms: it exists in a confused state in nature, where it is obscured by numerous irrelevant elements which add to the confusion by evoking their appropriate emotions, as a sunset produces a pleasurable sadness; it is visible in a purer state in the two-dimensional form of a picture, or in the three dimensions of a statue, but still obscured by the necessary irrelevance of representation and its accompanying emotions; or it is audible in poetry and again obscured by the emotional content of the words and the intellectual content of the phrase; finally it is heard in its purest form in music, where there need be no distraction of intellectual, representational, or other emotional elements; the transference of the aesthetic experience is—if successful—direct. Experience and expression are one.

It should be noted that this is not a claim that a work of art is more beautiful than nature. There is no question of competition, for a work of art is not a reproduction of nature, but the transference through some medium of an aesthetic emotion inspired directly or indirectly by nature.

To recapitulate: man has an aesthetic sense, of immensely varying degrees of development, which is sensitive to the quality of beauty, and a corresponding aesthetic emotion which is moved by this quality. Beauty is indefinable save in terms of the aesthetic emotion; that is, we recognize beauty because it moves us aesthetically. It is also subjective: one man is affected, another unmoved, and a third may be repelled. It takes innumerable forms: it may be visible or audible in nature or art, or it may be experienced as an emotion within an emotion. But the aesthetic is not a high intensity of some other emotion, a difference of quantity making a difference of quality, as water is changed into steam; even religious ecstasy is not aesthetic. Nor is a work of art the expression of such a concentration.

If it is impossible to define this abstract quality of beauty, it is almost as difficult to describe the aesthetic experience. Cecil Day Lewis writes of poetry: 'In despair of ever grasping this

capricious and untamed flyer, we are driven to define the nature
of poetry by its effects, upon us. Emily Dickinson, the American
poet, wrote: "If I read a book and it makes my whole body so
cold no fire can ever warm me, I know it is poetry. If I feel
physically as if the top of my head were taken off, I know this is
poetry. These are the only ways I know it." Professor Housman
in a recent lecture gave evidence of the hair-raising effect poetry
has upon him: "Experience has taught me, when I am shaving of
a morning, to keep watch over my thoughts, because, if a line of
poetry strays into my memory, my skin bristles so that the razor
refuses to act." I have known several people who share my own
sensation on approaching a passage of poetry where the strong
enchantment lies in wait—one of suffocation, followed by a
sense of physical lightening and relief: the same sensation as one
receives, for instance, at the entrance of the celestial *motif* in
Beethoven's A minor quartet, as though the world held its breath
waiting for an angel to appear. There can be little doubt that
this emotional disturbance in the reader is a reproduction of the
disturbance which was the poetical impulse of the writer; and
this reproduction is the first aim and effect of poetry. The first
test of poetry is an empiric one.' And Clive Bell writes of visual
art: 'The rapt philosopher, and he who contemplates a work of
art, inhabit a world with an intense and peculiar significance of
its own; the significance is unrelated to the significance of life.
In this world the emotions of life find no place. It is a world
with emotions of its own. . . . And let no one imagine, because he
has made merry in the warm tilth and quaint nooks of romance,
that he can even guess at the austere and thrilling raptures of
those who have climbed the cold, white peaks of art.'

Beauty exists in nature in such profusion and in such a confused
state that it is generally overlooked, save in its most obvious
manifestations, where again it is often obscured by irrelevant
elements that give rise to other emotions. The artist feels this
beauty intensely because he is able to isolate it, and he expresses
this aesthetic experience—which is not the same thing as the
reproduction of the cause of his emotion—in the simplified form
of a work of art.

Pleasurable emotions other than the aesthetic are aroused both
by natural phenomena and by works of art: for example, the joy
of living and the pleasure of recognizing the subject of a picture;
but it seems improbable that these add anything to the aesthetic
effect. A work of art, however, is composed of many elements,

and pleasure is to be derived from qualities other than the transferred aesthetic emotion of the artist.

Much of this is, of course, hypothesis, as any theory of aesthetic is bound to be, but it is at least a good working hypothesis; and at the worst it will serve as an aunt-sally to be knocked down by well-aimed criticism, and perhaps encourage the setting up of others in its place. What follows—the origin of the aesthetic sense, for it is clear that it must be a recent development—is also hypothesis, but there would seem to be biological foundation for it.

A baby first explores the world with its mouth and hands. Everything is strange, and it is interested in the taste and feeling of different shapes and substances. By experiment it learns that some things are more pleasant to taste and touch than others, and begins to distinguish the qualities of matter; whether a thing is hard or soft, rough or smooth, wet or dry, hot or cold. With experience it learns to recognize these qualities by sight as well as by touch, so that it is able to keep danger at a distance.

In the same way an animal by means of its senses recognizes the difference between what is friendly and unfriendly in its environment. The remoter senses of smell, hearing, and sight are more valuable than the intimate senses of touch and taste, for to see or hear danger is safer than to touch it, to smell poison is better than to taste it. An animal's senses serve only a biological purpose; they help it to keep alive. A rabbit is not interested in the scent of roses, the thrush's song, or the appearance of the stars; but it is vitally interested in the scent of a fox, the sound of a gun, or the sight of a dog.

The fundamental instinct in all life is that of self-preservation, and all animal behaviour is conditioned directly or indirectly by this blind instinct. It is most obvious in wild animals, where the struggle for existence is a continuous process of finding food and avoiding death, of hunting and being hunted. The instinct of self-preservation is also a manifestation of the creative principle; for preservation of self, reproduction of self, even the destruction of that which endangers self, are all aspects of creation.

Man, too, is engaged in a struggle for existence, but as he lives normally in the safer environment of a more or less reasonably ordered society, the self-preservative instinct has undergone a process of refinement, and manifests itself in new and not easily recognizable symptoms. The primitive struggle for existence

B

becomes a more sophisticated struggle for recognition (a point which is elaborated in the chapter on Art and Utility). At the same time, because man no longer is hunter and hunted the pressure on the physical senses becomes less urgent, so that they deteriorate until he depends mostly on the senses of sight and hearing, and a certain amount of energy is freed to develop in other directions.

If the fundamental instinct of life is self-preservation, the primitive emotion is fear—fear of destruction. And the corollary of fear is hate, and hate implies its antithesis, love. The most primitive forms of life act entirely from instinct: feeding, protecting, and reproducing themselves without any consciousness of their environment; but higher forms recognize the difference between friendly and unfriendly surroundings, and develop appropriate emotional reactions: fear and hatred of that which threatens, and a rudimentary affection for that which offers security.

Thus must have evolved the love of the child for its parents,* loyalty to the tribe, and to the institutions and gods which afforded protection. These emotions, varying in intensity from favour and disfavour to love and hatred, would become attached to a wider range of phenomena and experience; at first to those that gratified the coarser senses of smell, taste, and touch, and then to those that by their sound or appearance suggested a pleasurable physical contact. At the same time the senses of sight and hearing, owing to the safer environment, were less urgently exercised in self-preservation, so that a certain amount of sensuous energy was freed to develop in another direction—that of the disinterested appreciation of beauty; the recognition of beauty in sounds and appearance without any desire to touch or possess.†

This disinterested appreciation of beauty opened up an entirely new field for man's endeavour: the creation of works of art. Up till this time man's creative activities had been confined to the production of things that served an obviously biological purpose: food, tools, and shelter; many of his activities were, as they still are, creatively neutral, and at worst perversely destructive. But now the artist, the man with a highly developed

---

* The love of child for parent, and that of parent for child, are thus different manifestations of the same instinct of self-preservation. The parent sees the promise of immortality in his children; the child appreciates the security offered by the parents. This would explain why parental love is, on the whole, stronger and more lasting than that of child for parent.

† A parallel though possibly later sublimation of the love-hate complex is the ethical one: love of the good and hatred of evil.

aesthetic sense, began to create a new world of sounds and appearances, not because it helped him in his struggle for existence, but simply because he felt compelled to re-create his emotional experiences.

For the first time man created for the joy of creation, because his primitive emotions of love and hate had been sublimated into the love of the beautiful, and dislike of the ugly. The consequences to society were incalculable: man's instinctive energy could now flow in new creative channels, and the chances of its being frustrated and diverted to destructive ends were immeasurably reduced.

Art is not, as the metaphysicians say, the manifestation of some mysterious Idea of beauty, or God; it is not, as the aesthetical physiologists say, a game in which man lets off his excess of stored-up energy; it is not the expression of man's emotions by external signs; it is not the production of pleasing objects; and, above all, it is not pleasure; but it is a means of union among men, joining them together in the same feelings, and indispensable for the life and progress towards well-being of individuals and of humanity.

TOLSTOY: What is Art? (Trans. AYLMER MAUDE.)

The starting-point for all systems of aesthetics must be the personal experience of a peculiar emotion. The objects that provoke this emotion we call works of art. All sensitive people agree that there is a peculiar emotion provoked by works of art. I do not mean, of course, that all works provoke the same emotion. On the contrary, every work produces a different emotion. But all these emotions are recognizably the same in kind; so far, at any rate, the best opinion is on my side. That there is a particular kind of emotion provoked by works of visual art, and that this emotion is provoked by every kind of visual art, by pictures, sculptures, buildings, pots, carvings, textiles, etc., etc., is not disputed, I think, by anyone capable of feeling it. This emotion is called the aesthetic emotion; and if we can discover some quality common and peculiar to all the objects that provoke it, we shall have solved what I take to be the central problem of aesthetics. We shall have discovered the essential quality in a work of art, the quality that distinguishes works of art from all other classes of objects.

CLIVE BELL: Art.

The perception of purposeful order and variety in an object gives us the feeling which we express by saying that it is beautiful, but when by means of sensations our emotions are aroused we demand purposeful order and variety in them also, and if this can only be brought about by the sacrifice of sensual beauty we willingly overlook its absence.

Thus, there is no excuse for a china pot being ugly, there is every reason why Rembrandt's and Degas' pictures should be, from the purely sensual point of view, supremely and magnificently ugly.

This, I think, will explain the apparent contradiction between two distinct uses of the word beauty, one for that which has sensuous charm, and one for the aesthetic approval of works of imaginative art where the objects presented to us are often of extreme ugliness. Beauty in the former sense belongs to works of art where only the perceptual aspect of the imaginative life is exercised, beauty in the second sense becomes as it were super-sensual, and is concerned with the appropriateness and intensity of the emotions aroused. When these emotions are aroused in a way that satisfies fully the needs of the imaginative life we approve and delight in the sensations through which we enjoy that heightened experience because they possess purposeful order and variety in relation to those emotions. . . .

I have admitted that there is beauty in Nature, that is to say, that certain objects constantly do, and perhaps any object may, compel us to regard it with that intense disinterested contemplation that belongs to the imaginative life, and which is impossible to the actual life of necessity and action; but that in objects created to arouse the aesthetic feeling we have an added consciousness of purpose on the part of the creator, that he made it on purpose not to be used but to be regarded and enjoyed; and that this feeling is characteristic of the aesthetic judgment proper. . . .

We are so far obliged to protect ourselves from the implications of modern life that without a special effort it is hard to conceive the enormous quantity of 'art' that is annually produced and consumed. For the special purpose of realizing it I take the pains to write the succeeding paragraphs in a railway refreshment-room, where I am actually looking at those terribly familiar but fortunately fleeting images which such places afford. And one must remember that public places of this kind merely reflect the average citizen's soul, as expressed in his home.

The space my eye travels over is a small one, but I am appalled at the amount of 'art' that it harbours. The window towards which I look is filled in its lower part by stained glass; within a highly elaborate border, designed by someone who knew the conventions of thirteenth-century glass, is a pattern of yellow and purple vine leaves with bunches of grapes, and flitting about among these many small birds. In front is a lace curtain with patterns taken from at least four centuries and as many countries. On the walls, up to a height of four feet, is a covering of lincrusta walton stamped with a complicated pattern in two colours, with sham silver medallions. Above that a moulding but an inch wide, and yet creeping throughout its whole with a degenerate descendant of a Graeco-Roman carved guilloche pattern; this has evidently been cut òut of the wood by machine or stamped out of some composition—its nature is so perfectly concealed that it is hard to say which. Above this is a wall-paper in which an effect of eighteenth-century satin brocade is imitated by shaded staining of the paper. Each of the little refreshment tables has two cloths, one arranged symmetrically with the table, the other a highly ornate printed cotton arranged 'artistic-ally' in a diagonal position. In the centre of each table is a large pot in which every beautiful quality in the material and making of pots has been carefully obliterated by methods each of which implies profound scientific knowledge and great inven-tive talent. Within each pot is a plant with large dark green leaves, apparently made of india-rubber. This painful catalogue makes up only a small part of the inventory of the 'art' of the restaurant. If I were to go on to tell of the legs of the tables, of the electric-light fittings, of the chairs into the wooden seats of which some tremendous mechanical force has deeply impressed a large distorted anthemion—if I were to tell of all these things, my reader and I might both begin to realize with painful acute-ness something of the horrible toil involved in all this display. Display is indeed the end and explanation of it all. Not one of these things has been made because the maker enjoyed the making; not one has been bought because its contemplation would give any one any pleasure, but solely because each of these things is accepted as a symbol of a particular social status. I say their contemplation can give one no pleasure; they are there because their absence would be resented by the average man who regards a large amount of futile display as in some way inseparable from the conditions of that well-to-do life to which he belongs or aspires to belong. If everything were merely clean and service-able he would proclaim the place bare and uncomfortable.

The doctor who lines his waiting-room with bad photogravures and worse etchings is acting on exactly the same principle; in short, nearly all our 'art' is made, bought, and sold merely for its value as an indication of social status.

ROGER FRY : *Vision and Design.*

A postage stamp, the overture to *The Magic Flute*, No. 7 Acacia Grove, Guerlain's latest perfume, Leonardo's *Last Supper*, an innings by Don Bradman, Shakespeare's *Hamlet*, a performance of *Sylphides*, a dish of '*homard à la cardinal*', St. Paul's Cathedral, a Walt Disney cartoon—all these are (or can be) works of art.

There are other things that are not works of art. Niagara Falls is not a work of art, nor is the afterglow of the snows of Monte Rosa, nor the sound of breakers against a cliff, nor the dance executed by washing hanging on a clothes line in a stiff breeze, nor the scent of a pine wood on a summer day.

These two classes of phenomena are different in kind. The first are man-made and man-designed. They had to be conceived in the mind of a man (or group of men) and then made communicable to other men by the skill of the designer, working in some medium that could be perceived by the senses of other men—the eye, the ear, the nose, the palate.

The other set of phenomena—Niagara Falls, the sound of breakers and so on—are not man-made or man-designed. They may be equally beautiful or equally pleasurable. They may even be the result of design by God or the Laws of Nature or what you will, but they have not that double element in them of conception and parturition. They are not imagined first and then made manifest through the medium of visible materials, visible movements, audible sounds, perceptible smells.

ERIC NEWTON: *European Painting and Sculpture.*

Sailing to Byzantium

That is no country for old men. The young
In one another's arms, birds in the trees,
—Those dying generations—at their song,
The salmon-falls, the mackerel-crowded seas,
Fish, flesh, or fowl, commend all summer long
Whatever is begotten, born, and dies.
Caught in that sensual music all neglect
Monuments of unageing intellect.

An aged man is but a paltry thing,
A tattered coat upon a stick, unless
Soul clap its hands and sing, and louder sing
For every tatter in its mortal dress,
Nor is there singing school but studying
Monuments of its own magnificence;
And therefore I have sailed the seas and come
To the holy city of Byzantium.

O sages standing in God's holy fire
As in the gold mosaic of a wall,
Come from the holy fire, perne in a gyre,
And be the singing-masters of my soul.
Consume my heart away; sick with desire
And fastened to a dying animal
It knows not what it is; and gather me
Into the artifice of eternity.

Once out of nature I shall never take
My bodily form from any natural thing,
But such a form as Grecian goldsmiths make
Of hammered gold and gold enamelling
To keep a drowsy Emperor awake;
Or set upon a golden bough to sing
To lords and ladies of Byzantium
Of what is past, or passing, or to come.

W. B. YEATS: *Collected Poems.*

When forty winters shall besiege thy brow
And dig deep trenches in thy beauty's field,
Thy youth's proud livery, so gazed on now,
Will be a tatter'd weed, of small worth held:
Then being ask'd where all thy beauty lies,
Where all the treasure of thy lusty days,
To say, within thine own deep-sunken eyes,
Were an all-eating shame and thriftless praise.
How much more praise deserved thy beauty's use,
If thou couldst answer, 'This fair child of mine
Shall sum my count and make my old excuse',
Proving his beauty by succession thine!
    This were to be new made when thou art old,
    And see thy blood warm when thou feel'st it cold.

SHAKESPEARE.

CHAPTER II

THE FINE ARTS

ART is the expression in some medium of a particular emotional experience, the aesthetic, in such a way that the experience is communicated to others. Of course emotions other than the aesthetic, such as joy and sorrow, may be expressed in the same way; indeed it rarely happens that aesthetic emotion is transferred without the simultaneous expression of some other emotion; but the core and essence of a work of art is its expression of the original aesthetic experience of the artist. For example, the following lines convey the ordinary emotion of sadness, but they are poetry, that is a work of art, because to many people they express something more, Shakespeare's aesthetic experience:

> That time of year thou mayst in me behold
> When yellow leaves, or none, or few do hang
> Upon those boughs which shake against the cold,
> Bare ruined choirs, where late the sweet birds sang.

The noblest expressions of aesthetic emotion are generally considered to be Architecture, Sculpture, Painting, Poetry, and Music, and these are called the Fine Arts. It is of course impossible to make a finally exclusive catalogue; dancing for instance may be considered a fine art; pottery, carpentry, and textiles are all forms of art; and poetry must be extended to include prose as well as verse. But most of the arts other than the fine arts are primarily the province of the craftsman whose motive is the economic one of supplying a commodity for which there is a demand because of its utility as well as its beauty.* Great art, however, is not the product of conscious economic motives, though it may be the by-product, but is inspired and impelled by an aesthetic experience, and the artist will generally express himself in the medium of one of the fine arts. One of the char-

---

* There is a host of exceptions to this ruthless generalization: Limoges enamels, Bayeux tapestries, Persian carpets, Chinese porcelain, and medieval church screens, to mention only a few, were obviously often made by the artist from aesthetic rather than economic motives.

acteristics of the fine arts—with the exception of architecture—
is that they answer no material needs.

The mediums used by workers in the fine arts range from the
solid materials of the architect and sculptor—stone, brick, steel,
ferro-concrete, glass, wood and bronze—through the charcoal,
inks, and pigments of the painter, to the symbols and abstractions
of the poet and musician. It follows, therefore, that each art
has characteristics peculiar to itself.

It is clear that architecture, sculpture, and painting are visual
arts, that their appeal is in the first place to the eye. Of these
architecture is the purest form of visual art, for though the mind
may be distracted by romantic and historical associations, and
by a knowledge of the function a building has to perform, the
eye is not perplexed by any visual quality other than pure appearance. But in sculpture, and still more in painting, the eye is
confused and generally overpowered by the representational
element, so that instead of seeing a statue or a picture as a thing
in itself it sees the thing it is supposed to represent.

Poetry and music appeal to the ear. But because words both
by themselves and when combined in the phrase have inevitably
an intelligible meaning, the ear tends to concentrate on the thing
that is said rather than on the way in which it is said, on the
matter rather than on the manner. The notes in music however,
whether singly or in combination, have no rational significance,
so that music can be heard as pure sound. Music is indeed the
purest of the arts, for not only has it no function, but neither has
it—or at least it need not have—any element of representation or
rational meaning to distract the ear.

It is worth noting that the fine arts, as well as such subordinate
arts as those of the goldsmith and carpenter, appeal to the
remoter and finer senses of eye or ear, to the senses that can
appreciate beauty disinterestedly at a distance, while the coarser
arts of the cook and perfumer appeal to the more intimate and
more immediately physical senses of taste, smell, and touch.

The element of the visual arts is space, that of the aural arts is
time. A building and a statue are three-dimensional, a picture
is two-dimensional, though linear and aerial perspective and
chiaroscuro give the illusion of the third dimension to a painting;
and precisely because the third dimension is illusory the painter
has a far wider choice of subject than the sculptor, who must
treat depth in the same proportion as the length and height. In
a bas-relief the sculptor attempts to secure this advantage of the

painter by rapidly decreasing the scale of the depth as the horizontal plane recedes through middle distance and background
towards the imaginary horizon.

Because poetry and music are aural arts any visual imagery
they may describe or suggest is dependent on the imagination:
we do not see the images objectively, but in the mind's eye. But
again because the element of these arts is time they have the
advantage over the visual arts of continuity and progression.
Any poem or piece of music however short, a sonnet or a song
as well as an epic or a symphony, takes place in time, and it is
possible therefore to represent continuous action or a sequence of
ideas or emotions. It is true that in the visual arts, by selecting
the right moment of time, the events leading up to and following
the scene depicted may be suggested, and it is also possible to
suggest action by painting moving objects in a number of different
positions in the manner of the Futurist painters. The theatre
combines the continuity of poetry and the three-dimensional
quality of sculpture, the actors being seen in the round—especially
on the apron stage, and the cinema combines continuity with the
infinitely varied subject-matter of painting.

It should be remarked that in a sense the time element does
enter into sculpture and architecture. A painting can be seen
from one position because it is a flat pattern, but properly to
appreciate a sculpture we must walk round it and view it from all
angles. Our conception of a building is an even more complicated
affair, for not only must we walk round the outside, but we must
see the interior as well, so that our final impression is a complex
of external and internal appearances. The painter sometimes
rebels against the two-dimensional limits of his art, and in order
to work in three dimensions, and therefore in time, he super-
imposes a number of views of the same object seen from different
angles, as does Picasso in some of his portraits.

There are two other main ways of classifying the arts: as
functional and as representational. It has already been said that
one common characteristic of the fine arts is that—with the
exception of architecture—they answer no material needs. It
is true that a piano, a few pictures, and a few books are popularly
thought to be the irreducible apparatus of a certain position in
society, that painting can be exploited to increase the sale of
goods, and music to stimulate their production; but none of
these arts is really essential to bodily wants: poetry does not
teach us how to make a living, nor do any of them offer us food,

shelter, or warmth; life would be possible though nasty without them, and we should still have the same physical amenities, be as well fed, well clothed, and well housed. But without some form of building we should not be housed at all, and life would scarcely be tenable for more than a small fraction of the present population.

Architecture is a functional art; the first duty of a building is to provide shelter from the elements. There is a difference, however, between building and architecture; the meanest hovel is a building, as the most cacophonous metrical arrangement of words is verse, but the one would scarcely be dignified with the name of architecture or the other with the name of poetry. As poetry is great verse, so architecture is building that is aesthetically moving, and it is aesthetically moving not because it is functional but because it is beautiful. Though there is admittedly a relation between function and beauty in architecture they are by no means necessarily the same thing.

Finally, the arts may be classified as representational if they imitate or suggest some other thing, and as non-representational or abstract if there is no element of imitation: thus Botticelli's *Birth of Venus* is representational and a grandfather-clock is non-representational.* The most concrete of the arts, architecture, and the most abstract, music, are both essentially non-representational, for though a building may sometimes suggest natural or even man-made forms, and the musician may imitate sounds, these are the exceptions. St. Paul's Cathedral and a Mozart symphony have little or no resemblance to anything made by nature or by man.

Because sculpture is three-dimensional it is within limits potentially the most representational of the arts; the sculptor, for example, can make a model of a man's head almost with the precision that a mechanic makes a machine tool. The painter too, with his box of tricks, can suggest the illusion of reality over a wider field than the sculptor. And the poet working in the medium of words can represent anything under the sun, either indirectly by way of the imagination, or directly by imitating the sound or suggesting the quality of a thing onomatopoeically. Of course a sculpture and a painting are not necessarily representational, they may be a combination of shapes without rational

---

* Representation, it should be noted, is by no means necessarily the same thing as an exact copy. The *Birth of Venus*, for instance, can scarcely be commended for its realism. 'I have not tried to reproduce Nature,' said Cézanne, 'I have represented it.'

significance; but because the unit of speech and writing, the word, has a meaning irrespective of context there must always be an element of representation in poetry.

One of the main purposes of this book, however, is to attempt to show that representation is in itself an unimportant element in any of the arts, and that the thing that really matters is the expression; that the way in which a thing is expressed, whatever the medium, and not the thing expressed, whether a man, a landscape, an idea, or any emotion other than the aesthetic—that the way in which a thing is expressed is the essential element in every work of art.

Although, therefore, each art has a combination of qualities peculiar to itself there is one quality common to all works of art, that of moving us aesthetically as things in themselves, not by what they represent, but by what they are: or at least by a certain significant relationship between the two: a critical tension between the given, and in this sense unimportant, subject and the variable and therefore vital expression.

It is impossible to say what exactly is the secret of the elements in a work of art that makes them so powerfully moving; in the words of Housman, 'what it is in these six simple words of Milton—

Nymphs and shepherds dance no more—

that can draw tears to the eyes of more readers than one.' But it may be possible to find a clue.

All works of art—like everything else in the world—have the common characteristic of shape. This is most easily identified in the visual arts, as shape is most commonly conceived as a visual quality: a building, for example, has a well-defined three-dimensional shape, and this is the quality by which we remember and judge it. So too has a sculpture, though here the representational element competes with and partly obscures the property of pure shape. In a painting shape is still more difficult to isolate, partly because of the representational element, partly because its shape is ultimately the conventional one of the frame, and partly because it is an intricate pattern composed of a number of coloured shapes rather than one patently homogeneous shape.

Pure shape—its appearance, whether it looks beautiful or ugly —is the quality by which we must judge a building, and it is the essential quality by which we must judge all visual art, trying to isolate it from the competing interests of representation and literary content. The full appreciation of visual art depends on a sensitiveness to shape whether in three or two dimensions.

In the aural arts of poetry and music shape is more difficult to analyse because it is a quality in time that the ear cannot grasp until the whole has been heard, whereas the eye can see a shape, or at least one aspect of it, instantaneously. The shape of a work of art in the time element is a sequence, the successive arrangement of the parts in a pattern. That shape in this constructive sense is important can be appreciated by comparing Shakespeare's *Macbeth* with Webster's *White Devil*. The construction of *Macbeth*, its shape in time, augments the emotional expression because it intensifies the impact of the tragedy much as the correct timing of the boxer's blow increases its momentum. Thus, Duncan is murdered in Act II, Banquo in Act III, and Macbeth himself in Act V; if Act IV were omitted and the catastrophe of Macbeth's death followed immediately the climax of Banquo's murder the pattern would be wrong.* In *The White Devil*, however, the characters come and go speaking the loveliest poetry, but apparently waiting for the next accident to happen.

But shape is more than the arrangement of the major parts within the whole, the aspect on which the classical artist mainly insists; there is also the combination of the minor within the major parts on which the romantic tends to concentrate. Consider Shakespeare's sonnet:

> When in the Chronicle of wasted time
> I see descriptions of the fairest wights,
> And beauty making beautiful old rhyme
> In praise of Ladies dead and lovely Knights,
> Then, in the blazon of sweet beauty's best,
> Of hand, of foot, of lip, of eye, of brow,
> I see their antique pen would have expressed
> Even such a beauty as you master now.
> So all their praises are but prophecies
> Of this our time, all you prefiguring;
> And, for they looked but with divining eyes,
> They had not skill enough your worth to sing:
> > For we, which now behold these present days,
> > Have eyes to wonder, but lack tongues to praise.

* The pattern of all Shakespearean tragedy is the same: the interval between the climax of Act III and the catastrophe of Act V being bridged by a quiet Act IV in which the interest is focused on some new element, often on the secondary characters: in *Macbeth* on Malcolm and Macduff, in *Hamlet* on Ophelia and Laertes, in *Lear* on Gloucester and Edgar (see A. C. Bradley, *Shakespearean Tragedy*).

Here the construction as a whole is magnificent, making a splendid pattern in time. The octet, composed of two groups of four lines, is complete in itself, but leads logically and emotionally to the sestet which again is divided into two, the next four lines, and the final couplet which triumphantly clinches the meaning and completes the pattern. But within these four groups are the words and phrases which go to make them:

> And beauty making beautiful old rhyme—
> Then in the blazon of sweet beauty's best—
> So all their praises are but prophecies—

these too make a pattern in time, for the words are so selected and arranged—whether consciously or unconsciously does not matter here—that they have a beauty and a significance of their own depending on the order of the vowels and the combination of the consonants. Consider the parts played by the letters p and b both within the phrase and within the poem as a whole.

Because a building and a sculpture—at least one aspect of them —and a picture can be seen instantaneously, the pattern as a whole is more important than in poetry and music where the parts are isolated, for like the tableaux in a procession they must come in sequence and be judged separately, and maybe uncritically, with little reference to the whole. A bad poem may be memorable for one line, but a bad painting with one finely drawn hand will scarcely be remembered.

Shape in the element of time is most easily recognized as rhythm: we have only to read the sonnet quoted above, or to play a Beethoven sonata on the piano, breaking it up into arbitrary lengths, making pauses at random, and altering the speed at will, to make nonsense of it. Rhythm is an essential element in the aural arts at least.

Rhythm, the alternation of periods of exertion and repose, is the primitive form of emotional expression, particularly rhythmical *movement*, that is temporal rhythm, whether in dance, music, or words. It is also a characteristic of nature. The examples are obvious: the cycle of the seasons, the breaking of waves on the shore, the beating of the heart. But it should be noted that few natural rhythms are absolutely regular, they are rather variations about a norm, modifications of a regular pattern: the seasons do not succeed one another with predictable regularity, the waves break neither at equal intervals nor with equal emphasis, and the pulse quickens under the stress of emotion. Nor are the

rhythms of music and poetry a metronomic series: in music there
is a basic sequence of beats within which the rhythms may be
infinitely varied by the combination of notes and rests of different
time values; in verse the regularity of the foot sequence is broken
by the varying emphasis given to stressed and unstressed syllables,
the reversal and substitution of feet, and the shifting of the pause
and caesura about the line.

Absolute regularity, the repetition of a perfect sequence, is
non-rhythmical; its very perfection is the negation of rhythm.
For rhythm is the expression of life and of emotion: shifting,
various, vital, though subject ultimately to the restraint of an
imposed order. Sheer symmetry of sound is maddeningly
monotonous, a dead thing; it is indeed the symbol of death:
the ticking of the clock, the tolling of the passing-bell. At the
other extreme, random and unrelated sounds or movements
are emotionally impotent because they lack the momentum of
rhythmical progression. Rhythm is a compromise between law
and anarchy: an aesthetically satisfying sequence.

As the eye is more sensitive to shape considered as a whole, the
ear is more sensitive to shape considered as a rhythmical sequence:
the eye, that is, does not find it easy to see the rhythmical arrangement of masses, planes, lines, and colours in the visual arts where
there is no progression in time, though where there is this progression, as in dancing, the rhythm is apparent. But as a poem
or a piece of music may be considered as a shape in time much as
a building and a statue are shapes in space, so a building, a statue,
and a picture may be seen as rhythmical sequences in space.

Rhythm in space is analogous to that in time: an aesthetically satisfying sequence of line or form. A straight line, a circle,
and a sphere are no more rhythmical than the beat of a metro-
nome; they are the dead perfection of a logical process. So that
as temporal rhythm is a continual shifting of emphasis and beat
about a regular norm, linear and formal rhythm is a shifting of
emphasis and direction about symmetrical shapes: 'a compromise
between law and anarchy'. The difference in vitality can be
seen in a straight line or circle drawn by hand and one drawn
by ruler and compass; or compare the monotony of machine-
made carvings in a modern church with the animation of medieval
work; or examine the line in a good drawing and see how fluid
it is: insistent here, almost invisible there, never monotonous,
but varying in emphasis and direction throughout its length.
There is much the same sort of rhythm in colour: a change of

emphasis where there is a change of tone or in the intensity of a hue; a change of direction where the hue itself is altered.

So far an attempt has been made to show that rhythm is an essential factor in the visual arts as well as in poetry and music; that it is a function of shape, more obvious in poetry and music, and that it is the quality that gives variety and vitality to a work of art.

Since rhythmical expression is the natural way of expressing emotion it seems certain that the rhythmical element in a work of art is the product of the artist's emotional experience, and, other things being equal, the more profound the experience the more violent are the rhythms likely to be. But unrestrained rhythmical expression is rarely pleasant; some controlling element is necessary to resolve the competing rhythms into an aesthetically satisfying shape or pattern. This can most easily be appreciated in music, where a discord may be resolved by a conscious harmonizing process; or in painting, where the clash of violent complementary colours may be harmonized by the introduction of a grey composed of the two hues.

The harmonizing process is scarcely complete in this passage from Shelley:

> What is this? ye heavens for ever pure,
> At once intensely radiant and obscure!
> 　　Athwart the aethereal halls
> The lightning's arrows and the thunder-balls
> 　　The day affright,
> 　　As from the horizon round,
> 　　Burst with earthquake sound,
> In mighty torrents the electric fountains;—
> 　　Clouds quench the sun, and thunder-smoke
> Strangles the air, and fire eclipses Heaven.

But in the terrible imprecation of Lear there is no element of discord:

> Blow, winds, and crack your cheeks! rage! blow!
> You cataracts and hurricanoes, spout
> Till you have drenched our steeples, drowned the cocks!
> You sulphurous and thought-executing fires,
> Vaunt-couriers to oak-cleaving thunderbolts,
> Singe my white head! And thou all-shaking thunder,
> Smite flat the thick rotundity o' the world!
> Crack nature's moulds, all germins spill at once
> That make ingrateful man!

No doubt the harmonizing and integrating process is partly unconscious, the instinctive desire for order competing with the reckless profusion of creation; but the conscious mind is critical and it too recognizes the need for order, so that a work of art is the joint product of an emotional disturbance in the unconscious mind and a more or less conscious harmonizing and unifying process.

The shape of a work of art has been extended to mean a pattern made in time as well as in space; to mean not only the arrangement of the major elements within the whole, as the sequence of movements within a symphony, the scenes within a play, or the placing of a figure on a canvas, but also the arrangement of the smaller units within the parts, the pattern made by the letters within the word and by the words and notes within the phrase; and this shape, this arrangement is the product of the conflict between rhythmical expression with all that it implies of vitality and variety, the Romantic principle in art, and the Classical principle that controls, harmonizes and unifies.

Shape, however, is a word popularly used as an inclusive term to signify any pattern, whether beautiful or ugly, natural or man-made, deliberate or accidental. Form is the more critical word, implying the element of beauty, and is therefore the better word to use in this context.

Form then is a synthesis of all the elements that go to make the pure appearance and sound of a work of art, excluding that is the elements of function, representation, and rational significance; so that we may say that the essential element in a work of art is its form in the extended sense in which it has been defined, and that it is aesthetically moving by virtue of this quality. Beyond this analysis can scarcely go. We may agree that the essential element in a work of art, its form, is the product of rhythm and order, but what it is that makes a particular rhythm and a particular order aesthetically moving it is impossible to say.

Art is a human activity, consisting in this, that one man consciously, by means of external signs, hands on to others feelings he has lived through, and that other people are infected by these feelings, and also experience them. . . .

If people lacked this capacity to receive the thoughts conceived by the men who preceded them, and to pass on to others their own thoughts, men would be like wild beasts.

And if men lacked this other capacity of being infected by art,

c

people might be almost more savage still, and, above all, more separated from, and more hostile to, one another.

TOLSTOY: *What is Art?* (Trans. AYLMER MAUDE.)

Art is skill, that is the first meaning of the word. That meaning underlies all others. From that sense of the word art all the derivatives come—artful, artisan, artificer, artificial, artistry. It is thus that we speak of the arts of cooking, of dentistry and of building, the art of logic and the art of the geometer. When we speak of the art of painting or the art of music or the art of the poet we are really using the word in the same sense, the sense of skill. We mean the ability to use paint, to make music, to put words together so that something is made—a picture, a symphony or a poem. But in these arts we are so conscious of their appeal to the intelligence, to the sensibility of intelligent beings, so conscious of the fact that they offer us nothing useful, that is to say nothing which ministers to our immediate physical convenience, that we entirely forget the skill of the workman who made the picture or music or poem and think of his work as having no real material existence. Then we are tempted to say art is not the skill of the workman; it is the act of the creative mind; and physical skill, the will and ability to use tools and the very material itself are inessential to the thing called art.

On the other hand I say that to make a drain pipe is as much the work of an artist as it is to make paintings or poems. The making of drain pipes is a different art from that of the painter of pictures. It is a different art, that is all. Art abides entirely on the side of the mind. Yes, and the idea of a drain pipe must be as clear in the mind as the idea of a painting. There is no escape from mental responsibility. But the word art means skill: neither the painting nor the drain pipe would exist, either as pleasing objects or as useful ones, without the skill of their makers. All sorts of people have fine ideas, all sorts of people wish to serve their fellow-men by supplying them with things which please them or minister to their physical convenience, every man is potentially what is called an artist, but the fact remains, the artist is the person who actually has the skill to make things, to make, to bring into physical existence the things which abide in his mind. An artist is not simply a person with ideas. He is the person who has the skill to make his ideas manifest. He is not even a person with fine ideas or even fine skill; such a person is simply a better artist than others. Art itself is neither good nor bad; there is every kind of art, from the silliest and most inept to that which embodies the most refined sensibility in the most perfectly precise form.

ERIC GILL: *Art.*

If, then, an object of any kind is created by man not for use, for its fitness to actual life, but as an object of art, an object subserving the imaginative life, what will its qualities be? It must in the first place be adapted to that disinterested intensity of contemplation, which we have found to be the effect of cutting off the responsive action. It must be suited to that heightened power of perception which we found to result therefrom.

And the first quality that we demand in our sensations will be order, without which our sensations will be troubled and perplexed, and the other quality will be variety, without which they will not be fully stimulated.

It may be objected that many things in nature, such as flowers, possess these two qualities of order and variety in a high degree, and these objects do undoubtedly stimulate and satisfy that clear disinterested contemplation which is characteristic of the aesthetic attitude. But in our reaction to a work of art there is something more—there is the consciousness of purpose, the consciousness of a peculiar relation of sympathy with the man who made the thing in order to arouse precisely the sensations we experience. And when we come to the higher works of art, where sensations are so arranged that they arouse in us deep emotions, this feeling of a special tie with the man who expressed them becomes very strong. We feel that he has expressed something which was latent in us all the time, but which we never realized, that he has revealed us to ourselves in revealing himself. And this recognition of purpose is, I believe, an essential part of the aesthetic judgment proper.

ROGER FRY: *Vision and Design.*

A Racing Motor-Car, its frame adorned with great pipes, like snakes with explosive breath—a Roaring Motor-Car which seems to be running on shrapnel—is more beautiful than the *Victory* of Samothrace. . . .

The Past is balsam for prisoners, invalids, and men on their deathbeds who see the Future close to them.

We will none of it. We are young, strong, living—we are FUTURISTS.

Museums are cemeteries—public dormitories. We will permit flowers once a year before *La Gioconda*—but no more daily walking in these gloomy mausoleums, no more libations of living sensibility into cemetery urns.

We are out to glorify War—the only health-giver of the world —Militarism, Patriotism, the Destructive arm of the Anarchist, Ideas that kill, Contempt for Women. . . .

We are out to combat Moralism, Feminism and all Opportunist and Utilitarian meanness. . . .

We extol aggressive movement, feverish insomnia, the double-quick step, the somersault, the box on the ear. . . .

Poetry must be a violent onslaught. There is no masterpiece without aggressiveness. . . .

We shall sing of great crowds in the excitement of Labour, Pleasure, or Rebellion; of the nocturnal vibration of arsenals and workshops beneath their electric moons; of greedy stations swallowing smoking snakes; of factories suspended from the clouds by strings of smoke; of adventurous liners scenting the horizon; of broad-chested locomotives galloping on rails—giant steel horses bridled with long tubes; of aeroplanes with screws whose sound is like the flapping of flags and the cheers of a roaring crowd.

It is from Italy that we launch this Manifesto of Destructive, Incendiary Violence.

Italy has been too long the market-place of the Second-Hand Art Trade. We must free our country from its canker of professors, archaeologists, cicerones, antiquaries and second-hand dealers.

On then, Good Incendiaries! Fire the libraries! . . . Turn the floods into museums! Let the famous pictures float! . . . We cast our Challenge to the Stars!

                                 The First Futurist Manifesto (1909).

I have two or three times in my life composed from the wish rather than the impulse, but I never succeeded to any purpose. . . . All my poetry is the effect of easy composition, but of laborious correction. . . . The rough material of fine writing is certainly the gift of genius; but I as firmly believe that the workmanship is the united effort of pains, attention and repeated trial.

                                                         BURNS.

> O my Luve's like a red, red rose
>   That's newly sprung in June:
> O my Luve's like the melody
>   That's sweetly played in tune!
>
> As fair art thou, my bonnie lass,
>   So deep in luve am I:
> And I will luve thee still, my dear,
>   Till a' the seas gang dry:
>
> Till a' the seas gang dry, my dear,
>   And the rocks melt wi' the sun;
> I will luve thee still, my dear,
>   While the sands o' life shall run.

And fare thee weel, my only Luve,
  And fare thee weel a while!
And I will come again, my Luve,
  Tho' it were ten thousand mile.

                                        BURNS.

Sensibility, how charming!
  Thou, my friend, canst truly tell:
But distress, with horrors arming,
  Thou hast only known too well!

Fairest flower, behold the lily,
  Blooming in the sunny ray:
Let the blast sweep o'er the valley,
  See it prostrate on the clay.

Hear the wood-lark charm the forest,
  Telling o'er his little joys:
Hapless bird! a prey the surest,
  To each pirate of the skies.

Dearly bought the hidden treasure,
  Finer feelings can bestow;
Chords that vibrate sweetest pleasure,
  Thrill the deepest notes of woe.

                                        BURNS.

The artist's feeling for form and shape has given birth, in all
the arts, to a host of conventions that are on the face of them
fantastic. Why should poets have invented a shape called the
sonnet? Why should the ear have to be tickled with an elaborate system of rhymes? What is the virtue of fourteen iambic
pentameters if thirteen or fifteen would equally well express the
poet's thought? Why should Edward Lear, in recounting the
brief but poignant story of the old man of Aosta, have decided
to fit his story into the strange shape of a Limerick with its
attendant pattern of lines—long, long, short, short, long—and its
parallel pattern of rhymes—a, a, b, b, a? What gave birth to
the Sonata form? One can only answer that deep down in mankind is a thirst for something we have agreed to call aesthetic
pleasure, a thirst for order, harmony, balance, rhythm, pattern.

          ERIC NEWTON: *European Painting and Sculpture.*

If I am walking along the beach and my eye catches a sea-
worn and sun-bleached knot of wood whose shape and colour

strongly appeal to me, the act of identification (which may in any case have a psychological explanation) makes that object as expressive of my personality as if I had actually carved the wood into that shape. Selection is also creation. Nothing is so expressive of a man as the fetishes he gathers round him—his pipe, his pens, his pocket-knife—even the pattern of his suit. Art in its widest sense is an extension of the personality: a host of artificial limbs.

HERBERT READ: *Surrealism.*

Ode on a Grecian Urn

Thou still unravish'd bride of quietness,
    Thou foster-child of silence and slow time,
Sylvan historian, who canst thus express
    A flowery tale more sweetly than our rhyme:
What leaf-fring'd legend haunts about thy shape
    Of deities or mortals, or of both,
        In Tempe or the dales of Arcady?
What men or gods are these? What maidens loth?
    What mad pursuit? What struggle to escape?
        What pipes and timbrels? What wild ecstasy?

Heard melodies are sweet, but those unheard
    Are sweeter; therefore, ye soft pipes, play on;
Not to the sensual ear, but, more endear'd,
    Pipe to the spirit ditties of no tone:
Fair youth, beneath the trees, thou canst not leave
    Thy song, nor ever can those trees be bare;
        Bold Lover, never, never canst thou kiss,
Though winning near the goal—yet, do not grieve;
    She cannot fade, though thou hast not thy bliss,
        For ever wilt thou love, and she be fair!

Ah, happy, happy boughs! that cannot shed
    Your leaves, nor ever bid the Spring adieu;
And, happy melodist, unwearied,
    For ever piping songs for ever new;
More happy love! more happy, happy love!
    For ever warm and still to be enjoy'd,
        For ever panting, and for ever young;
All breathing human passion far above,
    That leaves a heart high-sorrowful and cloy'd,
        A burning forehead, and a parching tongue.

Who are these coming to the sacrifice?
    To what green altar, O mysterious priest,
Lead'st thou that heifer lowing at the skies,
    And all her silken flanks with garlands drest?
What little town by river or sea shore,
    Or mountain-built with peaceful citadel,
        Is emptied of its folk, this pious morn?
And, little town, thy streets for evermore
    Will silent be; and not a soul to tell
        Why thou art desolate, can e'er return.

O Attic shape! Fair attitude! with brede
    Of marble men and maidens overwrought,
With forest branches and the trodden weed;
    Thou, silent form, dost tease us out of thought
As doth eternity.   Cold Pastoral!
    When old age shall this generation waste,
        Thou shalt remain, in midst of other woe
Than ours, a friend to man, to whom thou say'st,
    'Beauty is truth, truth beauty,'—that is all
        Ye know on earth, and all ye need to know.

                                        KEATS.

CHAPTER III

IMITATION

IT would be interesting to know the reasons why the majority of people who pay any attention to such things admire, or think they ought to admire, a work of art. Perhaps the following analysis would not be far wrong:

Architecture: for its 'picturesqueness'. This may be because of its decoration or its unusual shape. Many people prefer their buildings—to look at—old or in ruins, and better still buried under ivy. They suggest a romantic past.

Sculpture and Painting: because they are 'life-like', or tell a story. Frankly they prefer a working model, or a picture paper.

Poetry: for the action, the story that is told. Some appreciate the thought or a moral. (The schoolboy sometimes says he reads Dickens and Shakespeare for the sake of 'the good grammar'.)

Music: for its rhythm and melody, a tune to dance to. Some people prefer songs, because then the music has more meaning.

It will be seen that the literary element is overwhelmingly strong: that people enjoy a good story. Such enjoyment is of course a natural and excellent thing, characteristic of children and primitive peoples; but a story however absorbing is not necessarily a work of art (though it well may be), and it is a pity that most adults should be emotionally arrested at the story stage.

One aspect of this appeal of a good story is the pleasure felt in recognizing an imitation of something we know. A child, for instance, will take a greater delight in a toy dredger if he has seen a real one at work, and a novel about life in Babylon is likely to have a smaller sale than one about modern London, Paris, or New York, because Babylonian customs are so foreign to our experience that it is not easy to relate them to anything we know.

Now, although people like to squeeze a story out of a building by way of its historical associations, they cannot reasonably complain that it is not a good likeness. For architecture is not a representational art, and the architect rarely attempts to

40

suggest a natural form in his building—nor is it expected of him; neither a cathedral nor a cinema is like anything in nature.

Nor at the other extreme is a symphony or a violin sonata like any noise in nature. Music, the most abstract of the arts, appeals to the ear by sounds that lack the immediate intellectual significance of words, so that it is a most unpromising literary medium. However, the composer can gratify the desire for a story either by writing songs in which music and words are complementary, or he can write 'programme' music which imitates sounds, a bird's song or a thunderstorm, or which suggests an action such as a battle or a sea voyage. But again the listener will not condemn a piece of music because it is not a good likeness, though he may reject unconsciously all music that does not more or less crudely represent a primitive emotion. In short, though people like to know what music is about, they do not expect it to be an accurate imitation of something else.

Any work of art appeals first to the physical senses: the so-called fine arts to the ear or eye, the sound or vision then being transmitted to the mind, where its development may be either conscious or unconscious, that is emotional or rational, or both processes may be involved. It follows then that the aesthetic emotion, the emotion moved by the disinterested contemplation of beauty as the emotion of terror or joy is moved by the terrible or joyful, may be directly affected without reference to the intellect or to the other emotions. To what extent, if any, the excitement of the other emotions and of the intellect stimulates the aesthetic emotion, so intensifying its response to a work of art, is a fascinating but probably insoluble problem. It is certain that music can be aesthetically moving without the intellect being involved; on the other hand sculpture, painting, and poetry are most affecting when their meanings are intellectually grasped; abstract visual art is rarely as satisfying as that where there is some element of representation, and poetry is more than an incomprehensible incantation, it must have some meaning, however slight. It is possible that the representational element, if it is not too insistent, merely helps us to appreciate the essential element in a work of art; that it affords an intelligible beginning to our experience. At any rate it is aesthetically irrelevant if it does not contribute by one means or another to our appreciation of the form.

The effect of music is almost entirely emotional, the intellect scarcely being involved. Literature, on the other hand, because it is composed of the significant sounds of words may have both emotional and intellectual consequences. Scientific exposition is, or should be, entirely an intellectual affair, and the reading of a novel is in the first place generally an intellectual process, most emotional effects being secondary, that is derived from an understanding of the action. For example, the emotion aroused in the reader's mind when the hero is in danger is derived from the recognition of his danger, and not directly from the words.

The appeal of music is generally direct to the emotions, its rhythm and melody acting as an exceedingly powerful emotional stimulant; but the direct effect of words, in so far as this can be divorced from the secondary effects which are the result of the intellectual content, is much less forcible. Though most people are susceptible to the emotions aroused by verbal associations, and to a well-marked rhythm such as,

Half a league, half a league, half a league onward,

few are moved by more subtle and varied rhythms, or by the complex music of the words themselves.

But whether the emotions are stirred directly as in music, or indirectly as in much literature, or by a combination of both processes, it does not follow that the aesthetic emotion is engaged; for the aesthetic sense is affected and the aesthetic emotion is moved directly by the form of a work of art, and only indirectly, if at all, by the action of other elements such as the representational on the other emotions and on the intellect.

The point is this: that music and literature may be intensely moving, the one directly evoking ordinary pleasurable emotions by its sound, the other indirectly by the representation of the story, and that these emotions may be mistaken for the aesthetic, whereas the aesthetic emotion is distinct from all the other emotions and is moved directly by the form.

For example, suppose we hear *God Save the King* superbly played by a symphony orchestra. Our knowledge of the literary content reinforces the ordinary emotions aroused by the tune; at the same time, if we can isolate the sensation from the overwhelming emotional effects of pride and patriotism, we may feel a pure aesthetic emotion derived from the form, that is from the sequence and the combination of the tones, rather than from any intellectual or other emotional content.

Next consider a passage of verse:

'How they'll greet us!' and all in a moment his roan
Rolled neck and croup over, lay dead as a stone;
And there was my Roland to bear the whole weight
Of the news which alone could save Aix from her fate,
With his nostrils like pits full of blood to the brim
And with circles of red for his eye-sockets' rim.

The rhythm is vigorous and is emphasized by the rhyme, but the
excitement aroused in the reader comes mainly from the story
which has first to be understood intellectually before it can re-
inforce the excitement produced directly by the rhythm and sound.
But excitement and pity are common enough emotions and must
not be confused with aesthetic appreciation of the form. 'The
way of saying it', not 'the thing said' will evoke the aesthetic
response if any.

Both music and literature are progressive in time, but while
the notes of music have no rational significance, words are com-
prehensible symbols, so that the epic poem, the drama, and the
novel can all represent continuous action. Literature therefore
is the natural medium for the representation of an action, and
the popular demand is for an exciting and realistic imitation
which, although it may in fact be impossible, must at least seem
probable. How often do we hear a portrait criticized as a bad
likeness, and a play or a novel as improbable. That the demand
is for realism and more realism is suggested by the popularity of
the cinema, where the moving picture with its enormous variety
is called in to give even greater realism to the spoken word. The
written word has not the immediate representational character
of a picture; for instance the Queen's description of Ophelia's
death in *Hamlet*:

There is a willow grows aslant a brook
That shows his hoar leaves in the glassy stream,

has not the objectivity of Millais's painting of the scene; but a
painting, though it may suggest, cannot imitate a continuous
action. The combination of the spoken word and the moving
picture is irresistible.

Because the majority want an exciting and realistic imitation
of life when they read, verse has little chance of popularity.
'Poetry's unnat'ral', said Mr. Weller, senior; people do not
speak in blank verse—as a matter of fact they often do—and they
certainly do not speak in rhyme, so that even a play in verse
with the most realistic trappings cannot compete in popularity

with a novel, still less with the cinema. And verse without a
story comes nowhere.

> Ah, sunflower weary of time,
> Who countest the steps of the sun,
> Seeking after that sweet golden clime
> Where the traveller's journey is done:
>
> And the youth pined away with desire,
> And the pale virgin shrouded in snow
> Arise from their graves, and aspire
> Where my sunflower wishes to go.

What has Blake's lyric to do with realism? And how many
people read it with pleasure?

It is not suggested that realism and great literature are in-
compatible. Literature must by its nature have some element of
representation, but the pursuit of realism for its own sake has
nothing to do with art. Realism is representation carried to
extremes, and representation is relevant in a work of art only as
it is an integral part of the author's expression. Literature is not
bad because it is realistic, but it is important to remember that
for the same reason neither is it good.

There is another and limited sense in which literature may be
representational. As the musician may imitate sounds, so by the
device of onomatopoeia may the writer. Not only this, but by
his rhythm as well as by his choice of words he may suggest the
quality of a thing. Good writing is far more suggestive of the
thing described than is generally realized, and this undoubtedly
may add to the aesthetic effect—but only because the representation is approximate, and an essential part of the expression.
Nobody expects imitation in this sense to be a good likeness.

Architecture and music are scarcely representational, literature
is representational at one remove, but sculpture and painting are
directly representational, and it is for this reason that they are
so misunderstood. Suppose we are looking at Frith's *Railway
Station*. The eye sees a pattern of line and colour which has an
immediate emotional effect because colours and shapes are in
themselves affective; for example, reds and straight lines will
tend to make us irritable and aggressive while greens and gentle
curves are soothing. This effect will probably be weak, and it
will be very weak compared with the secondary emotional effect
of the literary content. For the intellect at once grasps the
story—the bridal couple off on their honeymoon, the schoolboy

going back to school, the recruit on his way to join his unit, the forger arrested as he steps into the train—and all the appropriate emotions are aroused in the sympathetic spectator. Not only this, but the intellect appreciates the skill of the painter in imitating the scene so accurately. This is an extreme example to take, and in a landscape where the literary content is negligible the effect may be no more than the delight felt in recognizing a clever representation of a familiar scene.

There are then four possible reactions to looking at a picture, though of course the spectator may feel more than one. He may see it merely as a pattern of line and colour, as when he looks at a non-representational design or an abstract painting, and the effect will be mildly and directly emotional because of the affective qualities of the colours and shapes. If the picture is 'life-like' he will have the intellectual satisfaction of recognizing a clever imitation of something he knows, which may be accompanied by various emotions owing to association. If the literary content is high his emotions will be stirred in proportion to his intellectual grasp of the scene and his sympathy with the situation. Lastly his aesthetic emotion may be aroused by the beauty of the picture as a thing in itself, by its purely visual quality—by what Mr. Clive Bell would call 'significant form'—that has a meaning beyond that depicted, and which like poetry 'finds its way to something in man which is obscure and latent'.

Just as people may read narrative verse thinking they like poetry, whereas they only like the story, so they may think they admire painting when in fact they only like an illustration which is done far better in a photograph, or a facsimile which is no more art than the antics of a tight-rope walker—brilliantly clever and fascinating to watch, but the result simply of years of patient practice and a natural physical dexterity.

And because the skilful sculptor and painter can make such accurate copies it is natural to assume that the closer the imitation the greater the art, so that the visual arts are the easiest to appreciate for the wrong reason, and possibly the most difficult to appreciate for the right one. Yet, as Roger Fry says, 'ordinary people have almost no idea of what things really look like, so that oddly enough the one standard that popular criticism applies to painting, namely whether it is like nature or not, is one which most people are, by the whole tenor of their lives, prevented from applying properly'. This is because 'the needs of our actual life are so imperative, that the sense of vision becomes highly specialized in their service. With an admirable economy we learn to see only so much as is needful for our purposes; but this is in fact very little, just enough to recognize and identify each object or person; that done, they go into an entry in our mental catalogue and are no more really seen.'

To avoid misunderstanding, let it once again be admitted that there is a real and very great pleasure both in copying and in seeing an accurate copy. Just as 'poems very seldom consist of poetry and nothing else, and pleasure can be derived from their other ingredients', so there is much pleasure to be derived from the other ingredients of painting.

The point at issue here is that copying must not be confused with art, or the pleasure derived from seeing an accurate copy confused with aesthetic emotion. A coloured photograph is more accurate than a painting of the same subject, and a model railway far more life-like than any two-dimensional representation. Again, if the sculptor wished to be as life-like as possible he would work not in stone or bronze, but with coloured wax, glass eyes and real hair. The more closely Madame Tussaud's wax-works approximate to the original the greater the craftsmanship and the better they are as wax-works, but the further are they removed from art; the Chamber of Horrors is horrible, not because the figures are those of notorious criminals but simply because they are so life-like. This is true of all art, that when the reproduction coincides with the original, art is destroyed by the very perfection of craftsmanship, as the vital rhythm of a curve is annihilated in the perfect symmetry of the circle.

All art distorts, because the artist is creating, not copying; here he accentuates a line to complete a rhythm, there he adds a colour to balance or neutralize another area of colour, or he modifies a tone which is too insistent, or simplifies a form to give solidity; he may exaggerate features to add significance to the idea permeating his work, and subordinate surrounding objects to act as foils to the central theme. Even the Parthenon is full of distortions: the apparently horizontal lines are really curved, the columns are not vertical and are not even symmetrically spaced. Yet in spite of distortion the picture or sculpture may, and very often will, appear life-like to the spectator; but it is not a great work of art because it is life-like, but simply because it satisfies the aesthetic sense. On the other hand if the distortion is obvious it must not be condemned because of the distortion, because it is not true to life, but only if it is aesthetically displeasing.

This insistence on verisimilitude leads logically to another error. A schoolmaster who had been to see the Italian Exhibition in London some years ago said that for him 'a picture must have a beautiful subject, and be beautifully painted in beautiful colour'. He did not add whether the Italians satisfied his formidable demands, though he rather implied that they did not. Anybody would agree with his last two propositions, but what did he mean by a beautiful subject? If a work of art is to be merely a copy, then the ugly in nature will make an ugly copy; but if the aim of the artist is to create a form that expresses his aesthetic experience the question whether the original is beautiful or ugly is irrelevant. All that matters is that the work of art should be aesthetically satisfying. The artist knows the beauty latent in a superficially ugly or commonplace object. One of the most beautiful things in the Tate Gallery is van Gogh's picture of a yellow, rush-bottomed chair.

The Greeks are largely responsible for this tradition of beauty of subject, for it so happened that they did make superlatively beautiful statues of athletic bodies, and as Greek art set the standard since Renaissance times it was assumed that sculpture and therefore painting should follow the Greek model, just as tragedy according to the Neo-classical critics had to keep to the rules supposed to have been formulated by Aristotle. Incidentally, it is remarkable that Greek sculpture should have been so realistic while Greek drama was so highly stylized.

It will be as well to summarize the arguments of this chapter. The quality that most people look for in a work of art is imitation, either simple visual representation or the literary representation of anecdote and story. This is natural and admirable; but is this the finest and the final satisfaction to be derived from a work of art? It is suggested that the representation is relevant only as it contributes to a higher significance—the expression of the artist's aesthetic experience in the medium of the work of art, which must be considered as a thing in itself, and not as an imitation of something else.

Architecture and music, it will be admitted, are essentially non-representational and non-literary arts, so that the one must be judged by its appearance, the other by its sound, by what they are and not by what they represent. There seems therefore a good *prima-facie* reason for thinking that the representational arts of sculpture, painting and poetry have too a significance independent of representation.

The main difficulty in reaching an understanding on this
question is owing to the confusion between the beauty of nature
and the beauty of a work of art. Because nature is beautiful, it
is argued, the painter, the sculptor and the poet should imitate
what is beautiful in nature. This would mean that an accurate
copy of an ugly subject would itself be ugly. But is an accurate
copy of a beautiful subject necessarily beautiful? The accurate
imitation in music of natural sounds is vulgar and unpleasant;
or to take an extreme example, a life-like wax model of a beautiful
head in which all the features, colour, hair, etc., are accurately
represented is merely disturbing. On the other hand a photograph of the same head will be beautiful because it is a stylized
representation of the original in two dimensions and in varying
tones of grey. But it is only the representation of the natural
beauty. It is not the beauty of a work of art.

A work of art is the expression of the artist's aesthetic experience
and there seems no good reason why the beauty of this expression
should necessarily have anything to do with natural beauty.
Beauty in nature and beauty in art are different things, and each
must be judged by what it is and by no other consideration.
Just as we do not admire nature because it is like art, so we must
not admire art simply because it is like nature. This is obvious
if we pause for a moment to consider. Apart from sentimental
and sensuous reasons we admire natural beauty for its abstract
visual qualities. Thus a tree is beautiful because of its shape and
colour; its form is final, for it neither resembles nor represents
any other form. If then beauty in nature is the abstract quality
of form—the arrangement in space of certain coloured shapes—
it is not unreasonable to assume that the beauty of a picture or a
sculpture is the result of its purely visual qualities irrespective of
what it may represent.

This does not mean that a more or less accurate imitation of
nature cannot be a work of art, nor does it mean that the artist
should not imitate natural forms. Most sculpture and painting
are in fact representational, and this is only natural, for the artist
is generally inspired by what he sees, and with such a profusion
of forms to choose from there is no reason why he should not use
them, modifying them to suit his needs, rather than create new
abstract forms of his own.

It is possible also that elements other than pure form have
secondary aesthetic effects: that the ordinary emotional elements
as well as any intellectual content may intensify the aesthetic

response. In a poem, for example, a feeling of joy or sadness and the intellectual resolution of a simile or a metaphor may add to the aesthetic enjoyment, though that these elements are not essential is suggested by the arts of architecture, music and pottery. If there is this connection, however, the representational element may have a similar effect; there may be some aesthetic equation between the form of a work of art and the thing it represents in however stylized a fashion, a sort of contrapuntal relationship owing to the imposition of the one on the other. It should be noted that the introduction of the third dimension in painting is an elementary form of representation, and certainly the symbolic passing of time in Holst's *Saturn* is intensely moving.

Poetry in general seems to have sprung from two causes, each of them lying deep in our nature. First, the instinct of imitation is implanted in man from childhood, one difference between him and the other animals being that he is the most imitative of living creatures, and through imitation learns his earliest lessons; and no less universal is the pleasure felt in things imitated. We have evidence of this in the facts of experience. Objects which in themselves we view with pain, we delight to contemplate when reproduced with minute fidelity: such as the forms of the most ignoble animals and of dead bodies. The cause of this again is, that to learn gives the liveliest pleasure, not only to philosophers but to men in general; whose capacity, however, of learning is more limited. Thus the reason why men enjoy seeing a likeness is, that in contemplating it they find themselves learning or inferring, and saying perhaps, 'Ah, that is he.' For if you happen not to have seen the original, the pleasure will be due not to the imitation as such, but to the execution, the colouring, or some other cause.

Imitation, then, is one instinct of our nature. Next, there is the instinct for 'harmony' and rhythm, metres being manifestly sections of rhythm. Persons, therefore, starting with this natural gift developed by degrees their special aptitudes, till their rude improvizations gave birth to poetry.

ARISTOTLE: *The Poetics*. (Trans. S. H. BUTCHER.)

Then must we not conclude that all writers of poetry, beginning with Homer, copy unsubstantial images of every subject about which they write, including virtue, and do not grasp the truth? In fact, as we were saying just now, will not the painter, without understanding anything about shoemaking, paint what will be taken for a shoemaker by those who are as ignorant on the subject as himself, and who judge by the colours and forms?

Yes, certainly he will.

And just in the same way, I fancy, we shall assert that the poet, as well as the painter, lays on a species of colours, in the shape of verbs and nouns, to represent the several professions, of which he only understands enough to be able to imitate them; so that if he writes in metre, rhythm, and harmony, about shoemaking, or about generalship, or about any subject whatever, people who are as ignorant as himself, and who judge merely by the form of expression, look upon his poetry as very excellent. So powerful is the charm which these musical appliances naturally possess. For I suppose you know what a poor appearance the works of poets present when they have been stripped of their musical colouring, and are rehearsed in their proper nakedness. Doubtless you have observed the fact.

Yes, I have, he replied.

Does it not remind one of the withered appearance presented by the countenances of those who have once been blooming without being beautiful, whenever their bloom has deserted them?

Precisely so.

Now let me ask you to examine the following point. According to us, the maker of the image, that is, the imitator, understands only the appearance, and not the reality. Is it not so?

Yes.

Do not let us leave the matter half explained, but let us examine it satisfactorily.

Proceed.

A painter, by our account, will paint a bit and bridle, will he not?

Yes.

But the bridle and bit will be made by the saddler and the smith, will they not?

Certainly.

Then does the painter understand how the bit and bridle ought to be shaped? Or is it the case, that even the makers, the smith and the saddler, are ignorant on this subject, which is only understood by the rider, who knows how to use the things in question?

That is the true state of the case.

Then may we not assert that all things are in the same predicament?

What do you mean?

May we not assert that each single thing involves three particular arts,—the province of the first being to use the thing, of the second to produce it, of the third to imitate it?

Yes, we may.

Are not the excellence, beauty, and correctness of every manu-

factured article, or living creature, or action, to be tried only by
a reference to the purpose intended in their construction, or in
their natural constitution?

True, they are.

Hence the man who makes use of a thing must necessarily be
best acquainted with it, and must in the course of using it keep
the maker informed as to the success or failure of its performances.
For example, a fluteplayer, no doubt, informs a flutemaker
about the flutes which he employs in the exercise of his art, and
will direct him how they ought to be made; and the flutemaker
will submit to his directions.

Of course.

The one has a thorough acquaintance with good and bad
flutes, and conveys information upon which the other relies, and
will make accordingly: is not that the case?

Yes, it is.

Hence, the maker of the instrument will entertain a correct
belief with regard to its beauty or badness, by holding communication with the person who has a thorough acquaintance with the
subject, and by being compelled to listen to his instructions;
whereas the user of the same instrument will possess science on
these points.

Exactly so.

But which of the two will the imitator possess? Will he, by
actually using the things he describes, know scientifically whether
his productions are beautiful and right, or not; or will he entertain correct opinions from being compelled to put himself in
communication with the man of real knowledge, and to submit
to his directions as to the style in which he ought to work?

Neither.

That is to say, the imitator will neither know scientifically, nor
entertain correct opinions with reference to the beauty or badness
of the things which he imitates.

It seems not.

The poetical imitator will be charmingly wise upon the subjects
which he treats.

Not exactly.

However, he will go on imitating, notwithstanding his being
thoroughly ignorant as to what constitutes a thing good or bad.
Nay, apparently he will copy the vague notions of beauty which
prevail among the uninformed multitude.

Yes, what else can he copy?

Then, to all appearance, we are pretty well agreed so far as
this, that the imitative person knows nothing of importance
about the things which he imitates, and that therefore imitation
is an amusement and not a serious business; and that those who

cultivate tragic poetry in iambic or in epic verse are without exception in the highest possible degree imitators.

Exactly so.

PLATO: *The Republic.* (Trans. J. L. DAVIES and D. J. VAUGHAN.)

Poetry and picture are arts of a like nature, and both are busy about imitation. It was excellently said of Plutarch, poetry was a speaking picture, and picture a mute poesy. For they both invent, feign, and devise many things, and accommodate all they invent to the use and service of Nature. Yet of the two the pen is more noble than the pencil; for that can speak to the understanding, the other but to the sense. They both behold pleasure and profit as their common object; but should abstain from all base pleasures, lest they should err from their end, and, while they seek to better men's minds, destroy their manners. They are both born artificers, not made. Nature is more powerful in them than study.

BEN JONSON: Discoveries.

Be it fable or history that Love caused the first attempt of the creative Art, thus much is certain, that it was never weary of assisting the great old Masters; for although now the scope of Painting is enlarged so as to be more especially the art which imitates bodies upon flat surfaces, yet the wise Greek placed it within much narrower limits and confined it to the imitation of beautiful bodies. His Painter painted nothing but the beautiful; even the common type of the beautiful, the beautiful of an inferior kind, was to him only an accidental object for the exercise of his practice and for his recreation. The perfection of the object itself must be the thing which enraptures him: he was too great to require of those who contemplated him that they should be content with the cold satisfaction arising from the sight of a successful resemblance, or from reflection upon the skill of the artist producing it; to his art nothing was dearer, nothing seemed to him nobler than the object and end of Art itself.

'Who would paint you when nobody will look at you?' says the old epigrammatist of a very ugly man. Many modern artists would say, 'Be as ugly as it is possible to be, I will nevertheless paint you, though no one will willingly look at you, yet they will willingly look at my picture; not because it reproduces you, but because it is a proof of my skill which can so exactly imitate so hideous an object.' . . .

We smile when we hear that with the Ancients even the Arts were subjected to civil laws; but we are not always right when we smile. Unquestionably laws should exercise no power over sciences, for the end of science is truth. Truth is necessary for the soul, and it would be tyranny to exercise the slightest compulsion with respect to the satisfaction of this essential need.

The end of Art, on the other hand, is pleasure, and pleasure can be dispensed with; therefore it may always depend upon the law-giver what kind of pleasure he will allow, and what amount of each kind.

The plastic Arts especially, over and above the certain influence which they exercise upon the character of a nation, are capable of an effect which requires the vigilant supervision of the law. If beautiful men are the cause of beautiful statues, the latter, on the other hand, have reacted upon the former, and the state has to thank beautiful statues for beautiful men.

LESSING: *Laocoon*. (Trans. R. PHILLIMORE.)

Equally little can imitation, realism, serve, as many people think, as a measure of the quality of art. Imitation cannot be such a measure, for the chief characteristic of art is the infection of others with the feelings the artist has experienced, and infection with a feeling is not only not identical with description of the accessories of what is transmitted, but is usually hindered by superfluous details. The attention of the receiver of the artistic impression is diverted by all these well-observed details, and they hinder the transmission of feeling even when it exists.

To value a work of art by the degree of its realism, by the accuracy of the details reproduced, is as strange as to judge of the nutritive quality of food by its external appearance. When we appraise a work according to its realism, we only show that we are talking, not of a work of art, but of its counterfeit.

TOLSTOY: *What is Art?* (Trans. AYLMER MAUDE.)

In my youth all speculations on aesthetic had revolved with wearisome persistence around the question of the nature of beauty. Like our predecessors we sought for the criteria of the beautiful, whether in art or nature. And always this search led to a tangle of contradictions or else to metaphysical ideas so vague as to be inapplicable to concrete cases.

It was Tolstoy's genius that delivered us from this *impasse*, and I think that one may date from the appearance of '*What is Art?*' the beginning of fruitful speculation in aesthetic. It was not indeed Tolstoy's preposterous valuation of works of art that counted for us, but his luminous criticism of past aesthetic systems, above all, his suggestions that art had no special or necessary concern with what is beautiful in nature, that the fact that Greek sculpture had run prematurely to decay through an extreme and non-aesthetic admiration of beauty in the human figure afforded no reason why we should for ever remain victims of their error.

It became clear that we had confused two distinct uses of the word beautiful, that when we used beauty to describe a favourable aesthetic judgement on a work of art we meant something quite different from our praise of a woman, a sunset or a horse as beautiful. Tolstoy saw that the essence of art was that it was a means of communication between human beings. He conceived it to be *par excellence* the language of emotion. It was at this point that his moral bias led him to the strange conclusion that the value of a work of art corresponded to the moral value of the emotion expressed. Fortunately he showed by an application of his theory to actual works of art what absurdities it led to. What remained of immense importance was the idea that a work of art was not the record of beauty already existent elsewhere, but the expression of an emotion felt by the artist and conveyed to the spectator.
ROGER FRY: *Vision and Design.*

Painting went on in power till, in Raffael, it attained the zenith, and in him too it showed signs of a tendency downwards by another path. The painter began to think of overcoming difficulties. After this the descent was rapid, till sculptors began to work inveterate likenesses of perriwigs in marble,—as see Algarotti's tomb in the cemetery at Pisa,—and painters did nothing but copy, as well as they could, the external face of nature. Now, in this age, we have a sort of reviviscence—not, I fear, of the power, but of a taste for the power, of the early times. . . .

It is a poor compliment to pay to a painter to tell him that his figure stands out of the canvass, or that you start at the likeness of the portrait. Take almost any daub, cut it out of the canvass, and place the figure looking into or out of a window, and anyone may take it for life. Or take one of Mrs. Salmon's wax queens or generals and you will very sensibly feel the difference between a copy, as they are, and an imitation of the human form, as a good portrait ought to be. Look at that flower vase of Van Huysum, and at these wax or stone peaches and apricots! The last are likest to their original, but what pleasure do they give? None, except to children.
COLERIDGE: *Table Talk.*

If a man is insensible to poetry, it does not follow that he gets no pleasure from poems. Poems very seldom consist of poetry and nothing else; and pleasure can be derived also from their other ingredients. I am convinced that most readers, when they think that they are admiring poetry, are deceived by inability to analyse their sensations, and that they are really admiring, not the poetry of the passage before them, but something else in it, which they like better than poetry.

To begin with a very obvious instance. I have been told by devout women that to them the most beautiful poetry is Keble's. Keble is a poet; there are things in the *Christian Year* which can be admired by atheists; but what devout women most prize in it, as Keble himself would have wished, is not the poetry; and I much doubt whether any of them, if asked to pick out the best poem in the book, would turn at once to the Second Sunday after Easter. Good religious poetry, whether in Keble or Dante or Job, is likely to be most justly appreciated and most discriminatingly relished by the undevout.

A. E. HOUSMAN: The Name and Nature of Poetry.

But when we say the beautiful thing is that which being seen pleases we must remember that it is the *thing* which is seen. It is remarkably easy to look at a thing and not see it. Confronted by the painted portrait of a friend most people hardly, that is to say only with great difficulty, see the painting itself. They only see a reminder of their friend. They judge the thing as a likeness only and not at all as a painting. They are still entitled to say that the portrait pleases them or does not, but in that case they should remember that what they are saying is simply that it is or is not a pleasing portrait and that they have not said whether or no it is a pleasing painting.

'What I ask of a painting', said the French painter, Maurice Denis, 'is that it should look like paint.' But several centuries of insistence upon verisimilitude as being the highest quality of good painting have obfuscated our minds and filled us with the quite silly notion that everything reminiscent of natural appearance should be a faithful facsimile. We suppose that a portrait of a man of flesh and blood should produce the illusion that the man is standing before us. On the contrary it is better to say that things should look what they are—that a stone carving should look like stone, a painting like paint, instrumental music like the music of flutes or bassoons or whatever it is, the Tower Bridge like a work of iron engineering and not a medieval castle, and a work of the imagination like a work of the imagination. It may well be that some painters actually set out to produce illusions and to deceive the eye. Let us admit the fact, but let us also admit that there are other and possibly better and more normal kinds of painting. In any case we must be careful to distinguish between the thing seen and the thing of which it reminds us, neither confusing the one with the other nor judging of them as though they were identical.

ERIC GILL: Art.

CHAPTER IV

ART AND UTILITY

ARCHITECTURE differs from sculpture, painting, poetry, and music in serving primarily a useful purpose, so that a building has a value determined partly by its utility, partly by its appearance. For example, an efficient garage has an exchange value independent of aesthetic considerations, but a really bad picture, sentiment apart, will fetch no more than the value of the wood in the stretcher and a piece of waterproof canvas. On the other hand, a good picture may have a value out of all proportion to that of the materials from which it is made. Most manufactured articles have an exchange value which, from the demand side, is the sum of their value as materially useful things, and their value in appearance (or some other sensuous quality: taste, smell, etc.): carpets, curtains, clothes, dinner-services—the list might be prolonged almost indefinitely. But the things produced by man that have no value other than the aesthetic are severely limited, and are confined almost to the fine arts.

This is what Roger Fry means when he says that 'biologically speaking art is a blasphemy'; that is, the creation of things that serve no material purpose, and their appreciation for purely aesthetic reasons are unbiological, or contrary to life, because they have nothing to do with the struggle for existence, which, consciously or unconsciously, directly or indirectly, determines our thoughts and actions.

But works of art may be produced for biological reasons, as when a man paints a picture with the sole object of selling it. Again, works of art may be demanded for biological reasons because society allows a certain pre-eminence, which is only another aspect of the biological struggle for existence, to the man who is spacious in the possession of things, whether of dirt or pictures. Thus the wealthy and uncultured Roman demanded and got a life-like portrait bust, just as his counterpart in Victorian England demanded a life-like portrait in oils, or a clever copy of a beautiful scene, the possession of which had a publicity value and incidentally set the academic standard of the age. Or more obviously, commerce and industry have

recently enlisted the artist's help in the biological process of
selling goods. If the demand happens to be aesthetic as well as
biological, that is if the patrons are enlightened amateurs as well
as publicists, as were on the whole the Medici, the Roman
Catholic Church, and the eighteenth-century European aris-
tocracy, then the artist is free to express his emotional experience.
Only under such conditions of enlightened patronage, or if the
artist is like Cézanne independent of, or like Rembrandt impatient of patronage, is really useless, unbiological, and really
great art likely to be produced.

Roger Fry therefore makes a distinction between the biological
instinct to produce or possess something because it helps in the
struggle for existence, and the 'unbiological' instinct to create or
appreciate something useless but beautiful. But is the creation
of a work of art really an unbiological process?

It is clear that the hack painter's motives are biological, as are
those of the exploiter of the artist for prestige or snobbery, but it
seems odd that the creation of a real work of art should run
counter, that it too should not fundamentally be biological.
Indeed the act of creation, even of something useless, implies a
biological background. In brief, granted that the work of art
has no direct utility, though it may be exploited both by creator
and possessor for biological ends, has this peculiar creative
impulse itself any biological significance, and is the question of
any importance?

This has been partly answered already in the first chapter,
where it was argued that the aesthetic sense is a refinement of the
love-hate complex, love of what secures, and hatred of that
which threatens life in the desperate struggle for survival. But
this does not explain why men should go to such trouble in
producing works of art that have no material use.

In a civilized society the struggle for existence is no longer a
matter of brute force and primitive cunning,* yet the more man
becomes conscious of his environment and of his ultimate
annihilation, the more desperately does he engage oblivion.

> Nor dread nor hope attend
> A dying animal;
> A man awaits his end
> Dreading and hoping all.

* It is a different matter when the untrained, and therefore unfit and unstable
emotions of society are exploited; when the individual is seduced into concentrating
in the nation his instinct to survive; when self-preservation is perverted into the mass-
aggression of war.

An animal is unaware of its own mortality; 'man has created death', and his struggle for existence has become a much more complex process. It is not only the simple protection of his own life, the preservation of a friendly environment, the instinctive re-creation of himself in his children, the primitive display of strength, skill, and beauty, the extermination of the enemy. All these; but the rival of civilized man is more humanely and symbolically destroyed in the law courts, or annihilated in accordance with the rules of the game. This struggle for recognition leads to the acquisition of symbols that give prestige: money, titles, lands, works of art, blazers, the certificate for the prize vegetable; it leads to the sterile scribble on the wall, the barren keeping of records, to the monument, the mummy, and the pyramid. It produces tyrants and martyrs, bad verses and bad pictures. Finally it leads to the invention of mythologies in which the one is sacrificed that the many may survive, and which offer the hope of a personal immortality.

'Die two months ago, and not forgotten yet? Then there's hope a great man's memory may outlive his life half a year. But, by'r lady, he must build churches then, or else shall he suffer not thinking on.' But in one of his sonnets Shakespeare proudly writes:

> Not marble nor the gilded monuments
> Of Princes shall outlive this powerful rhyme;
> But you shall shine more bright in these contents
> Than unswept stone besmeared with sluttish time.
> When wasteful war shall statues overturn,
> And broils root out the work of masonry,
> Nor Mars his sword, nor war's quick fire shall burn
> The living record of your memory.
> 'Gainst death, and all-oblivious enmity
> Shall you pace forth, your praise shall still find room
> Even in the eyes of all posterity
> That wear this world out to the ending doom.
>   So till the judgment that yourself arise
>   You live in this, and dwell in lovers' eyes.

Here then we have it: 'death and all-oblivious enmity', 'or else shall he suffer not thinking on', 'the iniquity of oblivion'.

Man is still impelled by this tremendous instinctive will to survive, which is intensified by his knowledge of time and death, yet more subtle and less obvious in its manifestations because of the complexity of his activities and his environment. The fundamental instinct is self-preservation, often disguised as self-assertion; and because creation is the most powerful form of self-assertion—though destruction is the easiest—as well as a direct means of self-preservation, man is essentially creative. But the most creative of all activities is that of the artist or poet, 'the maker', who out of his imagination creates 'forms more real than living man, nurslings of immortality'. The self-preservative or self-assertive principle in man, therefore, exploits his aesthetic sense as a channel for a powerful discharge of creative energy, so that the work of art performs a profound biological function to the creator, and because the amateur identifies himself with it he too shares in the creative process.

It is not suggested that this self-assertive or power instinct is necessarily conscious in the artist any more than it is in the child or for that matter in any man—that Shakespeare, for instance, wrote with one eye on posterity. Nevertheless the artist's creative impulse is really the self-preservative principle on another plane, an attempt to project himself beyond the limits of his physical life.*

It is vitally important that this biological function of art should be recognized, for both the production and the appreciation of a work of art afford a powerful and socially desirable release of emotional energy, which if repressed may turn to destructive and anti-social activities—a perverted, but nevertheless biological process—or if not actively encouraged will leave the individual and society emotionally undeveloped and unsatisfied.

This must not be misconstrued as a defence of art on the grounds of its utility; a painting or a poem is there to be enjoyed, and the fact that its creation and appreciation have a biological function need not affect the enjoyment. Nor is it a pedantic attempt to foist 'Art' indiscriminately on everybody. But it is a plea for the intelligent education of the aesthetic sense, which must be latent in many people, in the belief that the more creative the outlets for man's instinctive self-assertion the more happiness and the fewer wars will there be in the world.

Sith, then, poetry is of all human learnings the most ancient and of most fatherly antiquity, as from whence other learnings

* It is an interesting fact that when a number of boys of more than average intelligence were asked whether they would rather have taken Quebec or written Gray's *Elegy* most of them considered the alternatives according to their survival value—whether Wolfe or Gray, the soldier or the poet, is best remembered by posterity.

have taken their beginnings; sith it is so universal that no learned nation doth despise it, nor no barbarous nation is without it; sith both Roman and Greek gave divine names unto it, the one of prophesying, the other of making, and that indeed the name of making is fit for him, considering that whereas other arts retain themselves within their subject, and receive, as it were, their being from it, the poet only bringeth his own stuff, and doth not learn a conceit out of a matter, but maketh matter for a conceit; sith neither his description nor his end containeth any evil, the thing described cannot be evil; sith his effects be so good as to teach goodness, and delight the learners of it; sith therein (namely in moral doctrine, the chief of all knowledges,) he doth not only far pass the historian, but for instructing is well nigh comparable to the philosopher, and for moving leaveth him behind him; sith the Holy Scripture, (wherein there is no uncleanness), hath whole parts in it poetical, and that even our Saviour Christ vouchsafed to use the flowers of it; sith all his kinds are not only in their united forms, but in their several dissections fully commendable; I think, and think I think rightly, the laurel crown appointed for triumphing captains doth worthily, of all other learnings honour the poet's triumph.

SIR PHILIP SIDNEY: Defence of Poesy.

Biologically speaking, art is a blasphemy. We were given our eyes to see things, not to look at them. Life takes care that we all learn the lesson thoroughly, so that at a very early age we have acquired a very considerable ignorance of visual appearances. We have learned the meaning-for-life of appearances so well that we understand them, as it were, in shorthand. The subtlest differences of appearance that have a utility value still continue to be appreciated, while large and important visual characters, provided they are useless for life, will pass unnoticed. With all the ingenuity and resource which manufacturers put into their business, they can scarcely prevent the ordinary eye from seizing on the minute visual characteristics that distinguish margarine from butter. Some of us can tell Canadian cheddar at a glance, and no one was ever taken in by sham suède gloves.

ROGER FRY: Vision and Design.

Art, all art, has this characteristic, that it unites people. Every art causes those to whom the artist's feeling is transmitted to unite in soul with the artist, and also with all who receive the same impression. But non-Christian art, while uniting some people together, makes that very union a cause of separation between these united people and others; so that union of this kind is often a source, not only of division, but even of enmity towards others. Such is all patriotic art, with its anthems, poems, and monuments; such is all Church art, *i.e.* the art of certain cults, with their images, statues, processions, and other local ceremonies. Such art is belated and non-Christian art, uniting the people of one cult only to separate them yet more sharply from the members of other cults, and even to place them in relations of hostility to each other. Christian art is only such as tends to unite all without exception, either by evoking in them the perception that each man and all men stand in like relation towards God and towards their neighbours, or by evoking in them identical feelings, which may even be the very simplest, provided only that they are not repugnant to Christianity and are natural to everyone without exception.

TOLSTOY: *What is Art?* (Trans. AYLMER MAUDE.)

Art embraces all making—all things made are works of art. But, in the twentieth century, the word art only means the 'fine' arts, the arts which are concerned with the making of those things which minister to mental satisfactions alone, whereas art in the general sense ministers to satisfactions both mental and physical. In the twentieth century the dilemma is becoming both obvious and tragic. On the one hand is seen the gradual emergence of the 'useful object' shorn of all 'art-nonsense', all factitious allurement or ornament or caprice, the true product of the machine—beautiful because truly functional, therefore satisfactory to the mind, therefore pleasing when seen—and at the same time the degradation of the workman from the position of a responsible craftsman to a sub-human condition of intellectual irresponsibility, with the consequent necessity of providing for his amusement and culture by means of state-controlled and state-censored cultural and educational organizations. On the other hand is seen the extraordinary development of the fine arts now that they are freed from their age-old entanglement with physical utility, and the extraordinary position of the 'artist' who, though he is responsible to no one but himself, is the only responsible workman left—he is the only workman whose power of choice is effective in the work of his hands.

On the one hand the twentieth century will witness the worship of human personality and sensibility in the arts of poetry, music, painting and sculpture; on the other will be seen the complete suppression of personality in the common workman as such—he will only be human in his 'spare time', the time when he is not working.

ERIC GILL: *Art.*

The present-day cleavage of artists into two groups, those who are so enslaved to their employers that they 'can't call their souls their own', and those unfettered spirits whose souls are so much their own that they are no use to anyone but themselves, is a comparatively new thing. It has led to the division of art into two kinds, known as 'commercial art' and 'fine art'—*i.e.* men who only work to please the man who pays them and men who have no one to please but themselves—though these latter always hope that they will happen to please someone else sufficiently to induce him to pay them enough to go on pleasing themselves without starving. Three-quarters of the films made, about a quarter of the books published, ninety per cent. of the music composed are 'commercial' in the true sense that they are created in order to be turned into money. The bulk of the remainder, the 'fine' works of art, are genuine attempts at self-expression without reference to the requirements of society. In some cases they succeed so well in impressing themselves on society that society begins to require them. In others they are so personal and so remote from average human experience that society, far from requiring them, complains of their uselessness, their unintelligibility or divorce from 'life'. That complaint, so often heard nowadays, is not a criterion of the genuineness or sincerity of the works of art in question. It is an index of the unfamiliarity of the language in which those works of art are couched. For a personal vision demands a personal set of idioms to express it. Usually a generation or so must pass before those idioms become understood and accepted by the average man and pass into general currency. The time-lag between the appearance of an unfamiliar artistic message couched in an unfamiliar artistic idiom, and its acceptance by the average man can only be reduced when the artist can be harnessed to a cause that the average man understands. Giotto was as violent an innovator as Picasso, but as Giotto's innovations were harnessed to Christianity (while Picasso's are harnessed to nothing more stable than Picasso) the average contemporary of Giotto, shocked though he may have been by the new Giottesque idiom, felt that he could at least understand the cause that idiom served, and could dimly see how the new idiom somehow served the cause in a new and valuable way. To-day the same phenomenon can be observed. The more the artist is willing to compromise between making what *he* wants (in Rembrandt's case, a study of light) and what his employer wants (in Banning Cocq's case a set of recognizable portraits) the more immediately acceptable his work will be. A cubist whose picture conveys nothing but the cubiness of things in general is apt to leave the average man cold and puzzled. But a cubist who uses his cubism to advertise the merits of A's petrol or B's beer is understood at once. A cubized egg is, to the average man, simply a bad egg; but a cubized glass of beer grasped in a cubized hand is interesting and arresting. The one is merely an artist's visual adventure, the other is a voyage of discovery that carries the spectator along with it and deposits him surprisingly at his destination. Once the artist has harnessed himself to society, society at once begins to regard him as a workman performing a useful function and not as a playboy amusing himself in a vacuum.

ERIC NEWTON: *European Painting and Sculpture.*

Art does affect the lives of men; it moves to ecstasy, thus giving colour and moment to what might be otherwise a rather grey and trivial affair. Art for some makes life worth living. Also, art is affected by life; for to create art there must be men with hands and a sense of form and colour and three-dimensional space and the power to feel and the passion to create. Therefore art has a great deal to do with life—with emotional life. That it is a means to a state of exaltation is unanimously agreed, and that it comes from the spiritual depths of man's nature is hardly contested. The appreciation of art is certainly a means to ecstasy, and the creation probably the expression of an ecstatic state of mind. Art is, in fact, a necessity to and a product of the spiritual life.

CLIVE BELL: *Art.*

There is, in fact, a path from phantasy back again to reality, and that is—art. The artist has also an introverted disposition and has not far to go to become neurotic. He is one who is urged on by instinctual needs which are too clamorous; he longs to attain to honour, power, riches, fame, and the love of women; but he lacks the means of achieving these gratifications. So, like any other with an unsatisfied longing, he turns away from reality and transfers all his interest, and all his libido too, on to the creation of his wishes in the life of phantasy, from which the way might readily lead to neurosis. There must be many factors in combination to prevent this becoming the whole outcome of his development; it is well known how often artists in particular suffer from partial inhibition of their capacities through neurosis. Probably their constitution is endowed with a powerful capacity for sublimation and with a certain flexibility in the repressions determining the conflict. But the way back to reality is found by the artist thus: He is not the only one who has a life of phantasy; the intermediate world of phantasy is sanctioned by general human consent, and every hungry soul looks to it for comfort and consolation. But to those who are not artists the gratification that can be drawn from the springs of phantasy is very limited; their inexorable repressions prevent the enjoyment of all but the meagre day-dreams which can become conscious. A true artist has more at his disposal. First of all he understands how to elaborate his day-dreams, so that they lose the personal note which grates upon strange ears and become enjoyable to others; he knows too how to modify them sufficiently so that their origin in prohibited sources is not easily detected. Further he possesses the mysterious ability to mould his particular material until it expresses the ideas of his phantasy faithfully; and then he knows how to attach to this reflection of his phantasy-life so strong a stream of pleasure that, for a time at least, the repressions are out-balanced and dispelled by it. When he can do all this, he opens out to others the way back to the comfort and consolation of their own unconscious sources of pleasure, and so reaps their gratitude and admiration; then he has won—through his phantasy—what before he could only win in phantasy: honour, power, and the love of women.

FREUD: *Introductory Lectures on Psycho-Analysis.*
(Trans. JOAN RIVIERE.)

To his Coy Mistress

Had we but world enough, and time,
This coyness, Lady, were no crime;
We would sit down and think which way
To walk and pass our long love's day.
Thou by the Indian Ganges' side
Shouldst rubies find: I by the tide
Of Humber would complain. I would
Love you ten years before the Flood,
And you should, if you please, refuse
Till the conversion of the Jews.
My vegetable love should grow
Vaster than empires, and more slow;
An hundred years should go to praise
Thine eyes and on thy forehead gaze;
Two hundred to adore each breast,
But thirty thousand to the rest;
An age at least to every part,
And the last age should show your heart.
For, Lady, you deserve this state,
Nor would I love at lower rate.

But at my back I always hear
Time's wingèd chariot hurrying near;
And yonder all before us lie
Deserts of vast eternity.
Thy beauty shall no more be found,
Nor, in thy marble vault, shall sound
My echoing song: then worms shall try
That long preserved virginity,
And your quaint honour turn to dust,
And into ashes all my lust:
The grave's a fine and silent place,
But none, I think, do there embrace.
　　　Now therefore, while the youthful hue
Sits on thy skin like morning dew,
And while thy willing soul transpires
At every pore with instant fires,
Now let us sport us while we may,
And now, like amorous birds of prey,
Rather at once our time devour
Than languish in his slow-chapt power.
Let us roll all our strength and all
Our sweetness up into one ball,
And tear our pleasures with rough strife
Thorough the iron gates of life:
Thus, though we cannot make our sun
Stand still, yet we will make him run.

ANDREW MARVELL.

PART TWO

CHAPTER V

ARCHITECTURE

IT seems a pity that a sixth-form boy in a Public School when asked what are the three Orders of Greek architecture should answer in all seriousness, 'Gothic, Platonic and Slavonic'. There is no great virtue, it is true, in knowing the names of the Greek Orders, or even in recognizing them, if there is no appreciation of Greek architecture; but it is a reasonable hypothesis that an acquaintance with the technique and terminology of architecture will stimulate an interest in it as an art, and possibly an interest in other forms of art as well.

Man's material environment is the work either of nature or of his own hands, and if he is to make the most of life he must sharpen his aesthetic sense and with it his social conscience, so that he refuses to tolerate mean buildings, squalid streets and sordid cities. And because buildings are a large part of our environment architecture may more easily be studied and appreciated than any other of the arts, and serve as an introduction to other forms.

It is not easy to define Architecture. It means something more than the science of building, just as poetry means something more than verse; and if poetry may be defined as 'great verse', because of its higher significance, so architecture for the same reason may be called the art of great—or, at any rate, of good—building. It has been called 'The Mother of the Arts', and certainly structure and design in the other arts are modifications or refinements of the structural masses of architecture. Sculpture is most nearly related to architecture, and its appreciation depends largely on the feeling for its architectonic qualities, just as an appreciation of architecture may depend ultimately on the imaginative perception of volume and solidity in natural forms, particularly in the bulk and related planes of hills and mountains.

Architecture is one of the visual arts, three-dimensional in space, and because of this last quality to some extent dependent on the time element, for the full appreciation of a building is a highly complex affair: a synthesis of the views from a number

66

of angles, both inside and out. Unlike the other visual arts, sculpture and painting, it is not representational: that is, the architect does not set out to represent natural forms save sometimes in the detail—a thirteenth-century Gothic capital, for instance—though he may be inspired by them; a Gothic nave inevitably reminds one of an avenue of trees. And sometimes buildings may be symbolic: medieval architecture by its vertical lines suggests spiritual aspiration; or more self-consciously the Einstein observatory by Erich Mendelsohn is designed to suggest the typical shape of optical instruments. But most buildings, sordid or lovely, are erected because they fulfil a material need. This is the main difference between architecture and the other arts, for whereas man could live on a lower plane of existence without sculpture, painting, poetry and music, he must burrow or build, or perish in the struggle for survival. Building, if not architecture, serves a biological purpose.

A building, then, is there because it answers a material need. If it does this as efficiently as possible is it necessarily beautiful, or is a building a compromise between efficiency and beauty? Stimulated by the machine age and particularly by the invention of the aeroplane there is a school of thought which argues that anything that expresses its function by its form is beautiful. Certainly the aeroplane is one of the loveliest of man's creations, and derives its form directly from its function. In the same way a lighthouse, a grain-elevator and a factory have well-defined functions, which of necessity determine their forms; to disguise their forms would be insincere, to depart far from them would lessen their efficiency. But even if these buildings are beautiful this does not establish functional form as the sole or even the main source of beauty in architecture. For function is not always so well defined; the function of a house is to be lived in, but how is the function of living to be expressed? The function of a church or temple is worship, but what is the inevitable form derived from this?

The vaguer the function of a building the more latitude has the artist in his design, and it would be pedantic to insist that the function of a house can be expressed only in one way. The most that can be said is that where efficiency is the primary consideration form must be derived from function, and the architect is right to make the most of these functional forms; but where efficiency is not so urgent, or where its definition is less precise, the emphasis on function may well be shifted towards more creative form. This does not mean that the architect is entitled to force his building into a preconceived design independent of its purpose, or to disguise its function with a mass of frivolous and irrelevant ornament; but it does mean that architecture is not to be confused with aeronautical or marine engineering, or with plumbing; that functional beauty is not the same thing as fitness for purpose, or the only source of beauty in architecture. Indeed in so far as form is absolutely determined by function, though there may be skill there can scarcely be art; for the artist is above all the maker, the creator, whose freewill is implied. If the form is predetermined the question of creation cannot arise.

To avoid misunderstanding let it once again be stated that all great art is sincere—in the sense that it is not merely superficial, but the expression of a genuine creative impulse; the disguising and falsification of functional form by such devices as sham façades, and decoration divorced from structure and design, as a buttress with nothing to support, are not always easily defensible.* But integrity in architecture does not necessarily imply the reduction of a building to a few simplified and emphatic functional forms.

Architectural forms are modified by environment, so that geology, climate, and the general culture of a people will help to determine them. Thus the sky-scrapers of New York are the result of many influences: geological—the hard rock; economic —the restricted area and high rents; scientific—the invention of ferro-concrete and the fast passenger-lift; and legislative—the Zoning Law. Flat roofs are easily constructed but only suitable for dry climates, while steeply pitched roofs are necessary where there is much rain or snow; horizontal lines are more effective in sunny countries and vertical lines in higher latitudes. Different architectural forms may be found quite close to one another; compare for instance the stone houses of the Cotswolds with the brick and half-timbered houses of the Vale of Evesham. Again the discovery of new building materials will modify old forms, and scientific invention and fresh needs will demand new ones, such as garages and airports. It would be interesting to trace the effect of scientific discovery—of railways and synthetic materials —on the de-localization of architectural forms.

* This should not be pedantically interpreted. Too austere and Puritanical a view might lead logically to the condemnation of much seventeenth-century art: poetry as well as architecture, Donne as well as Wren. After all, provided a building is fit for its purpose the ultimate test is its appearance, and if a little deception adds to the beauty—why not? The dome of St. Paul's is a lovely thing.

Photograph by "Country Life"

KING'S COLLEGE CHAPEL, CAMBRIDGE. 1446-1515

:ing page 68]

THE PANTHEON, ROME.   2ND CENTURY

S. MARK'S, VENICE.   11TH CENTURY

The artist cannot be fettered by rules; Shakespeare defied the canons of the pedants, and the Baroque architects ignored those laid down by Palladio. The true artist legislates for himself, and his work is not to be judged by the mechanism of an imposed body of laws; the only criterion is its success as a work of art. But there are certain general principles in all the arts that can be affirmed with some confidence. Thus, it has already been suggested that sincerity is an important quality in a work of art, and that ornament for its own sake without reference to the integrity of the work is a perilous device.

A good building will have good proportions; but it is almost as difficult to define proportion as it is to define beauty, and 'what is beauty I know not' said Dürer. Vitruvius established a system of proportion for the Roman Orders, but with it he reduced architecture to a mechanical science; and any attempt to base architecture on mathematical formulae is likely to lead to disaster. Proportion is an element in beauty, and the aesthetic sense, not the reason, is creator and judge.*

Unity is one of the most important elements in a building. The spectator should feel the influence of a harmonizing process that binds the parts into a significant whole. The Greeks subordinated and organized the parts of their buildings so that they formed a simple mass; but where, as in a medieval cathedral, there are two or more big masses, they must be harmonized and resolved into a larger unity if an uneasy feeling of conflict is to be avoided. This principle of unity applies to the parts as well as to the whole. Suppose, for instance, a house has a classical porch; if the entablature is insignificant, the supporting columns, as two identical features, will compete equally for attention; the entablature should resolve the duality and bind all three parts into a new and greater whole.

But the building may be part of a greater unity: a street, a square, or a town; and if the community has both civic and aesthetic sense it will insist that any new building shall harmonize with its environment. This does not imply a monotonous repetition of the same forms, and the stifling of individuality; contrast may emphasize the features of neighbouring buildings: a spire may set off the contours of a dome, and the dome in return act as a foil to the slender lines of the spire. What must

---

* 'The man who has eye and intellect will invent beautiful proportions, and cannot help it; but he can no more tell *us* how to do it than Wordsworth could tell us how to write a sonnet.'—RUSKIN.

be avoided is an aggressive appearance, as though the buildings were engaged in a perpetual struggle for existence in which only the biggest or most self-assertive would survive.

One more point; a footnote rather than a principle. It will be noticed that it is generally more satisfactory to emphasize the place where a member's function ends. Thus a wall that sinks into the ground without warning is less pleasing than one that marks its termination by some device such as a string-course or a different type of stone. Many examples of this principle will spring to the mind: the frieze and dado of interior walls, the capital and base of columns, the lintel over doors and windows. or the cornice of a classical building. This device is most obvious in the more formal designs of classical buildings; modern architects sometimes ignore it, as when they rely for their effect on the severity of their masses and dispense with a cornice. The musician recognizes the same principle when he defines the end of a sonata or a symphony with a coda; and in the same way Shakespeare emphasizes the conclusion of his sonnets and the scenes in his plays with a rhyming couplet.

Nearly all European buildings are derived ultimately from the Hellenic period of Greek architecture. The typical Greek building is the temple, and partly because religious ceremonies took place in front, partly because it was raised and isolated from other buildings, it was essentially meant to be seen from outside, so that it may be considered as a monument, almost as a statue, rather than a building. This statuesque appearance is emphasized by the fine marble of which it is built, by the simple proportions, unity of design, and subtle attention to detail. There were three Greek Orders of architecture: the Doric, Ionic and Corinthian, which are most easily distinguished by the capitals of their columns, though there are differences in the details of the entablature.

The Romans adopted the Greek Orders, and added two new ones: the Tuscan and the Composite. From the Etruscans they borrowed the arch, which the Greeks never used, and because they built in concrete as well as in stone and brick, they were able to develop its logical derivatives, the vault and dome. With this new material and principle of construction they could span great openings, erect buildings of several storeys, and extend the scope of architecture to include vast public buildings like the Colosseum, theatres and baths, as well as bridges and aqueducts.

The core of their buildings was concrete, but this they faced inside and out with their standardized five orders, which often bear little relation to the structure they conceal. Though their architecture is almost brutal in its impressiveness, the Romans had a fine civic sense, and they exported their formalized style to cover their empire with splendid public buildings and towns.

The Roman style of architecture was naturally practised at Byzantium, the capital of the Empire after A.D. 324, where it inevitably received an Oriental twist. The dome is characteristic of Eastern architecture, so that Byzantine buildings are a combination of the classical columnar style and the Oriental dome. The Romans had used the dome to cover only circular or polygonal compartments, but by means of pendentives the Byzantines adapted it to fit a square plan. To cover a large area they used a series of domes instead of the simple pitched roof of the Greeks, or the Roman system of vaulting. They also grouped a number of smaller domes about the great central dome, leaving them visible externally instead of covering them with a second roof. But in Byzantium many of the architects were Greeks, who for the sham Roman veneer substituted panels of marble and magnificent mosaics, while they took the column from the wall and made it structural again.

From the collapse of the Roman Empire in the west towards the end of the fifth century, until the end of the twelfth century, when the pointed arch was adopted, is the period of Romanesque architecture in Europe. The provinces were impoverished, but the early Christians, using the Roman ruins as quarries, built churches whose character was necessarily determined by the material used. Early Christian churches were an adaptation of the Roman basilica, or Hall of Justice, and were characterized by a nave flanked by columns supporting an entablature or semicircular arches, above which was a clerestory. On either side of the nave were aisles. The basilican plan was gradually modified to form a cross by the addition of transepts, and the prolongation of the sanctuary. The churches were roofed either with timber or by the simple Roman cross-vault. In some parts of Europe, notably near the Mediterranean, there is a strong Byzantine influence.

In England, Norman architecture is a form of late Romanesque introduced from France by Edward the Confessor. During the Roman occupation the buildings were similar to those of the rest of the Empire, and in the long Anglo-Saxon period (450–1050)

preceding the Norman most of the buildings were of timber which
has perished, and when stone was used there was no very definite
character, though they may often be recognized by such devices
as long and short work and pilaster strips.

Towards the end of the twelfth century the pointed arch superseded the round arch of Roman and Romanesque times, and this,
together with its vertical lines, is the most obvious characteristic
of Gothic architecture, which lasted until the end of the Middle
Ages. But more important than the pointed arch was the new
principle of construction. The Roman and Romanesque walls
were solid and thick enough to carry the dead weight of the roof,
but the function of the walls in a Gothic building was to enclose
rather than to support. Elasticity was given to the structure by
the use of thick mortar and relatively small stones, while vertical
and lateral thrusts were concentrated at recognized points and
neutralized by a counter-thrust. The essential structure is a
stone framework of piers, pillars, arches, vaulting ribs and buttresses, held in equilibrium by this thrust and counter-thrust of
the various members. The walls are scarcely necessary save to
enclose the space between the buttresses, and as the style developed most of this space was taken up by stained-glass windows
with elaborate tracery.

There are three main subdivisions of the Gothic style, each
covering approximately a century, though of course the development was continuous and without abrupt transition.

The Early English period of Gothic architecture (thirteenth
century) is characterized by tall and narrow lancet windows,*
bold foliated capitals, and dog-tooth decoration.

In the Decorated period (fourteenth century) the windows are
wider and less pointed, the tracery is more elaborate, the typical
ornament is the ball-flower, and the lierne rib is added to the
vaulting.

The Perpendicular style of the fifteenth century gets its name
from the perpendicular lines of the window tracery and the
panelling that covers the walls inside and out. The windows
are enormous, often with flattened four-centred arches and
strengthened by transoms. Fan-vaulting, as in King's College
Chapel, Cambridge, is characteristic. Perpendicular Gothic is
peculiar to England; on the Continent the Decorated style
developed into the Flamboyant.

* It is a reasonable generalization to make of Gothic architecture that the flatter
the arch, the bigger the window and the deeper the buttress, the later the style.

The word 'Gothic' was used by Sir Christopher Wren as a term of abuse synonymous with 'barbaric'; a style at odds with the classical tradition. Medieval architecture is in fact Romantic, dynamic rather than static, and the architect instead of concealing the stones rejoiced in their variety of shape and colour, and frankly displayed the vitality of his construction.

Renaissance architecture began in Italy in the fourteenth century, and was stimulated by the researches of Brunelleschi and Donatello into Roman methods, so making a break in the evolution of architecture, which had developed logically from the Greek to the late Gothic style. Now, however, it doubled back on itself and sought inspiration at its classical source. The Renaissance architects were artists primarily interested in design, unlike their medieval predecessors who were more concerned with construction, so they naturally turned to classical forms, but because they built in stone they utilized some of the Gothic technique of construction. They used the five Roman Orders, both constructively and decoratively, and the semicircular Roman arch, vault and cross-vault. They borrowed the Byzantine method of covering a square compartment with a dome and pendentives, and by increasing the height of the 'drum' made the dome the central feature. One of the greatest contributions of Renaissance architects was their rediscovery of the Roman civic sense in architecture, so that buildings were often designed as subordinate parts in the greater entity of street or town, as Wren planned to reconstruct London.

When the early Renaissance had lost its vigour the sixteenth-century Italian architect, Palladio, laid down rules for architecture based on the precepts of Vitruvius, a Roman of the late Augustan age, much as Seneca tried to reduce the writing of tragedy to a formula based on a misinterpretation of Aristotle. The Baroque style was the inevitable reaction from the tyranny of the pedants 'closely wed to musty laws lined out with wretched rule and compass vile'. The Renaissance style is formal and restrained; the parts are carefully related to one another, yet their functions are limited and well defined; but the Baroque architect, with a sweeping and theatrical gesture, models his building as a single unit, so that details are related directly to the whole, rather than indirectly by co-ordination with the other parts. Thus, a column instead of defining one storey of a building may unite the whole façade into a single feature.

Tudor, Elizabethan and early Jacobean architecture are

picturesque combinations of Gothic construction and Renaissance design, but by the middle of the seventeenth century the classical element had overwhelmed the medieval, owing largely to the work of Inigo Jones. His successor, Christopher Wren, was less formal and more adventurous; there is even a trace of Baroque influence in his buildings, though this style is rare in England, possibly because architecture was never sufficiently formalized to produce-a revulsion. The eighteenth century is the period of the late Renaissance or Georgian style: the formal, pleasant, but sometimes uninspired product of architects supplying a standardized commodity to the new upper and middle classes.

The Romantic Movement led only to an unintelligent copying of the more romantic and picturesque aspects of Gothic,* while the Industrial Revolution failed to inspire a new style in the nineteenth century. The towns were ringed with the ostentatious and meaningless villas of the industrialists, while their hearts were clotted with the mean dwellings of the poor; the civic sense was lost in a riot of *laisser-faire*, and all was a jumble of over-elaborate and misinterpreted revivals.

The twentieth century is left to clear up the architectural rubbish of the nineteenth, and aided by the new building materials, glass, steel and ferro-concrete, a new style characteristic of the machine is being evolved. In America the sky-scraper began as an elongated Renaissance building, but as great height is foreign to the genius of a classical building with its emphatic horizontal lines—to prevent the cornice looking ridiculously insignificant it had to be made of metal painted the colour of stone—a Gothic facing was applied to the steel framework. But to-day the architect supports his main mass by a number of flanking masses in something the same way as the Byzantine artist grouped his domes, and rejecting imitations of past styles the sky-scraper is Gothic only in its height and vertical lines, and classical only in its simplicity.

In Europe, as in parts of America, steel and ferro-concrete are often used to express projecting horizontal forms, such as balconies, that would be impossible in stone; as they are also used, some-times crudely or self-consciously, to emphasize the function of the building.

Although the motor-car leaves in its wake a refuse of semi-

---

* Gothic architecture was the spontaneous expression of a particular age, so that 'modern' Gothic is rarely significant. Classical architecture, on the other hand, with its emphasis on formal design seems to express something permanent in the mind of man.

detached suburb, and a litter of bungalow, there are signs of a stirring of the civic conscience, and planning has begun. But fine buildings and splendid cities depend ultimately on the citizen. When the man in the street sees the difference between design and decoration, between significant form and insignificant shape, his will be a better street, and he a citizen of no mean city.

The value of architectural enjoyment once it is learnt seems to us to be based upon two sets of considerations, practical and psychological. From the practical point of view we may think of it as an art with which three-quarters of the English race who live or work in towns are bound to come into everyday contact. An understanding of its principles makes the dullest town come alive, and indeed to the townsman the architectural sense fills very much the place of a countryman's knowledge of natural history and of agriculture. The countryman who knows nothing of either will soon become a clod who reacts only to beer, while the townsman who knows nothing of architecture, once tired of watching the crowd, may soon find himself reacting to nothing more exquisite or exact than the posters of the successive editions of the evening paper. For both townsman and countryman the pleasures of travel—not necessarily foreign travel—will be very much increased by some knowledge of architecture.

Psychologically we may see the art as one demonstrating discipline, synthesis, dignity and the subordination of parts to the whole. Its appreciation will encourage a sense of realism and discourage sentimentality without freezing the fancy or nipping playful impulses. Its enjoyment is inseparable from a realization of the pleasures and merits of craftsmanship, which, however, it will encourage the student to see as means not ends. As the art is now an active one, the amateur's interest will be able to develop, or at least to move, with the living practice of the art.

Architecture is inferior only to literature in convenience and in the fact that it is not an art which can be satisfactorily practised by the amateur.

The sociologist cannot but approve the study of architecture, as in England most of our social evils are either the cause or the effect of bad building, and, the age of palaces having passed, architectural embellishment seems now bound up with ideals of civic improvement and efficiency. . . .

C. and A. WILLIAMS-ELLIS: *The Pleasures of Architecture.*

The ancient Greek and Roman Architecture answer all the Perfections required in a faultless and accomplished Building;

such as for so many Ages were so renowned and reputed by the universal Suffrages of the civilized World, and would doubtless have still subsisted, and made good their Claim, and what is recorded of them; had not the Goths, Vandals, and other barbarous Nations, subverted and demolished them, together with that glorious Empire, where those stately and pompous Monuments stood; introducing in their stead, a certain fantastical and licentious Manner of Building, which we have since called Modern or Gothick. Congestions of heavy, dark, melancholy, and monkish Piles, without any just Proportion, Use or Beauty, compared with the truly ancient; so as when we meet with the greatest Industry, and expensive Carving, full of Fret and lamentable Imagery; sparing neither of Pains nor Cost; a judicious Spectator is rather distracted or quite confounded, than touched with that Admiration, which results from the true and just Symmetry, regular Proportion, Union, and Disposition; and from the great and noble Manner in which the august and glorious Fabricks of the Ancients are executed.

It was after the Irruption and Swarms of those truculent People from the North; the Moors and Arabs from the South and East, over-running the civilized World; that where-ever they fixed themselves, they soon began to debauch this noble and useful Art; when instead of those beautiful Orders, so majestical and proper for their Stations, becoming Variety, and other ornamental Accessories; they set up those slender and misshapen Pillars, or rather Bundles of Staves and other incongruous Props, to support incumbent Weights, and ponderous arched Roofs, without Entablature; and though not without great Industry (as M. D'Aviler well observed) nor altogether naked of gaudy Sculpture, trite and busy Carvings; 'tis such as gluts the Eye, rather than gratifies and pleases it with any reasonable Satisfaction: For Proof of this (without travelling far abroad) I dare report myself to any Man of Judgement, and that has the least Taste of Order and Magnificence; if after he has looked a while upon King Henry the VIIth's Chapel at Westminster, gazed on its sharp Angles, Jetties, narrow Lights, lame Statues, Lace, and other Cut-work, and Crincle-crancle; and shall then turn his Eyes on the Banquetting-hall built at Whitehall by Inigo Jones, after the Ancient Manner; or on what his Majesty's Surveyor, Sir Christopher Wren, has advanced at St. Paul's, and consider what a glorious object the Cupola, Porticoes, Colonades, and other Parts present to the Beholder, or compare the Schools and Library at Oxford with the Theatre there; or what he has built at Trinity college, in Cambridge, and since all these, at Greenwich and other Places; by which Time our Home-traveller will begin to have a just Idea of the ancient and

TEWKESBURY ABBEY.   12-14TH CENTURIES

S. PETER'S, ROME.   16TH CENTURY

Facing page 76]

Photograph by M. Tomlinson, National Buildings Record

BARNFIELD CRESCENT, EXETER. 18TH CENTURY

DER RUNDLING, LEIPZIG. 20TH CENTURY

modern Architecture: I say, let him well consider, and compare them judicially, without Partiality and Prejudice; and then pronounce which of the two Manners strikes the Understanding as well as the Eye, with the more Majesty and solemn Greatness; tho' in so much a plainer and simple Dress, conform to the respective Orders and Entablature; and accordingly determine to whom the Preference is due: Not as we said, that there is not something of solid, and odly artificial too, after a Sort: but then the universal and unreasonable Thickness of the Walls, clumsy Buttresses, Towers, sharp-pointed Arches, Doors, and other Apertures, without Proportion: nonsensical Insertions of various Marbles impertinently placed; Turrets and Pinnacles thick set with Monkies and Chimeras, and Abundance of busy Work and other Incongruities dissipate and break the Angles of the Sight, and so confound it, that one cannot consider it with any Steadiness, where to begin or end; taking off from that noble Air and Grandeur, Bold and graceful Manner, which the Ancients had so well, and judiciously established: but, in this Sort have they and their Followers ever since filled not Europe alone, but Asia and Africa besides, with Mountains of Stone, vast and gigantick Buildings indeed, but not worthy the Name of Architecture.

JOHN EVELYN: *An Account of Architects and Architecture.*

Gothic architecture is juggling in stone and glass. It is the convoluted road that ends in a bride-cake or a cucumber frame. A Gothic cathedral is a *tour de force*; it is also a melodrama.

CLIVE BELL: *Art.*

The principle of the Gothic architecture is infinity made imaginable. It is, no doubt, a sublimer effort of genius than the Greek style; but then it depends much more on execution for its effect. I was more than ever impressed with the marvellous sublimity and transcendent beauty of King's College Chapel. It is quite unparalleled. COLERIDGE: *Table Talk.*

But the moment that the conditions of weight are comprehended, both truth and feeling require that the conditions of support should be also comprehended. Nothing can be worse, either as judged by the taste or the conscience, than affectedly inadequate supports—suspensions in air, and other such tricks and vanities. Mr. Hope wisely reprehends, for this reason, the arrangement of the main piers of St. Sophia at Constantinople. King's College Chapel, Cambridge, is a piece of architectural juggling, if possible still more to be condemned, because less sublime. RUSKIN: *The Seven Lamps of Architecture.*

King's College Chapel

Tax not the royal Saint with vain expense,
With ill-matched aims the Architect who planned,
Albeit labouring for a scanty band
Of white-robed Scholars only, this immense
And glorious work of fine intelligence.
Give all thou canst; high Heaven rejects the lore
Of nicely-calculated less or more;
So deemed the man who fashioned for the sense
These lofty pillars, spread that branching roof
Self-poised, and scooped into ten thousand cells,
Where light and shade repose, where music dwells
Lingering, and wandering on as loth to die;
Like thoughts whose very sweetness yieldeth proof
That they were born for immortality.

                              WORDSWORTH.

A new Gothic building, or a new missal, is in reality little less
absurd than a new ruin. The Gothic architecture, sculpture,
and painting, belong to peculiar ages. The feelings that guided
their inventors are unknown to us.

                              CONSTABLE.

There was not, at that time, much to be seen in the Isle of
Thanet besides the beauty of the country, and the fine prospects
of the sea, which are nowhere surpassed except in the Isle of
Wight, or upon some parts of the coast of Hampshire. One
sight, however, I remember, engaged my curiosity, and I went
to see it—a fine piece of ruins, built by the late Lord Holland at
a great expense, which, the day after I saw it, tumbled down
for nothing. Perhaps, therefore, it is still a ruin; and if it is, I
would advise you by all means to visit it, as it must have been
much improved by this fortunate incident. It is hardly possible
to put stones together with that air of wild and magnificent
disorder which they are sure to acquire by falling of their own
accord.

                              COWPER: *Letters.*

For in one point of view Gothic is not only the best, but the
only rational architecture, as being that which can fit itself most
easily to all services, vulgar or noble. Undefined in its slope of
roof, height of shaft, breadth of arch, or disposition of ground
plan, it can shrink into a turret, expand into a hall, coil into a
staircase, or spring into a spire, with undegraded grace and
unexhausted energy; and whenever it finds occasion for change

in its form or purpose, it submits to it without the slightest sense of loss either to its unity or majesty,—subtle and flexible like a fiery serpent, but ever attentive to the voice of the charmer. And it is one of the chief virtues of the Gothic builders, that they never suffered ideas of outside symmetries and consistencies to interfere with the real use and value of what they did. If they wanted a window, they opened one; a room, they added one; a buttress, they built one; utterly regardless of any external appearance, knowing (as indeed it always happened) that such daring interruptions of the formal plan would rather give additional interest to its symmetry than injure it.

RUSKIN: *The Nature of Gothic.*

This rationalistic art is the art commonly called Renaissance, marked by a return to pagan systems, not to adopt them and hallow them for Christianity, but to rank itself under them as an imitator and pupil. In Painting it is headed by Giulio Romano and Nicolo Poussin; in Architecture, by Sansovino and Palladio.

Instant degradation followed in every direction,—a flood of folly and hypocrisy. Mythologies ill understood at first, then perverted into feeble sensualities, take the place of the representations of Christian subjects, which had become blasphemous under the treatment of men like the Caracci. Gods without power, satyrs without rusticity, nymphs without innocence, men without humanity, gather into idiot groups upon the polluted canvas, and scenic affectations encumber the streets with preposterous marble. Lower and lower declines the level of abused intellect; the base school of landscape gradually usurps the place of the historical painting, which had sunk into prurient pedantry,—the Alsatian sublimities of Salvator, the confectionery idealities of Claude, the dull manufacture of Gaspar and Canaletto, south of the Alps, and on the north the patient devotion of besotted lives to delineation of bricks and fogs, fat cattle and ditchwater.

RUSKIN: *Stones of Venice.*

A house is a machine to live in.

LE CORBUSIER.

All that has been achieved in the creation of new architectural form since the great autonomous efflorescence of mediaeval architecture and even during the most fruitful period of the baroque, down to the days of our own artistic exhaustion, is based in principle on the inherited forms and traditions of antique building art.

Precisely as there is no longer any connection between the

principle of the antique world with its simple load and support, and the Gothic principle with column and vault,—both in the matter of construction and of ornamental architectonic expression, —so must we clearly recognize the fact that the first iron girder inspired an exalted feeling of liberation akin to that which the mediaeval masters felt when they had conquered the antique principle of construction by means of the vault. It is only from this point of departure that one is able to realize that the decisive features of the new constructive principle must be discovered again and again.

The regulation of our static sensation in accordance with the tensile power of reinforced concrete instead of, as hitherto, with the principle of direct load and support, necessitates a long and gradual approach, and evolution. It is therefore particularly urgent to discover and emphasize this antithesis in order to be able to visualize the breadth and extent of this great change.

Out of the columns and marble beams of the Greek temple,
Out of the pillars and stone vaults of the Gothic cathedral,
Evolves the girder rhythm of iron halls.

The balancing of the load practised by the ancients, the elevation of the load practised by the mediaevals, are succeeded by the dynamic tension of construction in steel and concrete.

ERICH MENDELSOHN. (Trans. H. G. SHEFFAUER.)

In this connection, we hear a great deal of claptrap talked about the sky-scraper. The sky-scraper, for the most part, is a tall box. So far it has been nothing but that; except where, as in the Schiller Theatre Building in Chicago, or the famous Woolworth Building, some dreadful intervention of 'the beautiful' has converted it into an acre-high advertisement of the modern architect's fatuity.

It has been a fashion lately to admire the sky-scraper in its purely engineering capacity, along with other forms of simple engineering. But a box is always a box, however high. And when you think of the things that could have been done by a liaison of the artist's fancy, once more, with all these works of engineering genius, you wonder that there is not one single example which one can quote of such a structure.

In the case of a dynamic structure like an aeroplane there is neither any reason nor any need for the collaboration of engineer and artist. All such machines, except for their colouring, or some surface design, to modify their shape, develop in accordance with a law of efficient evolution as absolute as that determining the tiger, the wasp, or the swallow. They are definitely, for the artist, in the category of animals. When we come to the static cell-structures in which we pass our lives there is far more latitude and opportunity for his inventiveness.

WYNDHAM LEWIS: *The Caliph's Design.*

Upon the Duke of Marlborough's House at Woodstock

See, Sir, here's the grand approach,
This way is for his Grace's coach.
Here lies the bridge, and there the clock,
Observe the Lion and the Cock,
The spacious court, the colonnade,
And mark how wide the hall is made.
The chimneys are so well designed,
They never smoke in any wind.
This gallery's contrived for walking,
The window's to retire and talk in.
The council chamber's for debate.
And all the rest are rooms of State.
'Thanks, Sir,' I cried, ''tis very fine,
But where d'ye sleep and where d'ye dine?
I find by all you have been telling
That 'tis a house but not a dwelling!'

POPE.

Epitaph on Sir John Vanbrugh

Under this stone, reader, survey
Dead Sir John Vanbrugh's house of clay.
Lie heavy on him, earth, for he
Laid many heavy loads on thee.

ABEL EVANS.

F

CHAPTER VI

SCULPTURE

As sculpture is a visual and three-dimensional art it is, over a limited range of subjects, potentially the most mimetic of the arts. The sculptor, it is true, cannot reproduce a landscape or a large group of figures in full relief—though he may do so in bas-relief—but he can if he wishes, by using colour and suitable materials, make an accurate and realistic reproduction of a single figure or even of a small group. But if it is true that representation is irrelevant unless it contributes to the aesthetic effect, that 'creating a work of art is so tremendous a business that it leaves no leisure for catching a likeness or displaying address', that 'every sacrifice made to representation is something stolen from art', with what is the sculptor concerned?

It is true that he may use his medium simply to express, and probably because he has been commissioned to do so, a rational statement, as, 'Here is a statue of a famous man', much as the writer uses prose as a medium for the transference of ideas, the more lucidly he does so the better within limits being his style. We normally read prose for the sake of what is said, but poetry we read for the way in which it is said. There are of course exceptions to this: the prose of Sir Thomas Browne and Virginia Woolf, to mention only two writers, must be read as poetry rather than as prose. But as poetry has a higher significance than prose, so sculpture means more than the representation of men, whether famous or with no other memorial.

Obviously the sculptor is concerned with the modelling or carving of a three-dimensional shape, but so is the jobbing carpenter, the cobbler and the toy-maker. As an artist his business is to create three-dimensional form that is the expression of his aesthetic experience; form, which although it may be derived from and may clearly resemble a model, has a significance of its own, independent of and more profound than the thing it represents. Thus the statue of John the Baptist in Chartres Cathedral represents a man, but it is a great work of art not because it is a good or realistic copy, which it is not, being made of uncoloured stone and more slender than life, but because the form as a thing in itself is aesthetically moving. The representational element may, it is true, emphasize the aesthetic effect, but it is an accidental rather than an essential attribute, and it is beyond all doubt certain that the *accuracy* of representation has nothing to do with it whatever. In the same way a line of poetry—

In thrilling region of thick-ribbed ice—

has a significance independent of the literal meaning, which is simple enough, a significance which cannot be explained, but can only be felt.

Form has a more critical meaning than shape, at once more limited and more extended. Visual shape may be two or three dimensional, natural or artificial, accidental or deliberate, beautiful or ugly; thus the grain in a piece of wood is a two-dimensional, natural shape, the product of a law of nature, and probably beautiful; the shape of a broken bottle is three-dimensional, artificial and accidental, and may or may may not be beautiful. Form, on the other hand, implies the element of beauty; and there is a certain inevitability about it, as though, given certain premises, the thing, whether in nature or in art, must develop as it does according to a law implicit in its origin, like a healthy tree or a great tragedy.

In sculpture, then, form will mean a three-dimensional shape that is aesthetically moving. Whatever the medium, form is the work of art itself considered as a thing with an independent existence, to be looked at or listened to simply because its appearance or sound is aesthetically moving.

Few people are sensitive to shape even as a pattern in two dimensions. The tailor will look at the pattern in the cloth he is cutting, and for a similar reason a decorator will remark the pattern in a wall-paper. But will the tailor look at the wall-paper, and will the decorator really notice the pattern in his new suit? We look at certain things because it is our business to look at them, but most of the other shapes in the world pass unnoticed unless there is something curious or freakish about them. We rarely look at a thing because it is beautiful, and for no other reason, with no desire to touch or to possess it.

And if most people are insensible to two-dimensional shape, fewer still are imaginatively and disinterestedly aware of the third dimension of depth in space. It is not only that they could not describe or draw an Ionic capital, a Chippendale chair, or a cow's head, but they see three-dimensional shapes as a flat pattern. Thus if they draw a head they will trace an outline rather than try to model a solid shape composed of a series of related planes, and if they paint they will find one of their greatest difficulties is to give the effect of volume, so that three-dimensional objects will have razor-like edges and look no more solid than the canvas on which they are painted.

It may therefore come as a new experience to think consciously in terms of three-dimensional form: to feel the earth solid beneath the feet and reaching out over the horizon; to experience imaginatively the volume of the hills, the solidity of buildings and trees, even to realize a box as a three-dimensional object in space, the far side of which, although invisible, is just as real as the front. A building, a statue, and a vase are essentially masses conceived and created by the artist, a sequence of planes making a pattern in space, and it is as such that they should be looked at and judged. The architect must think in terms of mass; to the sculptor and potter three-dimensional form is a passion; and in some painters too, notably the Florentines—and more recently Cézanne—the desire to create three-dimensional form on a two-dimensional canvas is a reflection of the intense aesthetic experience produced by their perception of volume. The full appreciation of much visual art, and even perhaps of some poetry —that of Marvell and Keats for example—is dependent on this imaginative apprehension of volume.

All the mediums used in the fine arts have inherent qualities which, irrespective of what they may be made to represent, are capable of giving aesthetic pleasure. This is most obvious in music and architecture, where there is little or no question of representation; the essential quality in the sculptor's medium being the simple architectural one of mass, so that when his material is arranged in certain plastic sequences it becomes, like notes in music, the expression of the artist's aesthetic experience.

In architecture and pottery form can be studied in isolation, abstracted from the mimetic elements of sculpture, and here we can more easily realize the artist's passionate preoccupation with his material. 'Suppose, for example,' writes Roger Fry, 'that we are looking at a Sung bowl; we apprehend gradually the shape of the outside contour, the perfect sequence of the curves, and the subtle modifications of a certain type of curve which it shows; we also feel the relation of the concave curves of the

inside to the outside contour'; we realize that the precise thickness of the walls is consistent with the particular kind of matter
of which it is made, its appearance of density and resistance; and
finally we recognize, perhaps, how satisfactory for the display of
all these plastic qualities are the colour and the dull lustre of the
glaze.' It should be remembered that both architecture and
ceramics are functional arts, and that function therefore imposes
certain limits on their form, whereas abstract sculpture is form
in complete isolation with neither functional nor mimetic
qualities.

The sculptor then is primarily concerned with the creation of
three-dimensional form, with all that this implies in the balancing
of masses, the interrelation of planes, and the play of light and
shade. It follows therefore that the appreciation of sculpture is
largely dependent on an appreciation of formal, architectonic
qualities; that we must look at a statue with much the same
kind of vision that we look at a building, or a Chinese or Persian
bowl.

The Greeks were content to make the expression of the plastic
sequences of the perfectly developed human body the aesthetic
end of their art; they avoided violence and the dramatic, so that
both body and features were shown in repose. This has the
advantage that the vision is not distracted by any literary element,
by any attempt to tell a story, or by any irrelevant emotion, that
is by any emotion other than that produced by the contemplation
of the form.

The great anonymous sculptors of the Romanesque period, like
those at Chartres, were inevitably less realistic than the Greeks.
They had little anatomical knowledge, so that there is no question
of verisimilitude in their art; but by their peculiar formal
relationships they imposed a secondary spiritual significance
symbolic of that great age of faith. Such an emotional content
derived from the form, where formal relationships express a
psychological state, should not be confused with the reproduction
of emotion by facial expression. There is always the danger,
however, that form will be sacrificed to emotional expression,
and this is what happened as faith declined in the fourteenth
century, and plastic significance gave place to mere prettiness
and elegance of pose.

It was Donatello who, in the fifteenth century, combined the
Greek and Romanesque traditions. The Renaissance study of

classical models led him to conceive sculpture as an harmonious relation of forms, but with this dispassionate Greek conception he combined the plastic rhythms, derived from the Romanesque sculptors, expressive of character and the spiritual life. In the hands of Michelangelo these rhythms become more dynamic, even melodramatic and rhetorical; his titanic figures are convulsed in a single powerful rhythm—almost a spasm—reminiscent of Baroque building, with which indeed his sculpture has much in common.

Since Renaissance times artists have on the whole been so preoccupied with exploring the possibilities of painting that they have given less attention to the expensive practice of sculpture, while the demand has been largely the non-aesthetic one for realistic copies of public men in public places. Structural form gave place to the popular appeal of verisimilitude and sentiment, and it is only recently that artists such as Rodin, Maillol, Mestrovic, Eric Gill, Epstein and Henry Moore—to mention only a few— have returned to sculpture as an art concerned essentially with form.

A woman, a mountain, a horse—they are all the same thing; they are made on the same principles.

RODIN.

Appreciation of sculpture depends upon the ability to respond to form in three dimensions. That is perhaps why sculpture has been described as the most difficult of all arts; certainly it is more difficult than the arts which involve appreciation of flat forms, shape in only two dimensions. Many more people are 'form-blind' than colour-blind. The child learning to see, first distinguishes only two-dimensional shape; it cannot judge distances, depths. Later, for its personal safety and practical needs, it has to develop (by means of touch) the ability to judge roughly three-dimensional distances. But having satisfied the requirements of practical necessity, most people go no farther. Though they may attain considerable accuracy in the perception of flat form, they do not make the further intellectual and emotional effort needed to comprehend form in its full spatial existence.

This is what the sculptor must do. He must strive continually to think of, and use, form in its full spatial completeness. He gets the solid shape, as it were, inside his head—he thinks of it, whatever its size, as if he were holding it completely enclosed in the hollow of his hand. He mentally visualizes a complex form *from all round itself*; he knows while he looks at one side what the other side is like; he identifies himself with its centre of gravity, its weight; he realizes its volume as the space that the shape displaces in the air.

And the sensitive observer of sculpture must also learn to feel shape simply as shape, not as description or reminiscence. He must, for example, perceive an egg as a simple single solid shape, quite apart from its significance as food, or from the literary idea that it will become a bird. And so with solids such as a shell, a nut, a plum, a pear, a tadpole, a mushroom, a mountain peak, a kidney, a carrot, a tree-trunk, a bird, a bud, a lark, a ladybird, a bulrush, a bone. From these he can go on to appreciate more complex forms or combinations of several forms.

HENRY MOORE : *Art in England.*

They have indeed complete plastic freedom; that is to say, these African artists really conceive form in three dimensions. Now this is rare in sculpture. All archaic European sculpture —Greek and Romanesque, for instance—approaches plasticity from the point of view of bas-relief. The statue bears traces of having been conceived as the combination of front, back and side bas-reliefs. And this continues to make itself felt almost until the final development of the tradition. Complete plastic freedom with us seems only to come at the end of a long period, when the art has attained a high degree of representational skill and when it is generally already decadent from the point of view of imaginative significance.

ROGER FRY : *Vision and Design.*

If the Artist out of ever changing nature cannot use more than a single moment, and the Painter especially can only use this single moment with reference to a single point of view; if their works, however, are made not only to be seen but to be considered, and considered for a long time and repeatedly; then is it certain that this single moment, and the single point of view of this single moment, must be chosen which are most fruitful of effect. That alone is fruitful of effect which leaves free play to the power of imagination. The more we see, the more must we aid our sight by thought; the more we aid our sight by thought, the more must we believe that we see. But in all the gradations of a passion, there is no moment which has less this advantage than the moment of the highest degree of the passion. Beyond this there is nothing, and to show the eye the extremest point is to bind the wings of Fancy, and to compel her, inasmuch as her power cannot go beyond the impression on the senses, to busy herself with feeble and subordinate images, beyond which is that visible fullness of expression which she shuns as her boundary. When Laocoon sighs the imagination may hear him scream; but when he screams, then it can neither advance a step higher in this representation, nor descend a step lower without beholding him in a more tolerable and therefore in a less interesting condition: you either hear him groan for the first time, or you see him already dead.

Moreover, if this single moment obtains through Art an unchangeable duration, then it ought to express nothing which in our conception is transitory. All phenomena, the character of which we consider to be that they suddenly appear and suddenly disappear—that they can only be what they are for a moment—all such phenomena, be they agreeable or shocking, obtain, when prolonged by Art, so unnatural an appearance, that their impression becomes weaker with each repeated inspection, and ends in our feeling disgust or fear at the whole object.

LESSING : Laocoon.

Thoughts in a Garden

How vainly men themselves amaze
To win the palm, the oak, or bays,
And their uncessant labours see
Crown'd from some single herb or tree,
Whose short and narrow verged shade
Does prudently their toils upbraid;
While all the flowers and trees do close
To weave the garlands of repose!

Fair Quiet, have I found thee here,
And Innocence thy sister dear?
Mistaken long, I sought you then
In busy companies of men;
Your sacred plants, if here below,
Only among the plants will grow:
Society is all but rude
To this delicious solitude.

No white nor red was ever seen
So amorous as this lovely green.
Fond lovers, cruel as their flame,
Cut in these trees their mistress' name:
Little, alas! they know or heed
How far these beauties hers exceed!
Fair trees! wheres'e'er your barks I wound,
No name shall but your own be found.

JOHN THE BAPTIST.
CHARTRES CATHEDRAL
13TH CENTURY

Photograph by Alinari

BRONZE CHARIOTEER.
DELPHI
(*c.* 475 B.C.)

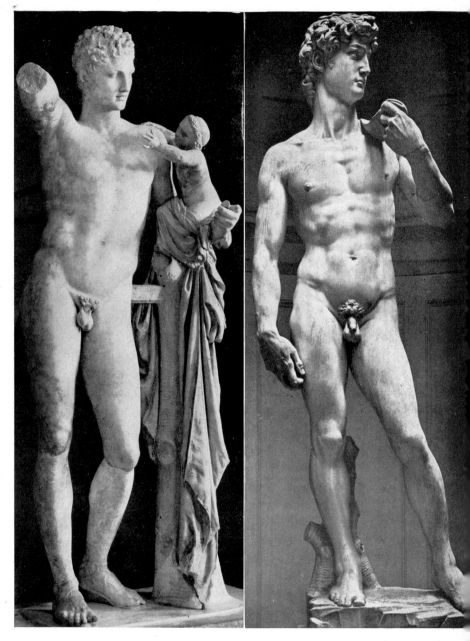

Photograph by Alinari

Photograph by A

HERMES.

DAVID.

BY PRAXITELES. *c.* 325 B.C.

BY MICHELANGELO. 1503

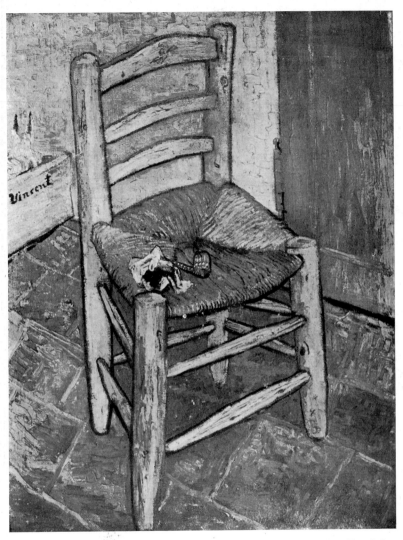

VAN GOGH.   THE YELLOW CHAIR

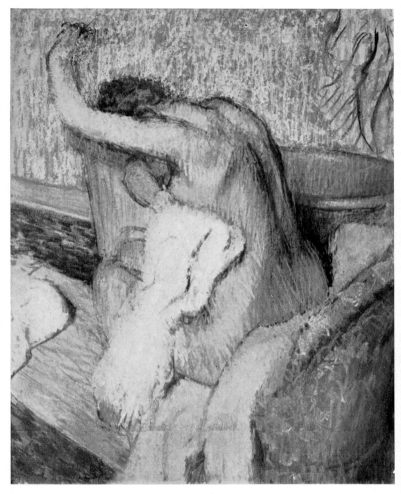

[*Facing page* 89

When we have run our passion's heat,
Love hither makes his best retreat:
The gods, that mortal beauty chase,
Still in a tree did end their race;
Apollo hunted Daphne so
Only that she might laurel grow;
And Pan did after Syrinx speed
Not as a nymph, but for a reed.

What wondrous life is this I lead!
Ripe apples drop about my head;
The luscious clusters of the vine
Upon my mouth do crush their wine;
The nectarine and curious peach
Into my hands themselves do reach;
Stumbling on melons, as I pass,
Ensnared with flowers, I fall on grass.

Meanwhile the mind from pleasure less
Withdraws into its happiness;
The mind, that ocean where each kind
Does straight its own resemblance find;
Yet it creates, transcending these,
Far other worlds, and other seas;
Annihilating all that's made
To a green thought in a green shade.

Here at the fountain's sliding foot,
Or at some fruit-tree's mossy root,
Casting the body's vest aside,
My soul into the boughs does glide;
There, like a bird, it sits and sings,
Then whets and combs its silver wings,
And, till prepared for longer flight,
Waves in its plumes the various light.

Such was that happy Garden-state
While man there walk'd without a mate:
After a place so pure and sweet,
What other help could yet be meet!
But 'twas beyond a mortal's share
To wander solitary there:
Two paradises 'twere in one,
To live in Paradise alone.

How well the skilful gard'ner drew
Of flowers and herbs this dial new!
Where, from above, the milder sun
Does through a fragrant zodiac run:
And, as it works, th' industrious bee
Computes its time as well as we.
How could such sweet and wholesome hours
Be reckon'd, but with herbs and flowers!

ANDREW MARVELL.

To Autumn

Season of mists and mellow fruitfulness!
  Close bosom-friend of the maturing sun;
Conspiring with him how to load and bless
  With fruit the vines that round the thatch-eaves run;
To bend with apples the moss'd cottage-trees,
  And fill all fruit with ripeness to the core;
    To swell the gourd, and plump the hazel shells
  With a sweet kernel; to set budding more,
And still more, later flowers for the bees,
Until they think warm days will never cease,
    For Summer has o'er-brimmed their clammy cells.

Who hath not seen thee oft amid thy store?
  Sometimes whoever seeks abroad may find
Thee sitting careless on a granary floor,
  Thy hair soft-lifted by the winnowing wind;
Or on a half-reap'd furrow sound asleep,
  Drowsed with the fume of poppies, while thy hook
    Spares the next swath and all its twined flowers;
And sometimes like a gleaner thou dost keep
  Steady thy laden head across a brook;
  Or by a cider-press, with patient look,
    Thou watchest the last oozings hours by hours.

Where are the songs of Spring? Ay, where are they?
  Think not of them, thou hast thy music too,—
While barred clouds bloom the soft-dying day,
  And touch the stubble-plains with rosy hue;
Then in a wailful choir the small gnats mourn
  Among the river sallows, borne aloft
    Or sinking as the light wind lives or dies;
And full-grown lambs loud bleat from hilly bourn;
  Hedge-crickets sing; and now with treble soft
  The redbreast whistles from a garden-croft;
    And gathering swallows twitter in the skies.   KEATS.

CHAPTER VII

COLOUR

MOST people are more sensitive to colour than to shape. Though few look at colours carefully—how many of us are really aware of the colours in our carpets or curtains, or of the colour of our friends' eyes?—yet an unusual colour will at once attract attention. Form is a more austere and quiet quality, characteristic of Classical art, while the flamboyancy of colour has more in common with Romanticism. Yet the device of camouflage suggests that the two are not unrelated, for camouflage is used to conceal objects, not only by harmonizing their colours with the background, but also by breaking up logical form into meaningless coloured shapes.

As the sculptor works in three dimensions, volume is a physical reality and colour an irrelevancy. But the painter, working on the two dimensions of his canvas, and wishing to create the illusion of three-dimensional form, must use colour, or at least different tones of grey, to suggest the third dimension of depth. Thus, colour is to the painter what the third dimension is to the sculptor. But it is, of course, more than this. Whether the painter's form is two or three dimensional, representational or abstract, the combination of colours and shapes has an emotional significance apart from any element of illusory depth. The painter's first concern is to create form, but form that is an aesthetically satisfying combination of shape and colour.

Some objects are self-luminous, like a candle or a red-hot poker, and they have their own characteristic colours, but all other colours are the effect of reflected light. The sun is self-luminous and its light is white, but this white light can be broken up into the colours of the spectrum or rainbow—red, orange, yellow, green, blue, violet. A red surface is one that reflects the red rays, but absorbs all the others; a white surface reflects all the rays; a black surface absorbs all the rays; and a neutral grey reflects part of all the rays in the same proportion that it received them. In practice there is no such thing as pure white or pure black, as no material will reflect or absorb all the rays, and a pure grey is extremely rare.

The word 'colour' is ambiguous; light blue, dark blue, bright blue, dull blue, are all different colours, yet they are all blue. It is convenient therefore to distinguish between hue, tone and intensity, three qualities that give a sort of three-dimensional property to colour.

Hue is the chromatic quality of a colour that we indicate by a name, such as yellow or red. If two hues (not complementary) are mixed, another hue is obtained. Thus yellow and red make orange.

Tone is the quality of lightness or darkness in a hue. Thus we talk of light or dark red; by adding white to red we can make it lighter, as by adding black we can make it darker, without changing the hue, because white and black are not hues.

Intensity refers to the brilliance or dullness of a hue. Pure red would contain no element of grey, while a dull red has a large amount of grey. Since a pure grey is not a hue, the intensity of a hue can be reduced by mixing with grey, again without altering the hue.

> Red and yellow make orange—a different hue.
> Red and white make light red—a different tone.
> Red and black make dark red—a different tone.
> Pure red is brilliant red—a different intensity.
> Red and grey make dull red—a different intensity.
> Red and green make grey—not a hue.

It will readily be seen that the number of colours is infinite; there is, indeed, an infinite number of hues between red and violet; an infinite number of tones of the same hue from almost white to almost black; and an infinite number of intensities of the same hue from the pure hue to almost pure grey.

Colours in pigment do not behave in the same way as colours in light. Thus the three primary hues in pigment are red, blue, and yellow; that is they cannot be made by mixing other hues.* But in light the primary hues are green, orange-red, and blue-violet; yellow, for instance, can be made by mixing orange-red and green lights, while blue and yellow lights make white. It was the discovery of the spectrum colours that led the nineteenth-century Impressionist painters to adopt a rainbow palette; that is, to use only the spectrum colours—and white—as they thought

---

* This is only approximately true, as low intensities of red, yellow, and blue can be made by mixing violet and orange, orange and green, green and violet. Again scientists now admit sea-green as a fourth primary hue.

that only by using the colours in sunlight could they hope to paint the true colours of nature.

Given red, yellow, and blue pigment, the painter can make any hue by mixing them in the right proportions; red and yellow make orange; violet is a mixture of red and blue.

The relations of hues to one another can be shown in the form of a circle, each hue gradually changing into its adjacent hues,

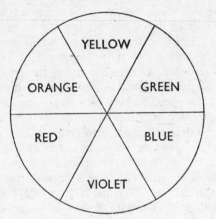

so that, for example, between the full intensities of yellow and orange there is any number of yellow-oranges and orange-yellows.

It is well known that if we look at a bright colour for some time, and then close our eyes, we see an after-image in a different colour. Thus, if we look at yellow we shall see a violet image. Yellow and violet are complementary colours, and if mixed in the right proportion they will make a neutral grey. Any diameter drawn on the colour circle will join two complementary colours, which when mixed will produce grey.

Until the Impressionists exploited the scientific discoveries of the nineteenth century, painters were generally content to make shadows a conventional brown; but the Impressionists saw that shadows were full of colour, and contained the complementary colour of that seen in the light. Thus, to represent a leaf-green in shadow, red-violet would be added to make a greyish green, while the shadows on a face will probably be a mixture of orange —approximately the colour in the light—and blue.

The colour of an object seen close at hand is called its local colour, but as it recedes the atmosphere interposes a veil, so that the local colour changes in hue, tone, and intensity. For example, the local colour of grass is a warm green, but distant hills are grey, grey-blue, or greyish purple, and eventually become indistinguishable from the sky. This expression of space by means of a change in the local colour is called aerial perspective; and as the Impressionists were mainly interested in painting transitory effects of light, they made the most of this device.

But Cézanne, who painted at the same time as the Impressionists, was obsessed by three-dimensional form, by the bulk and stability of things, so that out of colour he wanted to create something more permanent than Impressionist pictures of the fleeting effects of light. Cézanne is one of the greatest colourists in the history of painting, and the measure of his greatness can be appreciated if we realize how his colour seems to grow out of his form as naturally and inevitably as the bloom on bronze; that the colour is dependent on form rather than form on colour. 'He did not conceive his volumes in outline, geometrically,' writes Herbert Read, 'but in contrasted colours; and that is really the individual distinction of Cézanne: a sensibility to form expressed in colour. "To paint", he said, "was to register his colour sensations." Everything else—all values of atmosphere and perspective—is sacrificed to this end, sacrificed to the organization of his colour sensations. "When colour has its richness, form has its plenitude" is another of his more revealing aphorisms. This conception of form built up of colour, a colour synthesis, is perhaps a difficult one to realize, especially for people who are weak in colour sensibility; it is however the essential quality of Cézanne's art.'

It is difficult to say how highly the colour sense is developed in animals, but however this may be, it is certain that colour means little more to them than food or danger. Civilized man in his security does not need to worry about colour for these primitive biological reasons, and as there is no other urgent reason why he should, there must be millions of people who go through life scarcely aware of colour and certainly never looking at it. As an imaginative perception of volume is necessary for the full appreciation of natural forms, of architecture and sculpture, so the practice of looking at—not merely seeing—colour will be a new experience to many people unaware of the splendours in nature, and unable to see the beauty in great painting. It is a pity that we should through laziness and lack of exercise deny ourselves the pleasure to be derived from colour, and therefore from nature and visual art.

Colour is not peculiar to painting; for example, the Greeks and the medieval artists sometimes coloured their buildings and statues, though conventionally, and with little attempt at realism. 'Colour gives the eye a grip, so to speak, on shape, preventing its slipping off; we can look much longer at a coloured object than an uncoloured; and the colouring of architecture enables us to realize its details and its ensemble much more quickly and easily.'

And, in a sense, there is colour in music; the rich, warm tones of the 'cello could not be mistaken for the lighter and cooler colours of the violin and flute, while to many people a certain note or musical phrase will suggest a colour.

Words, too, are evocative of colours. Hard consonants and short, thin vowels suggest cold hues and light tones, whereas the softer consonants and long vowels suggest warm yellows, reds and ochres. (This, no doubt, is not accidental, for language is more onomatopoeic than is generally realized.) Shelley's shrill language is silvery and ice-green, the voice of the air and water, compared with the warm earth colours of Keats and Tennyson. Compare Shelley's *Skylark*—

> Hail to thee, blithe spirit!
>   Bird thou never wert,
> That from heaven, or near it,
>   Pourest thy full heart
> In profuse strains of unpremeditated art.
>
> Higher still and higher
>   From the earth thou springest
> Like a cloud of fire;
>   The blue deep thou wingest,
> And singing still dost soar, and soaring ever singest.

—with Keats's *Nightingale*:

> My heart aches, and a drowsy numbness pains
>   My sense, as though of hemlock I had drunk,
> Or emptied some dull opiate to the drains
>   One minute past, and Lethe-wards had sunk:
> 'Tis not through envy of thy happy lot,
>   But being too happy in thine happiness,—
>   That thou, light-winged Dryad of the trees,
>   In some melodious plot
> Of beechen green, and shadows numberless,
>   Singest of summer in full-throated ease.

The full appreciation of poetry—and prose—is dependent on a sensitiveness to colour sensations.

The eye can see only twenty odd per cent. of the colour waves that fly through space. We are totally colour-blind to the remainder. All waves that are longer than 36,000 to the inch (red), or shorter than 61,000 to the inch (violet), are invisible. There are waves longer than the red, called infra-red, unknown, and electric; and waves shorter than the violet, called ultra-violet, and Roentgen rays, which may be defined in musical analogy as covering three octaves, leaving about seven-eighths of an octave for the six colours which we can see. Our eyes are to the colour scale of nature as the child with its toy piano is to the master musician with a concert grand. Through the fluoroscope which retards the speed, the eye can see some of the ultra-violet rays; and the infra-red rays can be felt as heat.

E. A. AYERS.

If we were totally colour-blind we would see the landscape, flowers, people, and all other objects like a photograph in black and white, because colour-blind persons can see forms and light and dark perfectly well. Fortunately, it is very seldom that any one is totally colour-blind. Almost no-one is blind to yellow, blue, and violet. About one man in twenty, and one woman in two hundred are more or less blind to red or green, or both. . . .

Experiments show that when the object first comes within the field of vision, if we do not turn our eyes toward it, but continue looking straight ahead, we shall detect first its motion and something of its form as a mass of light and dark without colour. Then we shall see its colour, but the colour of a yellow or blue object can be detected at a wider angle than the colour of a red or a green object.

WALTER SARGENT: *The Enjoyment and Use of Color.*

It seems that in every country the words for the colours at the red end of the spectrum are of earlier appearance, more definite and more numerous than for those at the violet end. On the Niger it appears that there are only three colour words, red, white, and black, and everything that is not white or black is called red. . . . In this way as we pass from colours of long wave-length toward those of short wave-length we find the colour nomenclature becoming regularly less definite. . . .

Here again we may trace similar phenomena in Europe; the same greater primitiveness, precision and copiousness of colour vocabulary at the long wave-end of the spectrum has led to much controversy. Latin was especially rich in synonyms for red and yellow, very poor in synonyms for green and blue. The Latin tongue had even to borrow a word for blue from Teutonic speech. 'Caeruleus' originally meant dark. . . . Modern English bears witness that our ancestors, like the Homeric poets, resembled the Australian aborigines in identifying the colour of the short-wave end of the spectrum with entire absence of colour, for 'blue' and 'black' appear to be etymologically the same word.

HAVELOCK ELLIS: Psychology of Red.

Le Courrier du Livre reported the legibility of various combinations for reading at a considerable distance, the most legible print being black on a yellow background. The order of merit was found to be as follows:

1. Black on yellow.
2. Green on white.
3. Red on white.
4. Blue on white.
5. White on blue.
6. Black on white.
7. Yellow on black.
8. White on red.
9. White on green.
10. White on black.
11. Red on yellow.
12. Green on red.
13. Red on green.

It is noteworthy that in this list the customary black-on-white combination is sixth on the list. These results are interesting, although perhaps not final, owing to the many variables that enter such a problem.

M. LUCKIESH: Color and its Applications.

In the history of the world, colour has often been the sign by which nations accounting themselves the nobler have marked off their inferiors. The Sanskrit word for caste is 'varna', that is, 'colour', and this shows how their distinction of high and low caste arose.

E. B. TYLOR: Anthropology.

In nature there is neither colour nor line, only sun and shade. Give me a piece of charcoal and I will produce a beautiful picture.

GOYA.

When colour has its richness, form has its fullness.

CÉZANNE.

Cézanne gave to the forms of nature an exaggerated difference between every plane, or perhaps it would be clearer to say that

G

he multiplied those planes. At the same time in thus magnifying contour he made it more gradual, gave those planes an equality among themselves by employing marked changes of hue as well as of tone. On the other hand, by his use of strong contour lines at the farthest limit of his forms he enriched his colour relationships; since a coloured shape bounded by a darker line is stronger in colour than when it is seen without a boundary.

ADRIAN STOKES: *Colour and Form.*

At present I am busy with fruit trees in blossom: pinkish-red peach trees, whitish-yellow pear trees. I am not following any system in applying the colours. I lay them on the canvas with irregular strokes and then leave them as they are. Pasty places, one or two parts of the canvas uncovered, corners left quite unfinished, overpainting, roughness: in short the result—I have reason to believe—is disquieting and disturbing enough to cause no pleasure to people with fixed prejudices about technique. Anyway here is a sketch: the entrance to a Provençal orchard with its yellow fencing, its protecting row of black cypresses (against the Mistral), its characteristic vegetables in various shades of green, its yellow lettuce, onions and garlic and emerald-green leeks. As I always work right on the spot, I have tried to retain in the drawing what is essential. Then I fill in the surfaces bounded by the outlines—whether I succeed in expressing them or not, anyway I feel them—always in simplified tones, in such a way that everything belonging to the ground has the same violet kind of shade, that the sky has a bluish tinge, the foliage of the trees either blue-green or yellow-green, while in this case I have intentionally exaggerated the yellow or blue colour values.

VAN GOGH: *Letters.*

Partly because of its direct emotional effect upon us and partly because of its associations with various experiences, each colour has acquired a symbolism or mystic significance. Therefore its proper symbolic use in ancient art became an important matter. Usually each colour had a wide range of significance, and frequently for everything good which it symbolized it had a corresponding sinister meaning. . . .

Red, the most emotion-compelling colour, denotes ardent love, valour, energy, fire, and fervour. In its bad sense it typifies cruelty, wrath, and also sin, as in the expression, 'though your sins be as scarlet . . .'

In China, blue was attributed to the dead and red to the living.

WALTER SARGENT: *The Enjoyment and Use of Color.*

The rugged Pyrrhus, he whose sable arms,
Black as his purpose, did the night resemble
When he lay couched in the ominous horse,
Hath now this dread and black complexion smeared
With heraldry more dismal: head to foot
Now is he total gules; horridly tricked
With blood of fathers, mothers, daughters, sons,
Baked and impasted with the parching streets,
That lend a tyrannous and a damned light
To their lord's murder: roasted in wrath and fire,
And thus o'er-sized with coagulate gore,
With eyes like carbuncles, the hellish Pyrrhus
Old grandsire Priam seeks.

    O, beware, my lord, of jealousy;
It is the green-eyed monster, which doth mock
The meat it feeds on.

How all the other passions fleet to air,
As doubtful thoughts, and rash-embraced despair,
And shuddering fear, and green-eyed jealousy!

    Light thickens, and the crow
Makes wing to the rooky wood:
Good things of day begin to droop and drowse,
While night's black agents to their preys do rouse.

Go prick thy face and over-red thy fear,
Thou lily-livered boy. What soldiers, patch?
Death of thy soul! those linen cheeks of thine
Are counsellors to fear. What soldiers, whey-face?

    My way of life
Is fallen into the sear, the yellow leaf.

                   SHAKESPEARE

So, some tempestuous morn in early June,
    When the year's primal burst of bloom is o'er,
        Before the roses and the longest day—
    When garden-walks, and all the grassy floor,
        With blossoms, red and white, of fallen May,
            And chestnut-flowers are strewn—
So have I heard the cuckoo's parting cry,
    From the wet field, through the vext garden-trees,
    Come with the volleying rain and tossing breeze:
The bloom is gone, and with the bloom go I.

Too quick despairer, wherefore wilt thou go?
  Soon will the high Midsummer pomps come on,
    Soon will musk carnations break and swell,
  Soon shall we have gold-dusted snapdragon,
    Sweet-William with its homely cottage-smell,
      And stocks in fragant blow;
  Roses that down the alleys shine afar,
    And open, jasmine-muffled lattices,
    And groups under the dreaming garden-trees
And the full moon, and the white evening-star.
                MATTHEW ARNOLD: *Thyrsis.*

A casement high and triple-arched there was,
All garlanded with carven imageries
Of fruits, and flowers, and bunches of knot-grass,
And diamonded with panes of quaint device,
Innumerable of stains and splendid dyes,
As are the tiger-moth's deep-damasked wings;
And in the midst, 'mong thousand heraldries,
And twilight saints, and dim emblazonings,
A shielded scutcheon blushed with blood of queens and kings.

Full on this casement shone the wintry moon,
And threw warm gules on Madeline's fair breast,
As down she knelt for heaven's grace and boon;
Rose-bloom fell on her hands, together prest,
And on her silver cross soft amethyst,
And on her hair a glory like a saint:
She seemed a splendid angel, newly dressed,
Save wings, for heaven:—Porphyro grew faint:
She knelt, so pure a thing, so free from mortal taint.
                KEATS: *The Eve of St. Agnes.*

But the Quincunx of Heaven runs low, and 'tis time to close the five ports of knowledge; We are unwilling to spin out our awaking thoughts into the phantasms of sleep, which often continueth precogitations; making Cables of Cobwebs, and Wildernesses of handsome Groves. Besides, Hippocrates hath spoken so little, and the Oneirocritical Masters have left such frigid Interpretations from Plants, that there is little encouragement to dream of Paradise itself. Nor will the sweetest delight of Gardens afford much comfort in sleep; wherein the dullness of that sense shakes hands with delectable odours; and though in the bed of Cleopatra can hardly with any delight raise up the ghost of a rose.   SIR THOMAS BROWNE: *The Garden of Cyrus.*

For my own part, though I am always serious, I do not know what it is to be melancholy; and can therefore take a View of Nature in her deep and solemn Scenes, with the same Pleasure as in her most gay and delightful ones. By this means I can improve myself with those Objects, which others consider with Terror. When I look upon the Tombs of the Great, every Emotion of Envy dies in me; when I read the Epitaphs of the Beautiful, every inordinate Desire goes out; when I meet with the Grief of Parents upon a Tomb-stone, my Heart melts with Compassion; when I see the Tomb of the Parents themselves, I consider the Vanity of grieving for those whom we must quickly follow: When I see Kings lying by those who deposed them, when I consider rival Wits placed side by side, or the holy Men that divided the World with their Contests and Disputes, I reflect with Sorrow and Astonishment on the little Competitions, Factions, and Debates of Mankind. When I read the several Dates of the Tombs of some that died Yesterday, and some six hundred Years ago, I consider that great Day when we shall all of us be Contemporaries, and make our Appearance together.

ADDISON: *The Spectator.*

CHAPTER VIII

PAINTING

MUCH that has been said about sculpture applies equally to painting. But whereas the sculptor creates form in three dimensions, the painter is limited to two. It is true that the painter by various devices such as linear and aerial perspective can suggest the third dimension of depth, but his problem is fundamentally that of creating form on the two dimensions of his canvas or whatever material he is working on. This he does by the use of colour and line—black and white being considered as colours—so that a picture is a synthesis of a number of shapes whose content is the colour, and whose contours are determined by boundaries of varying degrees of definition. The design thus created may be representational, like the painting of a landscape or the portrait of a man, or it may be non-representational, like the pattern on a vase.

It has already been suggested that most people appreciate art for its mimetic qualities and for its literary content, that they like it to tell or anyway to suggest a story. However, if this were the true criterion by which to judge a work of art a bad novel would be superior to Tewkesbury Abbey, and a poor painting better than a Beethoven symphony. But it may be objected that different kinds of art should be admired for different reasons: that we do not read a poem for the same reason that we look at a building, and that they must be judged by different standards. This is true up to a point, but it is true beyond all question that Tewkesbury Abbey and a Beethoven symphony are great works of art not because of any literary content or mimetic quality, but because the appearance of the one and the sound of the other appeal directly to some obscure emotion in man, which for want of a better name we call the aesthetic. No work of art, whether building, sculpture, painting, poem, or music, is a work of art because it resembles something else or because it tells a story; it may do both, but in proportion as it sacrifices any of its essential quality to verisimilitude and story-telling the less its value as a work of art.

This essential quality has little or nothing to do with the thing said or described; it is the way in which the thing is expressed, its form: in architecture and sculpture the relation of planes and masses, in poetry the combination of words, in music the sequence of notes, in painting the disposition of shapes and colours. And this form or expression is independent of imitation and rational significance save as they serve as convenient vehicles for the transference of the experience.

Because painting can so easily represent material things it is natural to assume that the more accurate the representation the finer the picture. Copying is undoubtedly a pleasant occupation —as any child will tell us—and so is the recognition of a copy and the skill with which it is done; but after all there is nothing more clever in copying a landscape or a face than in forging a banknote or juggling with knives, and anyway a camera copies far more accurately. A good picture, it is true, may well be a good likeness, but so may a bad one. The point is that it is not a good picture *because* it is a good likeness.

Most pictures have a literary content. Thus European painting until late Renaissance times was concerned principally with the major incidents in the life of Christ: the Annunciation, the Nativity, the Last Supper, or the Crucifixion, and many people would maintain with Matthew Arnold that as 'all depends upon the subject' then, other things being equal, a picture of the Crucifixion is a greater work of art than a picture of a chair. The majority would probably agree as to the importance of the subject-matter, but they might disagree about its choice; Arnold demanded nobility, they might prefer excitement. So we get the problem picture, the illustration, and the anecdote in pictorial form, where the spectator's emotions are stirred by the events depicted. Thus the main emotion felt when looking at Turner's *Fighting Téméraire* is pity—probably self-pity—that the glory of the world passes. Or to take another example: the admirable illustrations of engines in children's books are thrilling, but our emotion is the result of our association of the picture with the emotion felt when we see a real engine hauling its load at sixty or seventy miles an hour.

It is of course an excellent thing that a picture should be enjoyed because of the story it tells, but it is not so good when the public and the patrons, mistaking anecdote and emotional display for art, force the artist to become raconteur and acrobat. The slope is slippery to the sentimental depths of the Victorian

Academician. Painting is not ultimately concerned with story-
telling any more than it is with copying; and the thrill derived
from situation is not the final pleasure to be derived from painting.
The artist cannot compete with the camera; the picture paper
and the cinema are more accurate and more thrilling—as the
public very well knows.

The poet may describe his emotions in words, or the musician
may suggest them in his music, but it is not so easy, nor would
it be desirable, for an architect to suggest an emotion such as
dejection or terror in his work. The painter may, however,
convey his emotions in a number of ways. He may paint a self-
portrait depicting his terror—not a very satisfactory solution—or
he may paint a dramatic scene which arouses a mild feeling of
terror in the spectator; or he may, like Watts, resort to allegory
and symbolism; or without restraint portray in a surrealist
picture the dream imagery associated with his state of mind.
But again, a work of art is something more than the transference
of a common emotion from the artist to the spectator or listener
through the medium of paint, words, or music; it is more than
the stimulation of our latent everyday emotions. The emotion
felt on hearing the second movement of Beethoven's Seventh
Symphony is no ordinary experience, nor are the words,

> We are such stuff
> As dreams are made on, and our little life
> Is rounded with a sleep,

merely the transference of the ordinary emotion of sadness. That
there may be this emotional transference, and in poetry almost
certainly will be, nobody will deny, but art would be a poor
thing if it meant nothing more than this. Music, poetry, painting,
and all great art are beyond the frontiers of everyday experience,
and the true aesthetic emotion once felt cannot be mistaken for
gratified curiosity or the pleasure derived from a story.

All great art has this immediate appeal to the aesthetic sense
by virtue of its significant expression, and though this appeal may
be accompanied by other emotional and intellectual elements
it distinguishes a work of art from all the other creations of man.

A painting is most powerfully moving when the combination
of shapes and colours imposes another and higher significance
on the primary meaning, which primary meaning is important
merely as the medium conveying the new significance. Thus
the literal meaning of a landscape or still-life is quickly grasped,

THE PARTHENON (450 B.C.)

CÉZANNE.   THE CARD-PLAYERS

Facing page 104]

PIERO DELLA FRANCESCA.   VIRGIN AND CHILD

" A WOMAN—

CÉZANNE. MONT SAINTE-VICTOIRE

Photograph by Anderson

DONATELLO. GATTAMELATA

—A MOUNTAIN—A HORSE " (*see page* 86)

BOTTICELLI.   THE   BIRTH   OF   VENUS

CONSTABLE.   SALISBURY   CATHEDRAL

and this recognition gives a feeling of pleasure; but the picture is a work of art only if the combination of shape and colour, that is its form, evokes an emotion independent of that produced by mere representation.

This combination of shape and colour is what Clive Bell calls 'significant form'; the quality that distinguishes a work of visual art; meaning much the same thing as A. E. Housman when he says that poetry, the element in verse that appeals directly to the aesthetic sense, 'is not the thing said, but a way of saying it'. Whether we call this quality 'significant form', 'the way of saying it', or 'expression' does not matter so long as we realize that the essential element in any work of art is its significance apart from any subsidiary meaning derived from representation. At the one extreme architecture, the most concrete of the arts, must be judged by its appearance; at the other extreme music, the most abstract of the arts, must be judged by its sound; representation is obviously irrelevant; their value as works of art depends on the significance of the expression. Because sculpture and painting lend themselves to representation it is more difficult to appreciate them for their purely formal qualities, and poetry has the additional difficulty that its raw material, words, has inevitably an intellectual content; but again it is the expression rather than the matter expressed that makes it aesthetically moving.

Architecture and sculpture derive much of their formal significance from the third dimension of depth; painting is limited to two dimensions, but because the artist can create the illusion of depth a picture acquires an added significance when it is seen not as a flat pattern, but as a series of related planes. The full appreciation of a picture therefore depends on the capacity to feel the emotional significance of three-dimensional form.

It may reasonably be objected that the acknowledged masterpieces of painting are representational, and that if abstract form were the essential quality in art, great painting would be abstract rather than representational. There are several answers to this. The arts of architecture, music, and ceramics are abstract, and much great graphic art is in fact abstract: the design on Oriental carpets, on pottery and textiles, for instance. And the paintings of the greatest periods are more abstract than the trivial productions of decadent ages, in the sense that they are obviously less concerned with representation than with form. We have only to compare the work of Giotto with that of, say, Landseer to see the truth of this. The architect and potter have a definite problem to solve, for their forms are limited by function, and it is possible that the painter too must have a definite problem: that of expressing his experience in terms of the visible world. Or again, it may be that painting is partly dependent on a harmonic or contrapuntal relationship between its form and some original, much as two melodies are harmonized in contrapuntal music, or as rhythm is a distortion of, or a variation on, a perfect sequence in space or time. Finally, there is a real and legitimate enjoyment in the associations aroused by representation, and in the stimulus of emotional transference, and as very few people are powerfully moved by pure form, abstract art would tend to become precious and esoteric. If the painter, like the poet, is to transfer an aesthetic experience, he can best do so through an intelligible medium, even though he runs the risk of being misunderstood.

This is an exceedingly complex and controversial subject; but it does seem certain that although representation may add to the enjoyment of looking at a picture, it is inadequate, however noble the subject may be, to account for the final ecstasy of great painting. It is the perfect combination of shape and colour, the form, the expression, the way of saying it rather than the thing said that distinguishes great painting from the second-rate.

The history of painting is that of a series of steep ascents followed by gradual declines. The peaks are those periods when artists, inspired by new ideals, subordinate representation to the creation of form; the decline is the age during which the inspiration works itself out, when artists elaborate the mannerisms of their great predecessors, and to make up for their lack of creative power rely more and more on representation; the trough before the next ascent is the logical conclusion of the decline where painting is nothing but dexterous copying and trivial anecdote. Very often the painters of the peak are rebels against the academicians of the preceding trough and the accepted artistic standards of society; but the painters of the decline by a process of compromise reconcile society with the new art, so that they become subject to the pressure of patrons who demand art as a visible sign of their social prestige. This will probably accelerate the pace of the decline towards a polished and insignificant realism, though the steepness of the descent will depend partly on the aesthetic sensibility of the patrons. Partly, however, it will depend on the artist's use of newly acquired knowledge which increases his power of accurate representation.

Thus a knowledge of anatomy, of linear and aerial perspective, the scientific study of colour, and the invention of the photograph are all powerful weapons in the hands of the painter, which if rightly used may lead to the creation of yet finer formal effects; if abused hastens the descent into a descriptive naturalism.

It must be understood that the following outline is a very broad generalization, and therefore only an approximately true account of the major rhythms in the history of painting, and that there are innumerable exceptions and minor oscillations within the series.

The great formal art of primitive and classical Greece degenerated into the uninspired copies of Greek masterpieces demanded by the more cultivated Romans, or into the brutal realism and vulgar sentiment required by the prosperous citizens of Imperial Rome.

Art, however, was rescued from such trivialities by a new movement that sprang from the eastern Mediterranean. There classical culture still lingered, but vitalized by its contact with the East a new art arose that was to become the basis of the European tradition. Though limited in subject-matter, and deriving their significance from simple forms with little suggestion of depth, the sixth-century Byzantine mosaics at Ravenna and Constantinople are some of man's finest 'monuments of his own magnificence'. In spite of the minor decline in the eighth century during the Iconoclast movement Byzantine art remained vigorous until the twelfth century.

In north-western Europe, where art was largely conditioned by the demands of architecture, the magnificent formal sculpture and stained glass of the Romanesque period declined in the fourteenth century into extravagance and sentiment, in the fifteenth century into the realism demanded by the rising middle classes.

In Italy the Byzantine tradition of flowing contours and superbly spaced two-dimensional form was carried on by Duccio at Siena. But at the same time—the early fourteenth century —there was a new development in Florence, where Cimabue and Giotto conceived form as something plastic, and contrived in their drawing to suggest the bulk and volume of solid things. This representation of depth must not be confused with naturalism, the mere imitation of solid objects. Abstract form in three dimensions, which is a series of related planes, is emotionally more significant than a flat design, so that this new conception of form was of immense importance. It became the characteristic of the Florentine school.

A century later this architectural form was still further developed by Brunelleschi who discovered the laws of perspective, and by Masaccio who gave to painting the structural unity that Donatello gave to sculpture. Piero della Francesca continued the work of the Florentine school, and then at the end of the fifteenth century Leonardo da Vinci applied to painting the knowledge he had gained from the scientific investigation of anatomy and colour, while Raphael achieved the perfect spatial harmony of three-dimensional form. At the same time Michelangelo exploited the possibilities of sculptural form in pictorial art, and to violent foreshortening and rhetorical gesture added the sweeping rhythm of Baroque design.

Art could go no further along these lines, and the succesors of the High Renaissance either emphasized the sentimentality latent in Raphael's work, or like Caravaggio made melodrama out of the dramatic art of Michelangelo.

The Venetian artists, however, were concentrating on another aspect of painting. Whereas the Florentines were interested in colour primarily as a function of three-dimensional form, and in nature as a background and pedestal for their figures, the Venetians loved colour for its own sake and saw in natural objects a beauty equal to that of the human figure. Giovanni Bellini and Giorgione created new colour harmonies and anticipated some of the work of the later landscape painters, while Titian contributed to Baroque art not only his exuberant colour but also the unifying element of one pervading colour.

In the seventeenth century Rubens took back with him from Italy this Baroque conception of painting and overwhelmed the native Flemish tradition of realism and pernickety detail with the robust luxuriance of his style.

At the same time the Dutch discovered new possibilities in painting. Their art reflected the contented and prosperous lives of the middle classes, who demanded highly finished pictures that would satisfy civic and national pride as well as their own vanity. The Florentines had a strong sculptural sense of form; their vision was modified by their sense of touch so that they felt imaginatively the substance and the boundaries of solid objects, and their figures have the clarity and definition of very high altitudes. But the Dutch saw more literally; they saw that solid form is softened by the surrounding atmosphere, and that objects instead of being isolated are united by the common element of air. By adding as it were a third dimension to the atmosphere Dutch painters like Vermeer—and in Spain, Velasquez—extended enormously the boundaries of art. The greatest of the Dutch painters, Rembrandt, is a lonely figure, for he refused to sacrifice to the popular demand his dramatic conception of painting and his power to see both physical and spiritual beauty in the superficially ugly.

In France the great painters of the seventeenth century are Poussin and Claude; in the eighteenth century, Chardin and Watteau; and nineteenth-century French painting is one of the most important in the history of art. But it was an English painter, Constable, who inspired the new movement. He refused to accept the conventional colours of the landscape painters of his day, and when he painted he tried to forget that he had ever seen a picture in his life. Like the Dutch he looked at nature without prejudice, studied the effects of atmosphere and light, and saw that shadows were not merely different tones of brown. His work inspired the French Impressionists who, influenced by the discovery of the photograph, set out to capture the fleeting effect of the snapshot. They saw the enormous importance of light in modifying form and local colour and, as Monet said, light became the principal subject in their pictures. Because sunlight can be split up into a number of colours they set their palettes with pigments approximating to the colours of the spectrum, and to make their painting more brilliant laid strokes of pure colour side by side so that they mixed, as it were, in the spectator's eye rather than on the canvas, and they carried this scintillating colour into the shadows, which they saw were really as full of colour as illuminated objects. This type of painting in which solid form is broken down by the disintegrating effect of light is as far as possible from the sculptural conception of the Florentines, and led inevitably to a weakening of formal design. Impressionism, like lyric poetry, is the record of a moment, of a fleeting effect of light that may never occur again; the Florentine style of painting resembles the massiveness of epic poetry, a memorial of what is permanent in the world.

Impressionism is a form of Realism; the representation of an everyday scene as the camera might have caught it, though of course this superficially careless snapshot effect may be more apparent than real. But the fact remains that the Impressionist

tried to give the illusion of reality: Manet by the careful gradua-
tion of his tones as in a photograph; Monet, Pissarro, Sisley, and
Renoir—in his earlier works—by reproducing the effects of light
and atmosphere.

Towards the end of the nineteenth century, however, there was
a revolt against Realism and therefore against Impressionism;
architecture was proclaimed the Mother of the Arts, and painting
once again, in the hands of Seurat, Gauguin and Cézanne,
turned towards the formal design of classical art. At the same
time van Gogh, the Dutchman intoxicated by the sun, freed
colour from all restraint and inspired the Fauve Movement led
by Matisse, Vlaminck, and Derain, which carried still further
the reaction against representation.

At the beginning of the twentieth century non-representational
painting developed along two lines: the rhythmical design of
Matisse influenced by Eastern art, and the Cubism of Picasso
which derived from the emphatic planes and monumental forms
of Cézanne.

The Futurists with their insistence on the power of the machine,
and the Dadaists who believed in 'the negation of all systems,
the destruction of all recognized values', are more interesting
politically than aesthetically. The Romantic combination of
the possible with the impossible in Chagall's paintings, and the
'disquieting stillness' of Chirico's art are more important as the
forerunners of the Surrealism of the twenties.

Surrealism, as its name suggests, is only another form of
Realism; a return to Realism by another path, that of the
dream-world, so that a Surrealist picture is the imitation of the
imagery of the unconscious mind. In the words of André Breton
it is 'psychic automatism. Dictation by thought without any
control by reason or any aesthetic or moral preoccupation'.
The Surrealist is fascinated by the fantastic, by 'the chance
meeting on a dissecting table of a sewing machine and an
umbrella'; at its worst Surrealism is the tediously academic
imitation of the disturbing, often horrible, imagery of nightmare,
neurosis and madness; a perverted Romanticism, or at any rate
Romanticism uncontrolled.

But painting has at the same time continued its development
in the opposite direction, by way of Picasso's Cubism towards
the classical ideals of simplicity and order, the rejection of the
accidental and ephemeral, and a concentration on what is
essential and permanent. The functional architecture of Le

Corbusier with its purposeful design and contempt for the merely
decorative is another aspect of this movement.

To-day, therefore, the layman is puzzled and often outraged
by the contradiction of the unbridled Romanticism of Surrealism,
and the perilously logical and pedantic Classicism of Functional-
Purism. Once again the province of painting, and of all art,
seems to lie between these extremes.

Let us take, first, the plastic arts, sculpture and painting; and
to bring into clear relief the Greek point of view let us contrast
with it that of the modern 'impressionist'. To the impressionist
a picture is simply an arrangement of colour and line; the
subject represented is nothing, the treatment everything. It
would be better, on the whole, not even to know what objects are
depicted; and, to judge the picture by a comparison with the
objects, or to consider what is the worth of the objects in themselves, or what we might think of them if we came across them
in the connections of ordinary life, is simply to misconceive the
whole meaning of a picture. For the artist and for the man who
understands art, all scales and standards disappear except that
of the purely aesthetic beauty which consists in harmony of line
and tone; the most perfect human form has no more value than
a splash of mud; or rather both mud and human form disappear
as irrelevant, and all that is left for judgement is the arrangement
of colour and form originally suggested by those accidental and
indifferent phenomena.

In the Greek view, on the other hand, though we certainly
cannot say that the subject was everything and the treatment
nothing (for that would be merely the annihilation of art) yet we
may assert that, granted the treatment, granted that the work
was beautiful (the first and indispensable requirement), its worth
was determined by the character of the subject. Sculpture and
painting, in fact, to the Greeks, were not merely a medium of
aesthetic pleasure; they were ways of expressing and inter-
preting national life. As such they were subordinated to religion.
The primary end of sculpture was to make statues of the gods
and heroes; the primary end of painting was to represent
mythological scenes; and in either case the purely aesthetic
pleasure was also a means to a religious experience.

G. LOWES DICKINSON: *The Greek View of Life.*

Well, is it your wish that we should pursue our usual course in
the outset of our investigation? We have, I believe, been in the
habit of assuming the existence, in each instance, of some one

Form, which includes the numerous particular things to which we apply the same name. Do you understand, or not?

I do understand.

Then let us, on the present occasion, take any one of those numerous things that suits your pleasure. For example, if this instance suits you, there are, of course, many beds and many tables.

Certainly.

But of Forms in connexion with these articles, there are, I believe, only two, one the Form of a bed, and one that of a table.

Yes.

Have we not also been accustomed to say that the manufacturer of each of these articles is looking at the Form while he is constructing the beds or the tables which we employ, or whatever it may be? For, of course, no manufacturer constructs the Form itself; because that is impossible.

Certainly it is.

But pray consider how you will describe the following workman.

To whom do you allude?

I allude to the workman who constructs all the articles which come within the province of the whole class of artisans.

You are talking of a marvellously clever man.

Wait a little, and you will have better reasons for saying so. Besides being able to construct all manufactured articles, the same artisan produces everything that grows out of the ground, and creates all living things, himself among others; and, in addition to this, heaven and earth and the gods and all the heavenly bodies and all the beings of the nether world are his workmanship.

What an extraordinarily ingenious person you are describing!

You are incredulous, are you? Then tell me;—Do you think that the existence of such an architect is a complete impossibility? or do you believe that in one way there could, and in another way there could not, be a manufacturer of such a variety of things? Do you not perceive that, in a kind of way, even you yourself could construct this multiplicity of objects?

Pray what is this way? he asked.

Far from being difficult, I replied; it is a rapid method, and admits of many variations. Perhaps the most rapid way of all would be to take a mirror, and turn it round in every direction. You will not be long in making the sun and the heavenly bodies, nor in making the earth, nor in making yourself, and every other living creature, and all inanimate objects, and plants, and everything that we mentioned just now.

Yes, we can produce so many appearances, but assuredly not truly existing things.

Right; and your observation is just to the point. Now, in my opinion, the painter also belongs to this class of architects. Does he not?

Certainly he does.

But I suppose you will say that all his creations are unreal. And yet the painter too, in a kind of way, constructs a bed. Or am I wrong?

Yes, the painter too constructs a bed in appearance.

But what of the manufacturer of beds? Did you not certainly say a minute ago, that he did not construct the Form, which, according to our doctrine, constitutes the reality of a bed,—but only a particular bed?

Yes, I did say so.

Consequently, if he does not construct what really exists, must we not say that he does not construct a real thing, but only something like the reality, but still unreal? And if anyone were to describe the work of the bed-wright, or of any other artisan, as perfectly real, his account of the matter would be, in all probability, untrue, would it not?

Yes, in the opinion of those who are versed in such discussions as these.

Then let us not be at all surprised at finding that things as substantial as a bed are shadowy objects when contrasted with reality.

True.

Should you like us to employ these illustrations in our inquiry into the real nature of an imitator?

If you please, he replied.

Well, here we have three sorts of beds; of which one exists in the nature of things; and this we shall attribute, if I am not mistaken, to the workmanship of God. If not, to whom can we attribute it?

We can only attribute it to Him, I think.

The second is made by the upholsterer.

Yes.

And the third is the production of the painter, is it not?

Be it so.

Thus we have three kinds of beds, and three superintendents of their manufacture,—the painter, the upholsterer, God.

Yes, three.

Now whether it was that God did not choose to make more than one bed, or that by a species of necessity He was precluded from making more than one in the universe, He has at any rate made only one, which is the absolute essential Bed. But two, or more than two, such beds have not been created by God, and never will be.

H

How so?

Because, if God had made only two, a single bed would again have made its appearance, whose Form would enter into the other two in their turn; and *this* would be the absolute essential Bed, and not the two.

You are right.

Knowing this, I should suppose, and wishing to be the real maker of the really existing bed, and not a certain indefinite manufacturer of a certain indefinite bed, God created a single such Bed.

It seems so.

Then are you in favour of our addressing Him as the Creator, for example, of this object?

Yes, he replied, it is but just to do so, seeing that by creation He has made both this, and everything else.

And what of the upholsterer? Must we not style him the artificer of a bed?

Yes.

May we go on to call the painter, the artificer and maker of this same article?

Certainly not.

Then, by your account, what is he with reference to a bed?

In my opinion he might most justly be styled the imitator of that of which the other two are artificers.

Well, then, do you call the author of that which is twice removed from the thing as it was created, an imitator?

Yes, exactly so.

Hence, since the tragedian is an imitator, we may predicate of him likewise, that he, along with all the other imitators, is the third in descent from the sovereign and from truth.

So it would appear.

Then we are unanimous as to the nature of the imitator. But answer me one question about the painter. Do you suppose that a painter attempts to imitate the originally created object, or the productions of the artificer?

The latter, he replied.

As they really exist, or as they appear? Define this further.

What do you mean?

I mean this: when you look at a bed sideways, or in front, or from any other position whatever, does it alter its identity at all, or does it continue really the same, though it appears changed? And so of everything else?

The latter is the true account: it appears different, but is not really changed.

Now this is the point which I wish you to consider. To which of the two is painting, in every instance, directed? Does it study to imitate the real nature of real objects, or the apparent nature of appearances? In other words, is it an imitation of a phantasm, or of truth?

Of the former, he replied.

The imitative art, then, is, I conceive, completely divorced from truth; and, apparently, it is enabled to effect so much, because it only seizes upon an object in a small part of its extent, and that small part is unsubstantial. For example, we say the painter will paint us a shoemaker, a carpenter, or any other craftsman, without knowing anything about their trades; and, notwithstanding this ignorance on his part, let him be but a good painter, and if he paints a carpenter and displays his picture at a distance, he will deceive children and silly people by making them think that it really is a carpenter.

No doubt he will.

Be that as it may, I will tell you, my friend, how I think we ought to feel in such cases. Whenever a person tells us that he has fallen in with a man who is acquainted with all the crafts, and who sums up in his own person all the knowledge possessed by other people singly, to a degree of accuracy which no one can surpass,—we must reply to our informant, that he is a silly fellow, and has, apparently, fallen in with a juggler and mimic, whom he has been deceived into thinking omniscient, because he was himself incapable of discriminating between science, and ignorance, and imitation.

That is most true.

PLATO: *The Republic*. (Trans. J. L. DAVIES and D. J. VAUGHAN.)

The painter will produce pictures of little merit if he takes the works of others as his standard; but if he will apply himself to learn from the objects of nature he will produce good results. This we see was the case with the painters who came after the time of the Romans, for they continually imitated each other, and from age to age their art steadily declined.

After these came Giotto the Florentine, and he,—reared in mountain solitudes, inhabited only by goats and such like beasts —turning straight from nature to his art, began to draw on the rocks the movements of the goats which he was tending, and so began to draw the figures of all the animals which were to be found in the country, in such a way that after much study he not only surpassed the masters of his own time but all those of many preceding centuries. After him art again declined, because all were imitating paintings already done; and so for centuries it continued to decline until such time as Tommaso the Florentine, nicknamed Masaccio, showed by the perfection of his work how those who took as their standard anything other than nature, the supreme guide of all the masters, were wearying themselves in vain.

LEONARDO DA VINCI: *The Notebooks*. (Trans. E. MCCURDY.)

Now, here's the point. It was perfectly clear donkeys' years ago that graphic Art (capital A), hit by the mechanical age, needed-a new idea. Heaven knows, it hasn't had one since somebody 2,000 years ago thought 'of painting pictures to frame and hang on the wall as a change from carpets. All the cubes, abstracts and surrealist ironmongery haven't really saved the situation. It was clear also that as the machinery for representing movement improved some intelligent lad would drop to it that the means were present for opening a new and exciting vista of possible Art (capital A). At present your conventional Artist who wishes to represent the beauty and character of a woman or a landscape discovers the emotional elements of shape and colour in the subject, and, following principles of selection and emphasis, puts them down in a clarified form. But the woman moves with charm, the trees bend in the breeze. There are emotional elements in the movements to be discovered, selected, emphasized and represented in heightened form, also. Why not?

In *Fantasia* Disney lifts the art of drawing movement right out of the 'comic' and essays for the first time serious studies on the higher plane. Walpurgis Night and the prehistoric sequences drive right to the foothills of the New Art of the Future.

Your stick-in-the-muds will scoff, no doubt. But I know what Leonardo would be up to if he were alive to-day. He would be in the back room inventing simplifications of animating processes and projection devices.

DAVID LOW: from a letter to *The New Statesman*.

Painting is the most beautiful of all arts. In it, all sensations are condensed, at its aspect everyone may create romance at the will of his imagination, and at a glance have his soul invaded by the most profound memories, no efforts of memory, everything summed up in one moment. Complete art which sums up all the others and completes them. Like music, it acts on the soul through the intermediary of the senses, the harmonious tones corresponding to the harmonies of sounds, but in painting, a unity is obtained which is not possible in music, where the accords follow one another, and the judgement experiences a continuous fatigue if it wants to reunite the end and the beginning. In the main, the ear is an inferior sense to the eye. The hearing can only grasp a single sound at one time, whereas the sight takes in everything and at the same time simplifies at its will.

Like literature, the art of painting tells whatever it wants, with the advantage of letting the reader immediately know the prelude, the direction, and the *dénouement*. Literature and music ask for an effort of memory to appreciate the whole. This last art is the most incomplete and the least powerful.

You may dream freely when you listen to music as well as when you look at painting. When you read a book you are the slave of the author's mind.

Sight alone produces an instantaneous impulse.

PAUL GAUGUIN: Notes on Painting.

When I sit down to make a sketch from nature, the first thing I try to do is, to forget that I have ever seen a picture.

CONSTABLE.

No man of Sense ever supposes that copying from Nature is the Art of Painting; if Art is no more than this, it is no better than any other Manual Labour; anybody may do it, and the fool often will do it best as it is a work of no mind.

WILLIAM BLAKE.

I have not tried to reproduce Nature: I have represented it.

CÉZANNE.

The ballet-girl is merely a pretext for the design.

DEGAS.

We must never forget that accurate representation of what the grocer thinks he sees was the central dogma of Victorian art. . . .

For either all works of visual art have some common quality, or when we speak of 'works of art' we gibber. Everyone speaks of 'art', making a mental classification by which he distinguishes the class 'works of art' from all other classes. What is the justification of this classification? What is the quality common and peculiar to all members of this class? Whatever it be, no doubt it is often found in company with other qualities; but they are adventitious—it is essential. There must be some quality without which a work of art cannot exist; possessing which, in the least degree, no work is altogether worthless. What is this quality? What quality is shared by all objects that provoke our aesthetic emotions? What quality is common to Sta. Sophia and the windows at Chartres, Mexican sculpture, a Persian bowl, Chinese carpets, Giotto's frescoes at Padua, and the masterpieces of Poussin, Piero della Francesca, and Cézanne? Only one answer seems possible—significant form. In each, lines and colours combined in a particular way, certain forms and relations of forms, stir our aesthetic emotions. These relations and combinations of lines and colours, these aesthetically moving forms, I call 'Significant Form'; and 'Significant Form' is the one quality common to all works of visual art.

CLIVE BELL : Art.

What I think has resulted from Mr. Clive Bell's book, and the discussions it has aroused on this point, is that the artist is free to choose any degree of representational accuracy which suits the expression of his feeling. That no single fact, or set of facts, about nature can be held to be obligatory for artistic form. Also one might add as an empirical observation that the greatest art seems to concern itself most with the universal aspects of natural form, to be the least preoccupied with particulars. The greatest artists appear to be most sensitive to those qualities of natural objects which are the least obvious in ordinary life precisely because, being common to all visible objects, they do not serve as marks of distinction and recognition.

ROGER FRY : Vision and Design.

Nature contains the elements, in colour and form, of all pictures, as the keyboard contains the notes of all music.

But the artist is born to pick, and choose, and group with science, these elements, that the result may be beautiful—as the musician gathers his notes, and forms his chords, until he brings forth from chaos glorious harmony.

To say to the painter, that Nature is to be taken as she is, is to say to the player, that he may sit on the piano.

J. M. WHISTLER : The Gentle Art of Making Enemies.

CHAPTER IX

MUSIC

OF all the arts, music is the most powerful emotional stimulant. There can be few people who are moved more by a great painting than by a dance or military band, or by a symphony orchestra, although the picture is, at least superficially, more definite in its statement. It is this power of evoking emotions, right or wrong, social or anti-social, that compelled Plato to regulate music in his ideal Republic. 'The introduction of a new kind of music', he says, 'must be shunned as imperilling the whole state; since styles of music are never disturbed without affecting the most important political institutions. The new style gradually gaining a lodgment, quietly insinuates itself into manners and customs; and from these it issues in greater force, and makes its way into mutual compacts; and from compacts it goes on to attack laws and constitutions, displaying the utmost impudence, until it ends by overturning everything, both in public and in private.'

On the whole people admire a work of art for its literary or its mimetic qualities; we like a story, a doll, or a model railway, and therefore a novel, narrative verse, or a pictorial anecdote. But music is limited both in its literary appeal and representational effects. 'It is the province of painting to describe,' says Beethoven. 'Poetry, too, can esteem itself happy in that respect, in comparison with music. On the other hand, mine spreads further into other regions, and it is not so easy to attain my empire.'

Music cannot have the same literary content as prose or verse, its reference to the intellect being limited because it cannot make a literal statement of fact. The composer cannot say in his music: 'My father had a small estate in Nottinghamshire: I was the third of five sons. He sent me to Emmanuel College in Cambridge at fourteen years old, where I resided three years, and applied myself close to my studies.' But by various devices the composer can insinuate a literary element into his work. Thus modern European music until the seventeenth century was mainly vocal, so that the words illustrated the meaning of the music; and as music was an essential part of much Greek dramatic poetry Plato could write, 'When there are no words it is difficult to recognize the intention of harmony or rhythm, or to see that any good object is imitated by them.'

Again 'programme' music is descriptive instrumental music; either more or less crudely onomatopoeic, as in the imitation of sounds such as guns, bells, birds,* or machinery; or more subtly as in Macdowell's *Sea Piece*, describing the voyage of the *Mayflower*, or Liszt's interpretation of Lamartine's poetry in *Les Préludes*. Liszt, who developed the principle of programme music, defines a literary 'programme' as 'any foreword in intelligible language added to a piece of pure instrumental music, by which the composer intends to guard the hearer against an arbitrary poetic interpretation, and to direct his attention in advance to the poetical idea of the whole, or to a particular part of it.'

But despite these devices the main appeal of music is directly to the emotions, not indirectly by way of the intellect. 'Music began as the simple exponent of joy and sorrow. The uneducated can scarcely believe that it has the power of expressing particular passions. We have learned to express the finer shades of feeling by penetrating more deeply into the mysteries of harmony.' Music, in short, is a means of expressing the whole compass of our feelings and emotions, from the most ignoble passion to the highest spiritual exaltation.

Not only this, but its expression is purer—that is, unmixed with elements not strictly relevant—than that of any other art. In literature, for instance, an emotion must be expressed in phrases that have an intellectual significance, however slight; and the words themselves are pregnant with associations, so that the original emotion of the author is modified both by the intellectual content and the emotional significance attached by the reader to various words. Thus Shakespeare's lyric—

> Fear no more the heat o' the sun,
> Nor the furious winter's rages;
> Thou thy worldly task hast done,
> Home art gone, and ta'en thy wages:
> Golden lads and girls all must
> As chimney sweepers come to dust.

* Plutarch tells a story of someone who, being asked to go and hear a man who exactly counterfeited the voice of a nightingale, replied: 'Sir, I have heard the nightingale itself.'

—although the thought is commonplace enough, does make definite statements of fact; while such words as 'heat', 'sun', 'winter', 'home', 'wages', 'golden', 'lads', 'girls', 'chimney sweepers', 'dust' have an accumulation of associations for the reader independent of the context. But the composer expresses the same emotion without any rational statement, and because notes lack the emotional overtones of words, without the intrusion of other feelings which are the result of associations attached to the expression.

The visual arts, too, in so far as they are representational are fraught with innumerable associations, and may evoke feelings that have nothing to do with the emotion that the artist is trying to express. For example, any painting of the Crucifixion will almost certainly evoke sensations connected with the life of Christ, or with religious experience; even a still-life has associations attached to the subject-matter, however humble. The painter or sculptor can dispense with these distractions by creating abstract form; but the author can only avoid them by writing gibberish, for as soon as he uses normal words associations begin to creep in.

It is not suggested that the proper concern of the painter is with abstractions, or of the poet with gibberish, or that painting and poetry are inferior to music; but it should be clear that music is a more direct, and therefore purer expression of emotion than representational painting or literature. The only pure form in art, that is expression free from functional, representational, or intellectual content, is abstract visual art, and music; the one is pure appearance, the other pure sound without counterpart in the external world of nature.

But the effect, even of these abstract arts, on the spectator or listener is not merely that of the transference of an everyday emotion such as love, joy, fear, or sorrow; aesthetically these emotions may be as unimportant as function, representation, and rational thought. The final and overwhelming effect of great art is concerned with none of these things; it is the result of the impact of the expression—of the way in which the thing is expressed, not of the thing expressed, whether thought, emotion, or tangible object—on the sensitive eye or ear. It is true that there would be no building without function, no literature without intellectual content, little painting without representation, and little music without ordinary emotional appeal, so that form is ultimately dependent on these elements as mediums for the transference of the artist's experience; but it is the form and not the other things that makes a work of art. What does the scene depicted matter in Giotto's *Bewailing of St. Francis*? What is the relevance of the thought in,

> Bring me my bow of burning gold,
> Bring me my arrows of desire?

And what is the third movement of Beethoven's Archduke Trio all about, and what emotion exactly is involved? These may be extreme examples to take, and other elements besides pure form may contribute to the pleasure derived from a work of art; but there can be no great art without great form, 'the expression of the logically inexpressible'.

This is what Walter Pater means when he writes, 'All art constantly aspires towards the condition of music. For while in all other kinds of art it is possible to distinguish the matter from the form, and the understanding can always make this distinction, yet it is the constant effort of art to obliterate it. That the mere matter of a poem, for instance, its subject, namely, its given incidents or situation—that the mere matter of a picture, the actual circumstances of an event, the actual topography of a landscape—should be nothing without the form, the spirit, of the handling, that this form, this mode of handling, should become an end in itself, should penetrate every part of the matter : this is what all art constantly strives after, and achieves in different degrees.' *

Music is essentially a sequence of musical tones, that is, of tones caused by the regular vibrations of some object such as the string of a lute. But the earliest approximation to music must have been the production of mere noise, or irregular vibrations, by the rhythmical beating of some primitive form of drum. A sense of rhythm seems to be latent in all living things, and judging by the effect of tom-toms, drums, military and jazz bands it would seem to be the most emotionally stimulating element in music. The sense of tone was probably acquired slowly by man, and savages to-day are musically still in the rhythmic stage, while in the East music has developed on rhythmic rather than tonal lines. The combination of rhythm, a sequence of noises, with tone implies melody, which is a series of tones or notes so arranged that the combination is emotionally significant. Thus

---

* *The Renaissance.*

the separate notes of the *Londonderry Air* are meaningless, but the melody as a whole is profoundly moving.

We know little about the music of the pre-Christian era, and Greek music like Greek tragedy was lost with the fall of the Roman Empire, so that music and drama had to be evolved again by the early Christian Church. But whereas classical literature was rediscovered at the time of the Renaissance, we still cannot tell how Greek music sounded. Unlike any other art, therefore, with the possible exception of painting, our music is uninfluenced by classical models. We know that the Greeks had certain musical instruments such as the kithara (guitar), the smaller lyre and the aulos, that their music was dramatic because it was an integral part of their tragedies, that they had a system of musical notation, and a number of modes or scales such as the Dorian, Phrygian, and the Lydian. Almost certainly they had developed a system of harmony, though this was probably simple, and confined to the simultaneous sounding of two notes, one vocal and the other an instrumental accompanient. The Greeks had all the essentials of modern music, but their art has perished.

Music was developed again, together with the drama, as part of the service of the early Christian Church. In the sixth century Pope Gregory the Great made a collection of the hymns sung in the churches, and this early music is called the Gregorian Chant, or plain-song; that is, melody sung in unison, but without any definite time-value attached to the notes. By the eleventh century, however, tunes were written in the metrical form to which we are now accustomed. Up till this date no system of exact musical notation had been invented, so that music could not be preserved in writing, but had to be remembered and passed on from generation to generation; but about this time a method was discovered, and by the fifteenth century the essentials of modern notation had been developed. The invention of the staff made it possible to indicate the exact pitch of a note, while symbols represented the time-value of notes and rests such as semi-breves, minims and crotchets; finally by the device of the bar line a sequence of notes could be divided into groups having the same time-value.

It is curious how slowly the sense of harmony has developed. In the seventh century the only concord was unison, either absolute unison when the same note was sung or played by two or more people, or octave unison when the tones were separated by the interval of an octave. By the fourteenth century the simultaneous sounding of the first and fifth notes of a scale was admitted as harmony, and since then more complex harmonies have been evolved.

Until the seventeenth century most music was written to be sung, either unaccompanied, or accompanied by simple instruments like the lute; and until Renaissance times, apart from folk-songs, nearly all music was religious. But in the fourteenth century some secular music was composed, and the two following centuries were the great age of madrigals, or part-songs, written generally for five to eight voices, but sometimes for as many as twelve; the age of Palestrina and William Byrd, when music was part of the life of the whole people, and all educated persons were expected to be able to sing.

During this period the art of counterpoint was evolved from harmony. Harmony is the concord produced when certain notes are struck at the same time, so forming a vertical arrangement of tones, but it will be continuous and horizontal if there is a sequence of notes in harmony. This continuous harmony may have only one melody, the harmonic support being given by other notes, which in themselves do not form a melody; but if two or more melodies of equal interest are interwoven, making the effect of the whole harmonious, there is counterpoint. 'It is no use hearing a madrigal *vertically*, one must learn to hear it *horizontally*, i.e. as counterpoint, a simultaneous confluence of independent melodies and rhythms. Only so can we begin to appreciate the beauty of this wonderful music, so intricate and subtle in texture, and yet so direct in utterance.'

But by the end of the sixteenth century this polyphonic contrapuntal music had become so ornate that there was a revolt against it, and a movement towards simpler forms, such as the recitative, an imitation of the rhythm and inflexion of dramatic speech, based on that assumed to have been practised by the Greeks. The seventeenth century, therefore, is the age of the oratorio, the masque, and the opera, the age of Monteverde and Purcell; unfortunately it is also the age when Puritanism emasculated English musical drama. Purcell died in 1695, and with him perished England's contribution to the music of Europe until the musical renaissance of the twentieth century.

Up till this time instruments had been subordinated to the voice, and little purely instrumental music had been written. But at the beginning of the eighteenth century, composers such as Domenico Scarlatti, J. S. Bach, and Handel began to write instrumental music. This was an epoch-making development, and ever since then European music has been instrumental rather than vocal.

The movement also implied the rapid evolution of musical instruments. It was in the eighteenth century, for instance, that the psaltery, the strings of which were plucked by a plectrum, became the harpsichord; while the pianoforte was evolved from the dulcimer, played by striking the strings with small hammers. The favourite Elizabethan instruments, the lute and viol, were finally superseded in the eighteenth century by the violin. The strings of the lute were plucked with the fingers, but the viol and its descendant, the violin, had the enormous advantage that, by means of the bow, a note could be prolonged indefinitely on their strings. Perhaps the most famous of all violin makers was Antonio Stradivari, who died in 1737.

The wood-wind instruments are descendants of the reed-pipe, the aulos of the Greeks. The flute, oboe, and clarinet were evolved during the Middle Ages, and by the end of the eighteenth century these instruments and the bassoon were all used in the orchestra. (According to Samuel Butler the oboe is a clarinet with a cold in its head, and the bassoon a clarinet with a cold in its chest.)

Of the brass instruments, the horn and the trumpet, both of ancient lineage, were used in the eighteenth-century orchestra, the trombone and tuba being later additions.

Finally the primitive drum was developed, and though it still remains primarily a rhythmical instrument, the adoption of soft-headed drum-sticks improved the sound, while it became possible to design a drum producing a definite tone; and later, by a device for tightening and slackening the skins, to vary the tone. In an orchestra there are generally two kettle-drums, tuned to the tonic and dominant notes of the scale, though these tones can be varied by altering the tension of the skin.

The composers of instrumental music in the first half of the eighteenth century belonged mainly to the later contrapuntal school, of which J. S. Bach and Handel were the last great representatives. In his fugues Bach brought to a climax the art of polyphonic instrumental music, but in the hands of lesser men instrumental polyphony became as elaborate and mechanical as the vocal polyphony of the late madrigal writers, so that we find his son, Philipp Emanuel Bach, leading a revolt against these 'dry and despicable pieces of pedantry', and composing a new type of instrumental music, which was fully developed by Haydn and Mozart into the sonata form.

In a fugue one simple theme is twisted and woven about itself in the formal and logical manner of counterpoint; but a sonata —music to be played, as opposed to a cantata, or music to be sung—is a sequence of two or more themes, or movements, whose treatment is harmonic rather than contrapuntal. The fugue is obviously a much more limited means of expression than the flexible sonata form, the combinations of which are infinite, and its evolution made possible the wonderful instrumental music of the late eighteenth and early nineteenth centuries, one of the greatest periods of man's creative activity.

Later musical forms are mostly derived from the sonata and, though it is impossible to classify exactly, it is approximately true to say that music composed in sonata form for one or for two instruments is called a sonata, and most instrumental trios, quartets, and quintets are simply sonatas for three, four, and five instruments respectively. The concerto is a sonata for one chief instrument with orchestra, and a symphony is a sonata written for a full orchestra.

The hour brought forth the man; Beethoven was the heir to this new musical form, which he further developed, and brought to such perfection that in his hands music became a language expressing the whole range of human emotions; an empire spreading further and further into other regions.

Is it not strange that sheep's guts should hale souls out of men's bodies?

SHAKESPEARE: *Much Ado About Nothing.*

In the evening our gentleman-farmer, and the two others, entertained themselves and the company with a great number of tunes on the fiddle. Johnson desired to have 'Let ambition fire thy mind' played over again, and appeared to give a patient attention to it; though he owned to me that he was very insensible to the power of music. I told him that it affected me to such a degree, as often to agitate my nerves painfully, producing in my mind alternate sensations of pathetic dejection, so that I was ready to shed tears; and of daring resolution, so that I was inclined to rush into the thickest part of the battle. 'Sir,' said he, 'I should never hear it, if it made me such a fool.'

BOSWELL: *Life of Johnson.*

It will generally be admitted that Beethoven's Fifth Symphony is the most sublime noise that has ever penetrated into the ear of man. All sorts and conditions are satisfied by it. Whether you are like Mrs. Munt, and tap surreptitiously when the tunes come —of course, not so as to disturb the others—or like Helen, who can see heroes and shipwrecks in the music's flood; or like Margaret, who can only see the music; or like Tibby, who is profoundly versed in counterpoint, and holds the full score open on his knee; or like their cousin, Fräulein Mosebach, who remembers all the time that Beethoven is 'echt Deutsch'; or like Fräulein Mosebach's young man, who can remember nothing but Fräulein Mosebach: in any case, the passion of your life becomes more vivid, and you are bound to admit that such a noise is cheap at two shillings. It is cheap, even if you hear it in the Queen's Hall, dreariest music-room in London, though not as dreary as the Free Trade Hall, Manchester; and even if you sit on the extreme left of the hall, so that the brass bumps at you before the rest of the orchestra arrives, it is still cheap.

'Who is Margaret talking to?' said Mrs. Munt, at the conclusion of the first movement. She was again in London on a visit to Wickham Place.

Helen looked down the long line of their party, and said that she did not know.

'Would it be some young man or other whom she takes an interest in?'

'I expect so,' Helen replied. Music enwrapped her, and she could not enter into the distinction that divides young men whom one takes an interest in from young men whom one knows.

'You girls are so wonderful in always having—— Oh dear! one mustn't talk.'

For the Andante had begun—very beautiful, but bearing a family likeness to all the other beautiful Andantes that Beethoven had written, and, to Helen's mind, rather disconnecting the heroes and shipwrecks of the first movement from the heroes and goblins of the third. She heard the tune through once, and then her attention wandered, and she gazed at the audience, or the organ, or the architecture. Much did she censure the attenuated Cupids who encircle the ceiling of the Queen's Hall, inclining each to each with vapid gesture, and clad in sallow pantaloons, on which the October sunlight struck. 'How awful to marry a man like those Cupids,' thought Helen. Here Beethoven started decorating his tune, so she heard him through once more, and then she smiled at her cousin Frieda. But Frieda, listening to Classical Music, could not respond. Herr Liesecke, too, looked as if wild horses could not make him inattentive; there were lines across his forehead, his lips were parted, his pince-nez at

right-angles to his nose, and he had laid a thick, white hand on
either knee. And next to her was Aunt Juley, so British, and
wanting to tap. How interesting that row of people was! What
diverse influences had gone to the making! Here Beethoven,
after humming and hawing with great sweetness, said 'Heigho',
and the Andante came to an end. Applause, and a round of
'wunderschöning' and 'pract' volleying from the German con-
tingent. Margaret started talking to her new young man;
Helen said to her aunt: 'Now comes the wonderful movement:
first of all the goblins, and then a trio of elephants dancing';
and Tibby implored the company generally to look out for the
transitional passage on the drum.

'On the what, dear?'

'On the *drum*, Aunt Juley.'

'No; look out for the part where you think you have done
with the goblins and they come back,' breathed Helen, as the
music started with a goblin walking quietly over the universe,
from end to end. Others followed him. They were not aggressive creatures; it was that that made them so terrible to Helen.
They merely observed in passing that there was no such thing
as splendour or heroism in the world. After the interlude of
elephants dancing, they returned and made the observation for
the second time. Helen could not contradict them, for, once at
all events, she had felt the same, and had seen the reliable walls
of youth collapse. Panic and emptiness! Panic and emptiness!
The goblins were right.

Her brother raised his finger: it was the transitional passage
on the drum.

For, as if things were going too far, Beethoven took hold of the
goblins and made them do what he wanted. He appeared in
person. He gave them a little push, and they began to walk in
major key instead of in a minor, and then—he blew with his
mouth and they were scattered! Gusts of splendour, gods and
demi-gods contending with vast swords, colour and fragrance
broadcast on the field of battle, magnificent victory, magnificent
death! Oh, it all burst before the girl, and she even stretched
out her gloved hands as if it were tangible. Any fate was titanic;
any contest desirable; conqueror and conquered would alike be
applauded by the angels of the utmost stars.

And the goblins—they had not really been there at all? They
were only the phantoms of cowardice and unbelief? One healthy
impulse would dispel them? Men like the Wilcoxes, or President
Roosevelt, would say yes. Beethoven knew better. The goblins
really had been there. They might return—and they did. It
was as if the splendour of life might boil over and waste to steam
and froth. In its dissolution one heard the terrible, ominous

note, and a goblin, with increased malignity, walked quietly over the universe from end to end. Panic and emptiness! Panic and emptiness! Even the flaming ramparts of the world might fall.

Beethoven chose to make all right in the end. He built the ramparts up. He blew with his mouth for the second time, and again the goblins were scattered. He brought back the gusts of splendour, the heroism, the youth, the magnificence of life and of death, and, amid vast roarings of a superhuman joy, he led his Fifth Symphony to its conclusion. But the goblins were there. They could return. He said so bravely, and that is why one can trust Beethoven when he says other things.

E. M. FORSTER: Howards End.

Beethoven's Ninth Symphony is considered a great work of art. To verify its claim to be such, I must first ask myself whether this work transmits the highest religious feeling? I reply in the negative, for music in itself cannot transmit those feelings; and I therefore ask myself next, Since this work does not belong to the highest kind of religious art, has it the other characteristic of the good art of our time,—the quality of uniting all men in one common feeling: does it rank as Christian universal art? And again I have no option but to reply in the negative; for not only do I not see how the feelings transmitted by this work could unite people not specially trained to submit themselves to its complex hypnotism, but I am unable to imagine to myself a crowd of normal people who could understand anything of this long, confused, and artificial production, except short snatches which are lost in a sea of what is incomprehensible. And therefore, whether I like it or not, I am compelled to conclude that this work belongs to the rank of bad art.

TOLSTOY: What is Art? (Trans. AYLMER MAUDE.)

That poetry has a bearing on conduct we can indeed understand, though we do not make poetry the centre of our system of education; but that moral effects should be attributed to music and to dancing, and that these should be regarded as of such importance as to influence profoundly the whole constitution of a state, will appear to the majority of modern men an unintelligible paradox.

Yet no opinion of the Greeks is more profoundly characteristic than this of their whole way of regarding life, and none would better repay a careful study. That moral character should be attributed to the influence of music is only one and perhaps the most striking illustration of that general identification by the

I

Greeks of the ethical and the aesthetic standards on which we have so frequently had occasion to insist. Virtue, in their conception, was not a hard conformity to a law felt as alien to the natural character; it was the free expression of a beautiful and harmonious soul. And this very metaphor 'harmonious', which they so constantly employ, involves the idea of a close connection between music and morals. Character, in the Greek view, is a certain proportion of the various elements of the soul, and the right character is the right proportion. But the relation in which these elements stand to one another could be directly affected, it was found, by means of music; not only could the different emotions be excited or assuaged in various degrees, but the whole relation of the emotional to the rational element could be regulated and controlled by the appropriate melody and measure. That this connection between music and morals really does exist is recognized, in a rough and general way, by most people who have any musical sense. There are rhythms and tunes, for example, that are felt to be vulgar and base, and others that are felt to be ennobling; some music, Wagner's, for instance, is frequently called immoral; Gounod is described as enervating, Beethoven as bracing, and the like; and however absurd such comments may often appear to be in detail, underlying them is the undoubtedly well-grounded sense that various kinds of music have various ethical qualities. But it is just this side of music, which has been neglected in modern times, that was the one on which the Greeks laid most stress. Infinitely inferior to the moderns in the mechanical resources of the art, they had made, it appears, a far finer and closer analysis of its relation to emotional states; with the result that even in music, which we describe as the purest of the arts, congratulating ourselves on its absolute dissociation from all definite intellectual conceptions,—even here the standard of the Greeks was as much ethical as aesthetic, and the style of music was distinguished and its value appraised, not only by the pleasure to be derived from it, but also by the effect it tended to produce on character.

G. LOWES DICKINSON : *The Greek View of Life.*

But we said, you know, that in the case of words we did not require dirges and complaints.

No, we do not.

Which then are the plaintive harmonies? tell me, for you are musical.

Mixed Lydian and Hyperlydian, and such as are like these.

These then must be discarded: for they are useless even to women that are to be virtuously given, not to say to men.

Quite so.

And you will grant that drunkenness, effeminacy, and idleness are most unbecoming things in guardians.

Undoubtedly they are.

Which of the harmonies then are effeminate and convivial?

The Ionian and the Lydian, which are called 'lax'.

Will you employ these then, my friend, in the training of men of war?

By no means: and if I mistake not, you have only the Dorian and the Phrygian left you.

I do not know the harmonies myself, I said; only see you leave me that particular harmony which will suitably represent the tones and accents of a brave man engaged in a feat of arms, or in any violent operation, who, if he fails of success or encounters wounds and death, or falls into any other calamity, in all such contingencies with unflinching endurance parries the blows of fortune; leave me also another harmony, expressive of the feelings of one who is engaged in an occupation not violent, but peaceful and unconstrained; —it may be, using persuasion and entreaty, addressing either a prayer to a god, or instruction and advice to a man; or, on the other hand, lending himself to the prayers or advice or persuasion of another, and after this succeeding to his wish; and not behaving arrogantly, but acting in all these circumstances with soberness and moderation, and in the same spirit acquiescing in every result. Leave me these two harmonies, the one violent, the other tranquil, such as shall best imitate the tones of men in adversity and in prosperity, in a temperate and a courageous mood.

Well, said he, you are recommending me to leave precisely those which I just mentioned.

Then we shall not require for our songs and instrumental accompaniments a variety of strings, or an instrument embracing all harmonies.

I believe not.

Then we shall not maintain the makers of harps or dulcimers, or any instrument that has many strings and serves for many harmonies.

Apparently not.

But will you admit into your city flute-makers and flute-players? or am I right in saying that the flute has more strings than any other instrument, and that the panharmonium itself is only an imitation of the flute?

Manifestly you are right.

Then you have the lyre and the guitar remaining, which will be of service in the town; while in the country the herdsmen will have some kind of pipe.

So at least the argument indicates to us.

Surely we are guilty of no innovation, my friend, in preferring Apollo and Apollo's instruments to Marsyas and *his* instruments.

No, I really think we are not.

Well, I protest, said I, we have been unconsciously purging the city, which we said just now was in too luxurious a condition.

PLATO: *The Republic.* (Trans. J. L. DAVIES and D. J. VAUGHAN.)

An ear for music is a very different thing from a taste for music. I have no ear whatever; I could not sing an air to save my life; but I have the intensest delight in music, and I can detect good from bad. . . .

The best sort of music is what it should be—sacred; the next best, the military, has fallen to the lot of the Devil.

COLERIDGE: *Table Talk.*

I even think that *sentimentally* I am disposed to harmony. But *organically* I am incapable of a tune. I have been practising 'God Save the King' all my life; whistling and humming of it over to myself in solitary corners; and am not yet arrived, they tell me, within many quavers of it. Yet hath the loyalty of Elia never been impeached.

LAMB: *A Chapter on Ears.*

Music and the sounds of instruments, says the lively Vigneul de Marville, contribute to the health of the body and the mind; they quicken the circulation of the blood, and dissipate vapours, and open the vessels, so that the action of perspiration is freer. He tells a story of a person of distinction, who assured him, that once being suddenly seized by violent illness, instead of a consultation of physicians, he immediately called a band of musicians; and the violins played so well in his inside, that his bowels became perfectly in tune, and in a few hours were harmoniously becalmed.

ISAAC D'ISRAELI: *Curiosities of Literature.*

Music resembles poetry: in each
Are nameless graces which no methods teach,
And which a master-hand alone can reach.
If, where the rules not far enough extend,
(Since rules were made but to promote their end)
Some lucky license answer to the full
The intent proposed, that license is a rule;
Thus Pegasus, a nearer way to take,
May boldly deviate from the common track;

Great wits sometimes may gloriously offend,
And rise to faults true critics dare not mend;
From vulgar bounds with brave disorder part,
And snatch a grace beyond the reach of art,
Which, without passing through the judgment, gains
The heart, and all its end at once attains.

POPE: Essay on Criticism.

Music to hear, why hear'st thou music sadly?
Sweets with sweets war not, joy delights in joy:
Why lov'st thou that which thou receiv'st not gladly,
Or else receiv'st with pleasure thine annoy?
If the true concord of well tuned sounds,
By unions married do offend thy ear,
They do but sweetly chide thee, who confounds
In singleness the parts that thou should'st bear:
Mark how one string, 'sweet husband to another,
Strikes each in each by mutual ordering;
Resembling sire and child and happy mother,
Who, all in one, one pleasing note do sing:
  Whose speechless song, being many, seeming one,
  Sings this to thee: 'Thou single wilt prove none.'

SHAKESPEARE.

And ever against eating Cares,
Lap me in soft Lydian Aires,
Married to immortal verse
Such as the meeting soul may pierce
In notes, with many a winding bout
Of linkèd sweetness long drawn out,
With wanton heed, and giddy cunning,
The melting voice through mazes running;
Untwisting all the chains that tie
The hidden soul of harmony.
That Orpheus self may heave his head
From golden slumber on a bed
Of heaped Elysian flowers, and hear
Such strains as would have won the ear
Of Pluto, to have quite set free
His half regained Eurydice.   MILTON: L'Allegro.

A Song for St. Cecilia's Day

From harmony, from heavenly harmony
    This universal frame began:
  When nature underneath a heap
    Of jarring atoms lay,

And could not heave her head,
The tuneful voice was heard from high,
  'Arise, ye more than dead!'
Then cold, and hot, and moist, and dry,
In order to their stations leap,
  And Music's power obey.
From harmony, from heavenly harmony
  This universal frame began:
  From harmony to harmony
Through all the compass of the notes it ran,
The diapason closing full in man.

What passion cannot music raise and quell?
  When Jubal struck the chorded shell,
  His listening brethren stood around,
  And, wondering, on their faces fell
  To worship that celestial sound.
Less than a God they thought there could not dwell
  Within the hollow of that shell,
  That spoke so sweetly and so well.
What passion cannot music raise and quell?

  The trumpet's loud clangour
    Excites us to arms,
  With shrill notes of anger,
    And mortal alarms.
  The double double double beat
    Of the thundering drum
Cries, hark! the foes come;
Charge, charge! 'tis too late to retreat.

  The soft complaining flute
  In dying notes discovers
  The woes of hopeless lovers,
Whose dirge is whispered by the warbling lute.

  Sharp violins proclaim
  Their jealous pangs, and desperation,
  Fury, frantic indignation,
  Depth of pains, and height of passion,
    For the fair, disdainful dame.

  But oh! what art can teach,
    What human voice can reach,
  The sacred organ's praise?
  Notes inspiring holy love,
  Notes that wing their heavenly ways
    To mend the choirs above.

Orpheus could lead the savage race;
And trees uprooted left their place,
    Sequacious of the lyre:
But bright Cecilia raised the wonder higher:
When to her organ vocal breath was given,
An angel heard, and straight appear'd,
    Mistaking earth for heaven.

As from the power of sacred lays
    The spheres began to move,
And sung the great Creator's praise
    To all the bless'd above;
So when the last and dreadful hour
This crumbling pageant shall devour,
The trumpet shall be heard on high,
The dead shall live, the living die,
And music shall untune the sky.

                        JOHN DRYDEN.

CHAPTER X
WORDS

THE same stone may add to the horror of a slum, to the inanity of a suburb, or to the beauty of a cathedral; and the same word may be used miraculously by Shakespeare, or squandered by any bungler in language. And as England is rich in the variety of her building-stones, so no country is richer in words. Though the basic element of English is Saxon most powerfully reinforced by words of Latin origin, yet the ancient civilizations, the near and far East, as well as western Europe have all paid tribute, so that the English language is a complex of Saxon, Celtic, Latin, Greek, Arabic and Indian, French, German and Dutch. The result is an enormous wealth of synonyms and near-synonyms capable of expressing the finest shades of meaning.

Consider the passage:

But the *iniquity* of *oblivion* blindly scattereth her poppy, and deals with the *memory* of men without *distinction* to *merit* of *perpetuity*.

The words in italics are Latin in origin—it is significant that they are all abstract nouns—the rest are Saxon.* The important words in the first clause are *iniquity, oblivion, blindly, scattereth, poppy*: two Latin abstract nouns, a Saxon adverb, verb, and concrete noun. The following are some of the synonyms for these words given in Roget's *Thesaurus*:

Iniquity:—wrong, injustice, unfairness, partiality, partisanship, vice, evil, wickedness, peccability, immorality, impropriety, obliquity, infamy, depravity, brutality, corruption, knavery, profligacy, atrocity, infirmity, fault, criminality, etc.

Oblivion:—non-existence, nullity, nihility, blankness, nothingness, annihilation, extinction, forgetfulness, obliteration.

Blindly:—ignorantly, unconsciously, darkly, uncomprehendingly, unwittingly.

* It is a fair generalization that pronouns, prepositions, and conjunctions are Saxon, while nouns, verbs, adjectives, and adverbs may be of Saxon, Latin, or other origin. Saxon nouns are generally short and concrete. Latin nouns often long and abstract.

Scattereth :—disperse, sow, disseminate, diffuse, shed, spread, bestrew, distribute, apportion, cast, sprinkle.

Poppy :—opiate, anodyne, opium, laudanum, mandragora, narcotic.

Sir Thomas Browne had an almost infinite number of word combinations at his disposal, yet he chose precisely this one.

The function of words is primarily to express a definite and literal meaning, much as the first function of brick and stone is to make a building that serves a useful purpose. At the same time the writer, whether engaged in exposition or persuasion, will, or should, try to make his prose—and the architect his building— as attractive as possible within the limits set by his problem. But beyond this prosaic function, words have in common with the raw material of the other arts another purpose to perform; to express, not so much by their denotation, or even by their connotation, as by the manner in which they are combined, an emotion experienced by the author and to transfer it to the reader so that a sequence of words assumes another and a higher significance than that of the literal meaning. Like notes in music they have in themselves, independent of their meaning, the power to express the logically inexpressible.

But unlike notes, which are meaningless without their context, words even in isolation may have a powerful emotional effect, though this is not to be confused with their significance in sequence. This is the result largely of association, for words inevitably accumulate a host of ancillary implications, often illogical and remote, an accumulation peculiar to every human being. Nouns, particularly concrete nouns, verbs, adjectives, and adverbs are most susceptible to these accretions, while particles and most pronouns have by themselves little power of suggestion. *Which*, *but*, and *to*, for instance, are emotionally neutral words, though the personal pronoun *I* is infinite in its implications, and some prepositions such as *beyond* are more than neutral. But it is very different when we come to concrete nouns. Consider the feelings and objects associated with these words chosen at random, all short and all Saxon :—*mother, night, sun, rose, ship.* It is impossible to think dispassionately of these words. Many abstract nouns also have vivid associations, such as *cunning, speed, hope, freedom* — again all Saxon; but other abstractions like *equivalence, reciprocity, concept* can normally be isolated and considered with detachment.

Verbs descriptive of sensuous activities are likely to have the most associations, while those connected with mental processes will probably have the fewest. Thus for most people there is more emotional content in *see, shatter, freeze, paint* than in *think, vacillate, assume*. On the whole adjectives being attached to nouns have more associations than adverbs, which modify not only verbs but also adjectives and other adverbs, while adverbs of number and degree involve a rational rather than an emotional process. To take extreme examples: *red, rough, cold* are powerfully attractive of associations, whereas *then, twice, very* have few or none. Adjectives and adverbs, like verbs, will generally have the most associations when their meanings are sensuous.

Because words have this power of attracting within their influence objects and emotions, not only logically but irrationally and from great distances, there is little writing the clear literal outline of which is not blurred by the emotional atmosphere surrounding the words. It is true that we can read stuff like this without emotion—save irritation or laughter at its fantastic pedantry—

'Dichotomized divisions of cosmological phenomena and corresponding speech',

but the simple words 'There is no road through the woods' are heavy with emotional associations. The meaning of a purely scientific statement, such as 'two and two make four', is no doubt the same for all who know the twice-times table, but even scientific statements must introduce words with an emotional charge, as 'a shilling is worth twelve pennies'. It may also be noted in passing that words combined to make a statement that is not objectively true set up in the minds of readers emotional stresses which vary with the fanaticism of their acceptance or with the vehemence of their rejection. That a shilling is worth twelve pennies is not even mildly provocative, but substitute Reds or Tories for shillings or pennies and scientific detachment is at an end.

Bad and inexperienced writers often cover their ineptitude or lack of matter by exploiting the recognized association value of words, relying for their effect on purple passages with a fine excess of emotional overtones and undertones. But such words and their associations are often stale and exhausted through overwork, so that they are too feeble to stir any deep emotion or even to attract much attention.

This exploitation of emotional associations is a characteristic

of Romantic art. Thus Keats writes, 'Darkling I listen', 'She
took me to her elfin grot', 'Faery lands forlorn', and the young
Tennyson:

> Where Claribel low-lieth
> The breezes pause and die,
> Letting the rose-leaves fall:
> But the solemn oak-tree sigheth,
> Thick-leaved, ambrosial,
> With an ancient melody
> Of an inward agony,
> Where Claribel low-lieth.

Some of the finest passages in literature, Shakespeare's
'insubstantial pageant faded', for example, as well as some of the
worst, owe much to these mysterious associations. The difficulty
is to preserve the freshness of such words or to restore them when
exhausted; after a Romantic period the good artist probably
avoids them, so that his writing may appear hard and flat in
comparison, like that of Dryden in the seventeenth century or
W. H. Auden to-day.

In music it would be precious to insist that one note considered
by itself is more beautiful than another, that C is better than B;
but some words are undoubtedly lovelier than others. Here
again, however, it is difficult to say how far the beauty or ugliness
is inherent in the word or derived from associations. 'Slug' is
an unpleasant word, and most people would admit that 'sun' is
pleasant; but to what extent is this due to the objects they
symbolize, rather than to a dispassionate appreciation of their
sound? We all have moments when we are at a loss how to
spell a familiar word, and the more we look at it the more remote
does it become; it is possible that we then see the word in its
nakedness, stripped of all its associations, and very odd it may
appear. It is easier to assess the music of words with little or
no emotional significance; thus *inspissation* is ugly, and *comparatively* is clumsy, but *only* is good, and *foremost* not unattractive.
Perhaps the foreigner ignorant of the language is the best judge
of the musical content of words. There is a story of an Italian
who knew no English, and ignorant therefore of the associations
attached to the word 'mother' considered it ugly, and the most
beautiful word he knew in the language to be 'cellar-door'.

One cause, perhaps, of the associations attached to words, and
of their musical properties, inherent or acquired, is their onomatopoeic quality. Far more words are onomatopoeic, that is by

their sound suggestive of the thing described, than is generally realized. Much onomatopoeia is a crude but none the less effective imitation of a sound, as in *crash, clatter, squelch, cuckoo, roar*; it may be less obviously suggestive as in *ripple, wobble, glitter, clumsy, monotony*; or it may be subtle like the ungainly *awkward*, and *angular*, the warm-toned *gold* and *ochre*, the cold *icy, frigid, freeze, silver* (*cold* itself is a failure; the German *kalt* and French *froid* are better); the swelling *pomp, pride, bombast, balloon, bud, burst, beauty*, or the gong-like resonance of *bronze*. Though it is dangerous to generalize, short vowels, sibilants, and gutturals suggest cold or harsh qualities; long vowels and liquids are warm and gentle, while the labials *p* and *b* suggest turgidity. And it is roughly true that the warmer the climate the softer the speech; perhaps the difference between the Yorkshire-man's and the Londoner's pronunciation of *a* has a climatic origin.

Onomatopoeia is the natural property of many words, but it should be remembered that the search for and discovery of onomatopoeic word combinations is a relatively simple affair, and by no means always a touchstone of fine writing, any more than alliteration and assonance, which may easily be overworked. Thus 'The mellow ousel fluted in the elm' is successful—Tennyson thought it his finest line—but

> The black-cap warbles, and the turtle purrs,
> The starling claps his tiny castanets,

is more questionable. It is significant that little of our best poetry is dependent on onomatopoeia.

It is clear that even before words are combined into the complex of phrases and sentences they are so impregnated with emotional qualities modifying their literal meanings that their significance can rarely be the same for more than one person. In combination the process is infinitely more intricate, and the speaker or writer by skilfully selecting his words can express far more than will be revealed by any logical analysis of their content. This is the reason of course why it is so difficult to translate any but the most emotionally colourless language.

The writer's choice will be affected, therefore, not only by the denotation and connotation of the words themselves, but also by their music and rhythm, and by their alliterative, assonantal, and onomatopoeic qualities, both in isolation and as a sequence of extreme complexity. Consider again the passage from 'Urn Burial':

'But the *iniquity* of *oblivion blindly scattereth* her *poppy*, and deals with the *memory* of *men* without distinction to *merit* of *perpetuity*.'

The literal meaning is simple enough: 'Men are not remembered according to their deserts.' We have already seen the enormous number of words that Sir Thomas Browne might have chosen instead of five of these. Why did he choose these words, and why did he combine them in this order? Possibly he did not think overmuch either about choice or order, though on the whole his style seems to be the result of deliberation. But whether consciously or unconsciously these words in this sequence best expressed his ideas.

The most important words are printed in italics. Of these *blindly*, *scattereth*, *poppy*, *men* are Saxon and so brilliantly allusive that their denotation disintegrates in the multiplicity of their associations. The rest are Latin abstract nouns, more sober yet sonorous, and still of immense emotional significance: *iniquity*, *oblivion*, *memory*, *merit*, *perpetuity*.

When combined into the sequence of the sentence the words assume a further significance: the alliteration and assonance of *memory*, *men*, *merit* imposes on the primary unity of sense a secondary one of sound; *oblivion* and *blindly* is a noble combination; the proud alliteration of *poppy* is completed in the final *perpetuity*, and the whole passage is integrated by the subtle assonance, the echoes and half-echoes of the vowels *o*, *u*, *i*, *e*. There is little trace of onomatopoeia, except for the astonishing impact of *scattereth*, which, in the middle of the sentence, bursts like the seed-pod of the poppy itself.

The order of the words is straightforward and unaffected, a contrast to the extreme complexity of the music; but emphasis is added by the antithesis *oblivion—perpetuity*; by repetition—the second half of the sentence merely repeats in other words the meaning of the first; and by the imposition of the vivid visual image of the metaphor with its attendant personification—*oblivion blindly scattereth her poppy*.

Finally there is the flawless rhythm in perfect harmony with the sense and with the music of the words, so that the whole passage is contrapuntal, the perfect combination of three themes; of meaning, rhythm, and music in the common element of words.*

Yet this is not all; so far the passage is merely a commonplace

---

* Great verse, that is poetry, adds a fourth theme to this counterpoint in words: the secondary or natural rhythm of the phrase mounted on the primary or conventional rhythm of the metre.

idea superbly phrased in language with rare overtones of meaning
derived from the emotional content of the words, singly and in
combination; but the consummation of great prose such as this,
of great verse and of all great art is when all the elements are
caught up, combined and transfigured in a single new significance
which cannot be expressed in words but can only be experienced.

The thing said is the nucleus of this expression, but it is the
way of saying it that is the poetry, the element common to all
great art.

'When *I* use a word', Humpty Dumpty said in rather a scorn-
ful tone, 'it means just what I choose it to mean—neither more
nor less.'

'The question is', said Alice, 'whether you can make words
mean different things.'

'The question is', said Humpty Dumpty, 'which is to be
master—that's all.' . . .

'You seem very clever at explaining words, Sir,' said Alice.
'Would you kindly tell me the meaning of the poem "Jabber-
wocky"?'

'Let's hear it,' said Humpty Dumpty. 'I can explain all the
poems that ever were invented—and a good many that haven't
been invented just yet.'

This sounded very hopeful, so Alice repeated the first verse:

> ''Twas brillig, and the slithy toves
> Did gyre and gimble in the wabe:
> All mimsy were the borogoves,
> And the mome raths outgrabe.'

'That's enough to begin with', Humpty Dumpty interrupted:
'there are plenty of hard words there. "*Brillig*" means four
o'clock in the afternoon—the time when you begin *broiling*
things for dinner.'

'That'll do very well', said Alice: 'and "slithy"?'

'Well, "*slithy*" means "lithe and slimy". "Lithe" is the
same as "active". You see it's like a portmanteau—there are
two meanings packed up into one word.'

'I see it now', Alice remarked thoughtfully: 'and what are
"*toves*"?'

'Well, "*toves*" are something like badgers—they're something
like lizards—and they're something like corkscrews.'

'They must be very curious creatures.'

'They are that', said Humpty Dumpty: 'also they make their
nests under sun-dials—also they live on cheese.'

'And what's to "*gyre*" and to "*gimble*"?'

'To "*gyre*" is to go round and round like a gyroscope. To "*gimble*" is to make holes like a gimlet.'

'And "*the wabe*" is the grass-plot round a sun-dial, I suppose?' said Alice, surprised at her own ingenuity.

'Of course it is. It's called "*wabe*", you know, because it goes a long way before it, and a long way behind it——'

'And a long way beyond it on each side,' Alice added.

'Exactly so. Well then, "*mimsy*" is "flimsy and miserable" (there's another portmanteau for you). And a "*borogove*" is a thin shabby-looking bird with its feathers sticking out all round —something like a live mop.'

'And then "*mome raths*"?' said Alice. 'If I'm not giving you too much trouble.'

'Well, a "*rath*" is a sort of green pig: but "*mome*" I'm not certain about. I think it's short for "from home"—meaning that they'd lost their way, you know.'

'And what does "*outgrabe*" mean?'

'Well, "*outgribing*" is something between bellowing and whistling, with a kind of sneeze in the middle: however, you'll hear it done, maybe—down in the wood yonder—and when you've once heard it you'll be *quite* content. Who's been repeating all that hard stuff to you?'

LEWIS CARROLL: *Alice Through the Looking Glass.*

A useful statement is a statement that can mean only one thing. And it is the nature of words to mean many things. Take the simple sentence 'Passing Russell Square'. That proved useless because besides the surface meaning it contained many sunken meanings. The word 'passing' suggested the transiency of things, the passing of time and the changes of human life. Then the word 'Russell' suggested the rustling of leaves and the skirt on a polished floor; also the ducal house of Bedford and half the history of England. Finally, the word 'Square' brings in the sight, the shape of an actual square combined with some visual suggestion of the stark angularity of stucco.

VIRGINIA WOOLF: *Death of the Moth.*

The Ballad of Dead Ladies

Tell me now in what hidden way is
   Lady Flora the lovely Roman?
Where's Hipparchia, and where is Thais,
   Neither of them the fairer woman?
   Where is Echo, beheld of no man,
Only heard on river and mere,—
   She whose beauty was more than human? . . .
But where are the snows of yester-year?

Where's Héloïse, the learned nun,
  For whose sake Abeillard, I ween,
Lost manhood and put priesthood on?
  (From love he won such dule and teen!)
  And where, I pray you, is the Queen
Who willed that Buridan should steer
  Sewed in a sack's mouth down the Seine? . . .
But where are the snows of yester-year?

White Queen Blanche, like a queen of lilies,
  With a voice like any mermaiden—
Bertha Broadfoot, Beatrice, Alice,
  And Ermengarde the lady of Maine,—
  And that good Joan whom Englishmen
At Rouen doomed and burned her there.
  Mother of God, where are they then? . . .
But where are the snows of yester-year?

Nay, never ask this week, fair lord,
  Where they are gone, nor yet this year,
Except with this for an overword,—
  But where are the snows of yester-year?

                                   D. G. ROSSETTI.

Bring the rathe primrose that forsaken dies,
The tufted crow-toe, and pale jessamine,
The white pink, and the pansy freaked with jet,
The glowing violet,
The musk-rose, and the well-attired woodbine,
With cowslips wan that hang the pensive head,
And every flower that sad embroidery wears:
Bid amaranthus all his beauty shed,
And daffodillies fill their cups with tears,
To strew the laureat hearse where Lycid lies.

                              MILTON: *Lycidas.*

            Not that fair field
Of Enna, where Prosérpine gathering flowers,
Herself a fairer flower, by gloomy Dis
Was gathered, which cost Ceres all that pain
To seek her through the world; nor that sweet grove
Of Daphne by Orontes, and the inspired
Castalian spring, might with this Paradise
Of Eden strive; nor that Nyseian isle
Girt with the river Triton, where old Cham,

Whom Gentiles Ammon call and Lybian Jove,
Hid Amalthea, and her florid son,
Young Bacchus, from his step-dame Rhea's eye;
Nor where Abassin kings their issue guard,
Mount Amara, though this by some supposed
True Paradise under the Ethiop line
By Nilus' head, enclosed with shining rock,
A whole day's journey high, but wide remote
From this Assyrian garden, where the Fiend
Saw, undelighted, all delight, all kind
Of living creatures, new to sight, and strange.

MILTON: Paradise Lost.

But I
Have never known my grandsire's furrowed face,
Nor seen his lofty house in Seistan,
Nor slaked my thirst at the clear Helmund stream;
But lodged among my father's foes, and seen
Afrasiab's city's only, Samarcand,
Bokhara, and lone Khiva in the waste,
And the black Toorkman tents; and only drunk
The desert rivers, Moorghab and Tejend,
Kohik, and where the Kalmuks feed their sheep,
The northern Sir; and this great Oxus stream,
The yellow Oxus, by whose brink I die.

MATTHEW ARNOLD: Sohrab and Rustum.

We do not sufficiently distinguish in our observations upon
language between a clear expression and a strong expression.
These are frequently confounded with each other, though they
are in reality extremely different. The former regards the
understanding. The latter belongs to the passions. The one
describes a thing as it is; the latter describes it as it is felt. Now
as there is a moving tone of voice, an impassioned countenance,
an agitated gesture, which affect independently of the things
about which they are exerted, so there are words, and certain
dispositions of words, which being peculiarly devoted to passionate
subjects, and always used by those who are under the influence
of any passion, touch and move us more than those which far
more clearly and distinctly express the subject matter. We
yield to sympathy what we refuse to description. The truth is,
all verbal description, merely as naked description, though
never so exact, conveys so poor and insufficient an idea of the
thing described that it could scarcely have the smallest effect, if
the speaker did not call in to his aid those modes of speech

K

that make a strong and lively feeling in himself. Then, by the contagion of our passions, we catch a fire already kindled in another, which probably might never have been struck out by the object described. Words, by strongly conveying the passions, by those means which we have already mentioned, fully compensate for their weakness in other respects.

> BURKE: *An Enquiry into the origin of our ideas of the Sublime and Beautiful.*

There are two very natural propensities which we may distinguish in the most virtuous and liberal dispositions, the love of pleasure and the love of action. If the former be refined by art and learning, improved by the charms of social intercourse, and corrected by a just regard to economy, to health, and to reputation, it is productive of the greatest part of the happiness of private life. The love of action is a principle of a much stronger and more doubtful nature. It often leads to anger, to ambition, and to revenge; but, when it is guided by the sense of propriety and benevolence, it becomes the parent of every virtue; and, if those virtues are accompanied with equal abilities, a family, a state, or an empire may be indebted for their safety and prosperity to the undaunted courage of a single man. To the love of pleasure we may therefore ascribe most of the agreeable, to the love of action we may attribute most of the useful and respectable qualifications. The character in which both the one and the other should be united and harmonized would seem to constitute the most perfect idea of human nature. The insensible and inactive disposition, which should be supposed alike destitute of both, would be rejected, by the common consent of mankind, as utterly incapable of procuring any happiness to the individual, or any public benefit to the world. But it was not in *this* world that the primitive Christians were desirous of making themselves either agreeable or useful.

> GIBBON: *Decline and Fall of the Roman Empire.*

The dignity of the snow-capped mountain is lost in distinctness, but the joy of the tourist is to recognize the traveller on the top. The desire to see, for the sake of seeing, is, with the mass, alone the one to be gratified, hence the delight in detail.

And when the evening mist clothes the riverside with poetry, as with a veil, and the poor buildings lose themselves in the dim sky, and the tall chimneys become campanili, and the warehouses are palaces in the night, and the whole city hangs in the heavens, and fairy-land is before us—then the wayfarer hastens home; the working man and the cultured one, the wise man

and the one of pleasure, cease to understand, as they have ceased
to see, and Nature, who, for once, has sung in tune, sings her
exquisite song to the artist alone, her son and her master—her
son in that he loves her, her master in that he knows her.

WHISTLER: *The Gentle Art of Making Enemies.*

Where then shall Hope and Fear their objects find?
Must dull suspense corrupt the stagnant mind?
Must helpless man, in ignorance sedate,
Roll darkling down the torrent of his fate?
Must no dislike alarm, no wishes rise,
No cries invoke the mercies of the skies?
Inquirer cease! petitions yet remain,
Which Heaven may hear, nor deem Religion vain.
Still raise for good the supplicating voice,
But leave to Heaven the measure and the choice;
Safe in His power, whose eyes discern afar
The secret ambush of a specious prayer,
Implore His aid, in His decisions rest,
Secure whate'er He gives, He gives the best.
Yet when the sense of sacred presence fires,
And strong devotion to the skies aspires,
Pour forth thy fervours for a healthful mind,
Obedient passions, and a will resign'd;
For love, which scarce collective man can fill;
For patience, sovereign o'er transmuted ill;
For faith, that, panting for a happier seat,
Counts death kind Nature's signal of retreat:
These goods for man the laws of Heaven ordain,
These goods He grants, who grants the power to gain;
With these celestial Wisdom calms the mind,
And makes the happiness she does not find.

SAMUEL JOHNSON: *The Vanity of Human Wishes.*

But when from a long-distant past nothing subsists, after the
people are dead, after the things are broken and scattered, still,
alone, more fragile, but with more vitality, more unsubstantial,
more persistent, more faithful, the smell and taste of things
remain poised a long time, like souls, ready to remind us, waiting
and hoping for their moment, amid the ruins of all the rest;
and bear unfaltering, in the tiny and almost impalpable drop of
their essence, the vast structure of recollection.

And once I had recognized the taste of the crumb of madeleine
soaked in her decoction of lime-flowers which my aunt used to
give me (although I did not yet know and must long postpone

the discovery of why this memory made me so happy) immediately
the old grey house upon the street, where her room was, rose up
like the scenery of a theatre to attach itself to the little pavilion,
opening on to the garden, which had been built out behind it
for my parents (the isolated panel which until that moment had
been all that I could see); and with the house the town, from
morning to night in all weathers, the square where I was sent
before luncheon, the streets along which I used to run errands,
the country roads we took when it was fine. And just as the
Japanese amuse themselves by filling a porcelain bowl with
water and steeping in it little crumbs of paper which until then
are without character or form, but, the moment they become
wet, stretch themselves and bend, take on colour and distinctive
shape, become flowers or houses or people, permanent and
recognizable, so in that moment all the flowers in our garden
and in M. Swann's park, and the water-lilies on the Vivonne
and the good folk of the village and their little dwellings and the
parish church and the whole of Combray and of its surroundings,
taking their proper shapes and growing solid, sprang into being,
town and gardens alike, from my cup of tea.

MARCEL PROUST: *Swann's Way*. (Trans. C. K. SCOTT MONCRIEFF.)

April is the cruellest month, breeding
Lilacs out of the dead land, mixing
Memory and desire, stirring
Dull roots with spring rain.
Winter kept us warm, covering
Earth in forgetful snow, feeding
A little life with dried tubers.
Summer surprised us, coming over the Starnbergersee
With a shower of rain; we stopped in the colonnade,
And went on in sunlight, into the Hofgarten,
And drank coffee, and talked for an hour.
Bin gar keine Russin, stamm' aus Litauen, echt deutsch.
And when we were children, staying at the archduke's,
My cousin's, he took me out on a sled,
And I was frightened. He said, Marie,
Marie, hold on tight. And down we went.
In the mountains, there you feel free.
I read, much of the night, and go south in the winter.

T. S. ELIOT: *The Waste Land*.

'Tis not enough no harshness gives offence,
The sound must seem an echo to the sense:
Soft is the strain when Zephyr gently blows,
And the smooth stream in smoother numbers flows;

But when loud surges lash the sounding shore,
The hoarse, rough verse should like the torrent roar:
When Ajax strives some rock's vast weight to throw,
The line too labours, and the words move slow;
Not so when swift Camilla scours the plain,
Flies o'er th'unbending corn, and skims along the main.

POPE: Essay on Criticism.

In the course of our conversation, something cropped up which suggested a line of one of his poems, 'The Golden Year', and I quoted it.

'Go on,' said Tennyson, who seemed to like to know that anyone quoting him knew more than the bare quotation.

I happened to know that poem, and went on to the end of the lyrical portion. There I stopped.

'Go on,' he said again, so I spoke the narrative bit at the end, supposed to be spoken by the writer:—

> 'He spoke; and, high above, I heard them blast
> The steep slate-quarry, and the great echo flap,
> And buffet round the hills, from bluff to bluff.'

Tennyson listened attentively. When I had spoken the last line he shook his head and said:—

'No!'

'Surely that is correct?' I said.

'No!'

There was in this something which I did not understand, for I was certain that I had given the words correctly. So I ventured to say:—

'Of course one must not contradict an author about his own work; but I am certain those are the words in my edition of the poem.'

He answered quickly:—

'Oh, the words are all right—quite correct!'

'Then what is wrong?'

For answer he said:—

'Have you ever been on a Welsh mountain?'

'Yes! On Snowdon!'

'Did you hear them blast a slate quarry?'

'Yes. In Wales, and also on Coniston in Cumberland.'

'And did you notice the sound?'

I was altogether at fault and said:—

'Won't you tell me—explain to me? I really want to understand.'

He spoke the last line, and further explanation was unnecessary.

The whole gist was in his pronunciation of the word 'bluff',
twice repeated. He spoke this word with a sort of quick pro-
pulsive effort, as though throwing the word from his mouth. 'I
thought anyone would understand that', he added.

It was the correct muffled sound which the exploding charge
makes in the curves of the steep valleys.

This is a good instance of Tennyson's wonderful power of
onomatopoeia.

BRAM STOKER: *Personal Reminiscences of Henry Irving.*

Then Sir Bedivere returned again, and took the sword in his
hand; and then him thought sin and shame to throw away that
noble sword, and so efte he hid the sword, and returned again,
and told to the king that he had been at the water, and done his
commandment. What saw thou there? said the king. Sir, he
said, I saw nothing but the waters wappe and waves wanne.

SIR THOMAS MALORY: *Le Morte d'Arthur.*

And answer made the bold Sir Bedivere:
'I heard the ripple washing in the reeds,
And the wild water lapping on the crag.' . . .

And answer made the bold Sir Bedivere:
'I heard the water lapping on the crag,
And the long ripple washing in the reeds.' . . .

Dry clash'd his harness in the icy caves
And barren chasms, and all to left and right
The bare black cliff clang'd round him, as he based
His feet on juts of slippery crag that rang
Sharp-smitten with the dint of armed heels—
And on a sudden, lo! the level lake,
And the long glories of the winter moon.

TENNYSON: *The Passing of Arthur.*

The Lotos blooms below the barren peak:
The Lotos blows by every winding creek:
All day the wind blows low with mellower tone:
Thro' every hollow cave and alley lone
Round and round the spicy downs the yellow Lotos-dust is blown.

TENNYSON: *The Lotus Eaters.*

On Wenlock Edge the wood's in trouble;
  His forest fleece the Wrekin heaves;
The gale, it plies the saplings double,
  And thick on Severn snow the leaves.

'Twould blow like this through holt and hanger
   When Uricon the city stood:
'Tis the old wind in the old anger,
   But then it threshed another wood.

Then, 'twas before my time, the Roman
   At yonder heaving hill would stare:
The blood that warms an English yeoman,
   The thoughts that hurt him, they were there.

There, like the wind through woods in riot,
   Through him the gale of life blew high;
The tree of man was never quiet:
   Then 'twas the Roman, now 'tis I.

The gale, it plies the saplings double,
   It blows so hard, 'twill soon be gone:
To-day the Roman and his trouble
   Are ashes under Uricon.
                    A. E. HOUSMAN: *A Shropshire Lad.*

The Leaden Echo

How to keep—is there ány any, is there none such, nowhere
      known some, bow or brooch or braid or brace, láce, latch
  .   or catch or key to keep
Back beauty, keep it, beauty, beauty, beauty, . . . from vanishing
      away?
Ó is there no frowning of these wrinkles, rankèd wrinkles deep,
Dówn? no waving off of these most mournful messengers, still
      messengers, sad and stealing messengers of grey?
No there's none, there's none, O no there's none,
Nor can you long be, what you now are, called fair,
Do what you may do, what, do what you may,
And wisdom is early to despair:
Be beginning; since, no, nothing can be done
To keep at bay
Age and age's evils, hoar hair,
Ruck and wrinkle, drooping, dying, death's worst, winding
      sheets, tombs and worms and tumbling to decay;
So be beginning, be beginning to despair.
O there's none; no no no there's none:
Be beginning to despair, to despair,
Despair, despair, despair, despair.

The Golden Echo

               Spare!
There is one, yes I have one (Hush there!);
Only not within seeing of the sun,
Not within the singeing of the strong sun,
Tall sun's tingeing, or treacherous the tainting of the earth's air,
Somewhere elsewhere there is ah well where! one,
Óne. . . . .

G. M. HOPKINS.

Dread stood at the door, and this doom heard,
How the king had commanded constables and sergeants
To fetter Sir False, and to bind all his fellows.
Then went Dread away, and gave warning to False,
Bade him flee for fear, and his fellows go with him.

Then False in his fear fled fast to the friars;
And Guile too was going, aghast for his life,
But met with some merchants, who made him abide,
Shut him in their shops, to show forth their ware,
And apparelled him as a 'prentice, the people to serve.

WILLIAM LANGLAND: Piers Plowman.

CHAPTER XI

PROSE

Le Maître de Philosophie. Sont-ce des vers que vous lui voulez écrire?

M. Jourdain. Non, non : point de vers.

Phil. Vous ne voulez que de la prose?

M. J. Non, je ne veux ni prose ni vers.

Phil. Il faut bien que ce soit l'un ou l'autre.

M. J. Pourquoi?

Phil. Par la raison, Monsieur, qu'il n'y a, pour s'exprimer, que la prose ou les vers.

M. J. Il n'y a que la prose ou les vers?

Phil. Non, Monsieur. Tout ce qui n'est point prose est vers, et tout ce qui n'est point vers est prose.

M. J. Et comme l'on parle, qu'est ce que c'est donc que cela?

Phil. De la prose.

M. J. Quoi! quand je dis : 'Nicole, apportez-moi mes pantoufles, et me donnez mon bonnet de nuit', c'est de la prose?

Phil. Oui, Monsieur.

M. J. Par ma foi, il y a plus de quarante ans que je dis de la prose, sans que j'en susse rien ; et je vous suis le plus obligé du monde de m'avoir appris cela.

MOLIÈRE : *Le Bourgeois Gentilhomme.*

It may come as a shock to many people besides M. Jourdain that all their lives they have spoken prose. To others prose is simply the opposite of poetry. The antithesis of poetry, however, is not prose but science, for the appeal of poetry is to the emotions, where it is subject to the most various interpretations, the literal meaning being almost irrelevant ; whereas science appeals—if it is good science—to the intellect, and is concerned with matters of fact. This, be it noted, does not mean that science is inferior to poetry, any more than green is inferior to its complementary colour, red ; nor does it mean that science is not a proper subject for poetry. It simply means that science is concerned with what a man thinks, poetry with what a man feels.

The appeal of prose, however, may be either to the intellect or to the emotions ; it may express either what a man thinks, or what a man feels, or, of course, both. As the vehicle for the conveyance of rational thought or facts it is the servant of science, and itself a job that may well be tackled by a skilled engineer in words; as the vehicle for the transference of an emotional experience it is a medium for the artist.

Prose differs from poetry, superficially at least—or better, it differs from verse, in being unmetrical. Unmetrical, not unrhythmical, for rhythm is the quickening element, the life-bringer, in prose—as in all art. Whether there is any *essential* difference, a difference of kind rather than of degree, between great prose and great verse, that is between great prose and poetry, is another matter.

In parenthesis it may be observed that metrical writing—verse—may be the expression of thought rather than of feeling. Thus Erasmus Darwin (1731–1802) wrote *The Botanic Garden*, an emotionally-toned text-book of botany in verse:

> And the young rose, in beauty's damask pride,
> Drinks the warm blushes of his bashful bride;
> With honey lips, enamoured woodbines meet,
> Clasp with fond arms, and mix their kisses sweet.
> What beaux and beauties crowd the gaudy groves,
> And woo and win their vegetable loves.

And the didactic and satirical writing of the eighteenth century is an affair of the intellect and spleen rather than of the sort of feeling that is the stuff of poetry:

> All Nature is but Art, unknown to thee;
> All Chance, Direction which thou canst not see;
> All Discord, Harmony not understood;
> All partial Evil, universal Good:
> And, spite of Pride, in erring Reason's spite,
> One truth is clear, WHATEVER IS, IS RIGHT.

'Meaning is of the intellect, poetry is not.' And though prose is mainly an affair of the intellect, it is by no means necessarily so.

Because prose, spoken or written, is the normal medium of communication between men it is, like architecture, to some extent conditioned by its function. It has already been suggested that where visual form is determined absolutely by function, as in an aeroplane and possibly in a lighthouse and grain-elevator, there is no room for the artist, because there is no free will, no latitude for choice; the form is predetermined by the function.

This is the province of science and the engineer, not of art and the artist. But there are very few architectural forms that are determined absolutely by function, and though the form of most buildings must ultimately be limited by function the architect can normally so modify his forms that they convey what he wishes to express.

The function of prose is primarily a mechanical one: to act as a vehicle for the transference of ideas from one man to others, much as a lorry transports goods from one place to another, and in so far as the expression is absolutely determined by the function, that is if there is one way of conveying a rational idea that is more efficient than any other, prose is the province of the scientist, not of the artist.

But is there such an absolute prose? Prose whose form is determined absolutely by its function? 'Keep off the grass' and 'Trespassers will be prosecuted' are admirably functional, and no doubt it would be difficult to improve on Defoe's opening of *Robinson Crusoe*:

> I was born in the year 1632, in the City of York, of a good family, though not of that county; my father being a foreigner of Bremen, who settled first at Hull.

But it is not the only way. There are even many alternative ways of saying *yes*: *all right, very good, the answer is in the affirmative, even so, O.K.*, etc., and as soon as words are combined into the larger units of phrases and sentences the expression may be infinitely varied.

Yet it remains approximately true that when the object is the transference of a rational idea from one mind to another, as in scientific exposition, a business letter *, a military order, or a

---

* It should be noted that the strange and hideous jargon called business English is neither business-like nor is it English. It is shorter and less ambiguous to say: 'Thank you for your letter of July 29th' than 'We are in receipt of your favour of the 29th ult. for which we thank you.'
But see Sir Alan Herbert's *What A Word!*—from which the following 'lyric' is taken.

> I heard the happy lark exult,
> Too soon, for it was early ult.;
> And now the land with rain is rinsed—
> Ah, mournful is the month of inst.;
> Love, like a lizard in the rocks,
> Is hungry for the suns of prox.
>
> Boy Cupid with his catapult
> Could find but sorry sport in ult.;
> But through the woods, with bluebells chintzed,
> My lady comes to me in inst.:
> And O may Cupid speed the clocks,
> For she will marry me in prox.!

legal document, the form is—or should be—largely determined
by the function; the words should be simple, unemotional, and
as few as possible, the phrasing straightforward and unambiguous,
the sentences and paragraphs well-defined units, and the whole
a logical construction. Such prose is likely to be a scientifically
efficient aggregation of words, much as a modern bridge is a
scientific aggregation of steel parts, rather than a work of art:

Although we derive our names for Arithmetic and Geometry
from the Greeks, we must not forget that the Hindus independently
cultivated these subjects, and it is from the Hindus that we
derive our present numerical notation. The forms 1, 2, 3, etc.,
for the numbers are our copies of a variety of symbols used by
the Hindus in their writings, and have in modern times replaced
both the Greek method of using the letters of their alphabet
for this purpose and the clumsy Roman numerals I, II, III,
IV, etc.

But it is a different matter if the writer's object is persuasion,
for the expression will be modified by the choice of emotionally-
toned words, and by devices such as inversion and repetition the
emphasis will be concentrated at the most effective points. The
subject may still be one for rational analysis, but the expression
is no longer merely an intellectual process, and though such
prose may be competently written by the skilful craftsman, it
will be better written by the artist.

To be honoured and even privileged by the laws, opinions, and
inveterate usages of our country, growing out of the prejudice of
ages, has nothing to provoke horror and indignation in any man.
Even to be too tenacious of those privileges is not absolutely a
crime. The strong struggle in every individual to preserve
possession of what he has found to belong to him, and to distinguish him, is one of the securities against injustice and despotism
implanted in our nature. It operates as an instinct to secure
property, and to preserve communities in a settled state. What
is there to shock in this? Nobility is a graceful ornament to the
civil order. It is the Corinthian capital of polished society.
Omnes boni nobilitati semper favemus, was the saying of a wise and
good man. It is, indeed, one sign of a liberal and benevolent
mind to incline to it with some sort of partial propensity. He
feels no ennobling principle in his own heart who wishes to level
all the artificial institutions which have been adopted for giving
a body to opinion and permanence to fugitive esteem. It is a
sour, malignant, and envious disposition, without taste for the

reality, or for any image or representation of virtue, that sees with joy the unmerited fall of what had long flourished in splendour and in honour. I do not like to see anything destroyed, any void produced in society, any ruin on the face of the land.

In this passage by Burke the manner rather than the matter is emotional, and though it may not be remarkable for its logic, even his opponents would have to admit that it was well done.

But the subject-matter itself may be emotional, and then the writer will normally express himself in words that correspond to the emotion; both matter and manner, subject and expression, will be emotional. He may however secure an effect by a sort of inverted shock tactics, by deliberate understatement, by the use of prosaic and unemotional words and rhythms:

'Please go out of the room,' the doctor said. Catherine winked at me, her face grey. 'I'll be right outside,' I said.
'Don't worry, darling,' Catherine said. 'I'm not a bit afraid. It's just a dirty trick.'
'You dear, brave sweet.'
I waited outside in the hall. I waited a long time. The nurse came to the door and came over to me. 'I'm afraid Mrs. Henry is very ill,' she said. 'I'm afraid for her.'
'Is she dead?'
'No, but she is unconscious.'
It seems that she had one haemorrhage after another. They couldn't stop it. I went into the room and stayed with Catherine until she died. She was unconscious all the time, and it did not take her very long to die.

ERNEST HEMINGWAY: *A Farewell to Arms.*

Emotion is so personal that there can be no formula for its expression, no functional combination of words to describe so elusive and intimate a thing. Each man must struggle to express himself as best he can by choosing those words, both singly and in combination, that most effectively by their literal meaning explain, and by their overtones and undertones of meaning suggest the emotion he is trying to describe. And partly determining and partly determined by the choice and order of words is the vitalizing and integrating rhythm which itself suggests the thing expressed.

The holes were already dug, and they set to work. Winterborne's fingers were endowed with a gentle conjuror's touch in spreading the roots of each little tree, resulting in a sort of caress

under which the delicate fibres all laid themselves out in their
proper directions for growth. He put most of these roots towards
the south-west; for, he said, in forty years' time, when some
great gale is blowing from that quarter, the trees will require
the strongest holdfast on that side to stand against it and not fall.

'How they sigh directly we put 'em upright, though while
they are lying down they don't sigh at all,' said Marty.

'Do they?' said Giles. 'I've never noticed it.'

She erected one of the young pines into its hole, and held up
her finger; the soft musical breathing instantly set in, which was
not to cease night or day till the grown tree should be felled—
probably long after the two planters had been felled themselves.

THOMAS HARDY: The Woodlanders.

Here is the final frontier between prose as a science and prose
as an art. Art is the transference from the artist to other men
of an emotion—of the aesthetic emotion, the emotion within the
emotion—not by the mechanism of representation or description,
not as the cargo is carried in a steamer, but by a sort of chemical
metamorphosis of the medium itself, so that it is charged with a
significance that has little or nothing to do with the thing described
or represented. The meaning is not only conveyed by the
medium, the medium *is* the meaning. In music it is evident
that medium and meaning are one. It is not so obvious in prose,
poetry, and painting because it is obscured by descriptive and
representational elements.

When prose takes on this new and independent significance,
in such language as, 'They that are delivered from the noise of
archers in the places of drawing water', it assumes much of the
power of poetry, which in its extended sense may be taken to mean
the quality common to all great art of moving us aesthetically
by virtue of its significant expression.

It is perhaps because prose serves primarily a utilitarian
purpose that most people are deaf to its potential beauty. They
think of poetry as a form of art remote from everyday experience,
and written in a strange jargon of its own; but prose they
recognize as part of the business of life. It is used and abused
in speech, letters, newspapers, novels and text-books, and few
people ask more of it than a more or less literal meaning. Clarity
is indeed one of the great virtues of a prose style, though it is a
virtue rarely acquired, and great prose is often simple and austere;
but in addition there is the innate grace and energy of its rhythm,
which reinforces the literal and particular meaning, and may

impose another of its own. The merely correct and academic may be a consummate piece of craftsmanship, but it is a dead thing confined within a single meaning, and bears much the same relation to great prose as does a photograph to a fine painting.

The effect of prose on the ear and on the mind is only less complex than that of verse. With their intimate associations the precise and literal meanings of words disintegrate and assume a multitude of new and elusive values; there is the open music of the vowels, the subtle pluck and shock of the consonants, and unifying the minor themes the great harmony of the rhythm which inspires the whole.

The following passage is from Sir Thomas Browne's *Urn Burial:*

Now since these dead bones have already outlasted the living ones of *Methuselah*, and in a Yard under Ground, and thin Walls of Clay, outworn all the strong and specious buildings above it, and quietly rested under the drums and tramplings of three Conquests; What Prince can promise such diuturnity unto his Relics, or might not gladly say, *Sic ego componi versus in ossa velim*?

Consider the undertones and overtones of meaning suggested by such words as *dead, bones, living, Methuselah, walls, clay, buildings, drums, tramplings, conquests.* Next consider the repetition of the short *e* in *dead, already, rested, conquests*; the liquids in *already outlasted the living ones of Methusaleh, walls of clay, all, buildings, quietly, tramplings*; the sonorous *walls, outworn, all,* and the final triumph of the rolling *r's*; the powerful percussion of the consonants in *drums* and *tramplings,* and the tremendous crash of *conquests.*

Finally there is the profound rhythm like a deep sea ebbing, then swelling in *already outlasted, yard under ground, thin walls, outworn all,* then falling away until at last it breaks in the foam and thunder of *drums and tramplings of three conquests.*

How each word is an integral part of the music and rhythm may be appreciated by abstracting one or substituting another. Consider, for instance, the significance of *quietly.*

No doubt such a passage is an extreme example to take; it is a style 'compounded too curiously of foreign words, and nourished not on the evergreen pastures of the moment, but on the dried bents and clovers of Latinity'; it is prose on the ultimate precipice beyond which there can be no advance, perilously poised and

ready to tumble into caricature. Nevertheless all great prose has
its peculiar music and rhythm and, when it is not confined by
its function to a precise and limited exposition, its own verbal
associations, all of which impose on the literal meaning another
more pregnant and in a sense independent of the primary
significance.

The art of writing great prose cannot be taught any more than
can the writing of poetry; it is the creation of the artist. But
most people with any aptitude can learn the craft of writing.
Though the rarer elements of style still elude them, they can at
least become competent and critical workers in words; they can
construct good prose even if they cannot create great prose.

Words are the raw material of prose, and have been discussed
in the preceding chapter. The craftsman will search for the
right word, the word that best expresses what he has to say, not
only by its literal meaning, but also by its sound and its powers
of suggestion. And he will not choose more words than are
necessary to express his meaning, for the indolent word and the
redundant phrase obscure the sense much as superfluous ornament
and unarticulated members puzzle the eye and corrupt the
integrity of a building.

The richer the language the less need is there for words that
limit and refine the meaning of other words. The precise noun
or verb needs no auxiliary to support it. A careless, sentimental,
or over-analytical and enervated style is often betrayed by the
prodigal use of modifying words—particularly of epithets, while
sincere and vigorous writing is remarkable for its restraint.
Compare the following passages:

As I walked through the wilderness of this world I lighted on
a certain place where was a den, and laid me down in that place
to sleep; and, as I slept, I dreamed a dream. I dreamed, and
behold I saw a man clothed with rags standing in a certain place,
with his face from his own house, a book in his hand, and a great
burden upon his back. I looked, and saw him open the book,
and read therein; and, as he read, he wept and trembled; and,
not being able longer to contain, he brake out with a lamentable
cry, saying, 'What shall I do?'

BUNYAN: *The Pilgrim's Progress.*

On his way at last to gaze on the abode of the new hero or
demigod of poetry, Gaston perceives increasingly, as another
excellence of his verse, how truthful, how close it is to the minute

fact of the scene around; as there are pleasant wines which, expressing the peculiar quality of their native soil, lose their special pleasantness away from home. The physiognomy of the scene was changed; the plain of La Beauce had ruffled itself into low green hills and gently winding valleys, with clear, quick water, and fanciful patches of heath and woodland. Here and there a secular oak tree maintained a solitude around it. It was the district of the 'little river Loir'—the Vendomois; and here, in its own country, the new poetry, notwithstanding its classic elegance, might seem a native wild flower, modest enough.

WALTER PATER: *Gaston de Latour.*

Here he (Fra Angelico) was an innovator, for his eye dwells on gentle aspects, and in his landscape backgrounds he introduces pleasing forms of mountains and verdant meadows multicoloured with the budding flowers of spring. Indeed, all his painting is flower-like, but this delicate naturalism does not determine its character. It is the soulful quality of his work which gives it supreme distinction.

ANON.

There are various devices whereby the craftsman can make his work more memorable, and after all this is likely to be his immediate concern. Though simile and metaphor are essential neither to poetry nor to prose—'the rogue never hazards a metaphor', said Johnson of Swift—the flash generated by the fusion of ideas or images may illuminate an obscurity, and at the same time stimulate interest by the revelation of similarity in dissimilarity and the satisfactory resolution of a discord.

Assonance and alliteration, if not overdone, may add a grace to language. 'The beauty of the contents of a phrase, or of a sentence', writes Stevenson, 'depends implicitly upon alliteration and upon assonance. The vowel demands to be repeated; the consonant demands to be repeated; and both cry aloud to be perpetually varied. You may follow the adventures of a letter through any passage that has particularly pleased you; find it, perhaps, denied a while, to tantalize the ear; find it fired again at you in a whole broadside; or find it pass into congenerous sounds, one liquid or labial melting away into another.' *

And much may be done to secure attention, without being aggressive, by the right ordering of words within the sentence. According to Quintilian, 'there is sometimes an extraordinary

* *The Art of Writing.*

L

force in some particular word, which, if it be placed in no very conspicuous position in the middle part of a sentence, is likely to escape the attention of the hearer and to be obscured by the words surrounding it; but if it be put at the end of the sentence is urged upon the reader's sense and imprinted on his mind.' Consider the order of the words in the following extract from Synge's *Riders to the Sea*:

It isn't that I haven't said prayers in the dark night till you wouldn't know what I'd be saying; but it's a great rest I'll have now, and it's time, surely. It's a great rest I'll have now, and great sleeping in the long nights after Samhain, if it's only a bit of wet flour we do have to eat, and maybe a fish that would be stinking.

When the ideas to be conveyed are matter of fact, the choice and order of the words within the sentence, and the arrangement of the sentences within the paragraph, will be rationally determined, for they are all devices to help the reader to grasp the meaning. Such prose will be a logical construction, a series of smaller and greater units, sentences and paragraphs, each complete in itself, and each contributing to the final unity of the work.

But when the expression is one of feeling, the process is more complex. The writer—the good writer, that is—does not use the words merely descriptively, as a mechanism to convey his meaning; as in poetry the words and the meaning are one. It follows that the sentence and paragraph are determined, not by a logical process imposed from without, but by a force from within; because the words in their rhythmical combination *are* the meaning, not merely symbols of the meaning, the sentence and the paragraph are impelled by this higher significance, which is the direct expression of the author's emotion.

There are, therefore, two kinds of unity: the one imposed by the literal meaning, the other inseparable from the meaning. There is little danger that the second kind of prose will lack variety, for it is vitalized as well as integrated by its rhythm; but there is no guarantee that functional or semi-functional prose, cut into lengths and bound by logic, will be anything but awkward and monotonous. This is a danger that must be avoided even though the remedy itself be a somewhat mechanical process. Variety can be imparted by varying the structure of the sentences: they may be long or short, loose or periodic, simple, compound, or complex, classically balanced, or romantically luxuriant; the combinations are endless and if intelligently used should help to produce the necessary variety without any sacrifice of unity.

But when all is said and done the conscious construction of prose is only the beginning of style; it may be an excellent instrument for the transference of thought and even of a limited range of feelings, and that indeed is much. But the craftsman lays down his pen when he hears the words of the illiterate Vanzetti, which, one is almost tempted to say, are worth all the laboured pages of Pater:

If it had not been for these thing, I might have live out my life, talking at street corners to scorning men. I might have die, unmarked, unknown, a failure. Now we are not a failure. This is our career and our triumph. Never in our full life can we hope to do such work for tolerance, for joostice, for man's onderstanding of man, as now we do by an accident. Our words, —our lives—our pains—nothing! The taking of our lives—lives of a good shoemaker and a poor fish peddler—all! That last moment belong to us—that agony is our triumph!

If then the power of speech is as great as any that can be named —if the origin of language is by many philosophers considered nothing short of divine—if by means of words the secrets of the heart are brought to light, pain of soul is relieved, hidden grief is carried off, sympathy conveyed, experience recorded, and wisdom perpetuated,—if by great authors the many are drawn up into unity, national character is fixed, a people speaks, the past and the future, the East and the West are brought into communication with each other,—if such men are, in a word, the spokesmen and prophets of the human family—it will not answer to make light of Literature or to neglect its study: rather we may be sure that, in proportion as we master it in whatever language, and imbibe its spirit, we shall ourselves become in our own measure the ministers of like benefits to others—be they many or few, be they in the obscurer or the more distinguished walks of life—who are united to us by social ties, and are within the sphere of our personal influence.

CARDINAL NEWMAN: *Idea of a University.*

I never knew a writer yet who took the smallest pains with his style and was at the same time readable. Mr. Walter Pater's style is, to me, like the face of some old woman who has been to Madame Rachel and had herself enamelled. The bloom is nothing but powder and paint and the odour is cherry-blossom. Mr. Matthew Arnold's odour is as the faint sickliness of hawthorn.

SAMUEL BUTLER: *Note Books.*

That style is therefore the most perfect, not, as fools say, which is the most natural, for the most natural is the disjointed babble of the chronicler; but which attains the highest degree of elegant and pregnant implication unobtrusively; or if obtrusively, then with the greatest gain to sense and vigour. Even the derangement of the phrases from their (so-called) natural order is luminous for the mind; and it is by the means of such designed reversal that the elements of a judgement may be most pertinently marshalled, or the stages of a complicated action most perspicuously bound into one. . . .

Ordinary writers, in ordinary moments, content themselves with avoiding what is harsh, and here and there, upon a rare occasion, buttressing a phrase, or linking two together, with a patch of assonance or a momentary jingle of alliteration. To understand how constant is this preoccupation of good writers, even where its results are least obtrusive, it is only necessary to turn to the bad. There, indeed, you will find cacophony supreme, the rattle of incongruous consonants only relieved by the jaw-breaking hiatus, and whole phrases not to be articulated by the powers of man.

R. L. STEVENSON: *The Art of Writing.*

Good prose, to say nothing of the original thought it conveys, may be infinitiely varied in modulation. It is only an extension of metres, an amplification of harmonies, of which even the best and most varied poetry admits but a few.

LANDOR.

I wish to state here most dogmatically (leaving to another occasion a more detailed defence of this dogma), that the distinction between Poetry and Prose is not and never can be a formal one. No minute analysis and definition of 'feet', no classification of metre, no theory of cadence or quantity, has ever resolved the multiple rhythms of Poetry and the multiple rhythms of Prose into two distinct and separable camps. The most that can be said is that Prose never assumes a regular, even beat, but this is a negative criterion of no practical value. That there is a surface distinction between Poetry and Prose must, I think, be admitted; but it is like the surface distinction between sea and land—one is liquid and wavy, the other solid and indented; but why distinguish the surfaces of things when the things themselves are so palpably different?

The distinction between Poetry and Prose is a material distinction; that is to say, since we are dealing with mental things, it is a psychological distinction. Poetry is the expression of one form of mental activity, Prose the expression of another form.

Poetry is creative expression; Prose is constructive expression. That, in a sentence, is the real distinction—a distinction which will become clearer as we proceed.

By 'creative' I mean *original*. In Poetry the words are born or reborn in the act of thinking. The words are, in Bergsonian phraseology, a becoming; they develop in the mind *pari passu* with the development of the thought. There is no time interval between the words and the thought. The thought is the word and the word is thought, and both the thought and the word are Poetry.

'Constructive' implies ready-made materials; words stacked round the builder, ready for use. Prose is a structure of ready-made words. Its 'creative' function is confined to plan and elevation—functions these, too, of Poetry, but in Poetry subsidiary to the creative function.

Does it follow that Poetry is solely an affair of words? Yes: an affair of words conditioned by the emotion they express. An affair of one word, like Shakespeare's 'incarnadine', or of two or three words, like 'shady sadness', 'incense-breathing Morn', 'a peak in Darien', 'soft Lydian airs', 'Mount Abora', 'star-inwrought', or of all the words necessary for a thought like the *Divine Comedy*.

Prose, too, is an affair of words, but not of words in themselves, but only of words as so much dead material given life, *which life is rhythm*. Paradoxical as it may seem, we now see that Poetry may inhere in a single word, in a single syllable, and may therefore in an extreme case be without rhythm; Prose, however, does not exist except in the phrase, and the phrase always has rhythm of some kind.

HERBERT READ: *English Prose Style*.

We laid down certain rules to help us in the way of straight Prose:—

(1) Almost always prefer the concrete word to the abstract.

(2) Almost always prefer the direct word to the circumlocution.

(3) Generally use transitive verbs, that strike their objects; and use them in the active voice, eschewing the stationary passive, with its little auxiliary *is's* and *was's*, and its participles getting into the light of your adjectives, which should be few. For, as a rough law, by his use of the straight verb and by this economy of adjectives you can tell a man's style, if it be masculine or neuter, writing or 'composition'.

The authors of that capital book *The King's English*, which I
have already recommended to you, add two rules:—

(1) Prefer the short word to the long.
(2) Prefer the Saxon word to the Romance.

But these two precepts you would have to modify by so long a
string of exceptions that I do not commend them to you.   In
fact I think them false in theory and likely to be fatal in practice.
For, as my last lecture tried to show, you no sooner begin to
philosophize things instead of merely telling a tale of them than
you must go to the Mediterranean languages: because in these
man first learnt to discuss his 'why' and 'how', and these
languages yet guard the vocabulary.

Lastly we saw how, by experimenting with rhythm, our prose
'broke its birth's invidious bar' and learnt to scale the forbidden
heights.

Now by attending to the few plain rules given above you may
train yourselves to write sound, straightforward, work-a-day
English.   But if you would write melodious English, I fear the
gods will require of you what they ought to have given you at
birth—something of an ear.   Yet the most of us have ears, of
sorts; and I believe that, though we can only acquire it by
assiduous practice, the most of us can wonderfully improve our
talent of the ear.

SIR A. QUILLER-COUCH: On the Art of Writing.

Then Sir Bedivere took the king upon his back, and so went
with him to that water side.   And when they were at the water
side, even fast by the bank hoved a little barge with many fair
ladies in it, and among them all was a queen, and all they had
black hoods, and all they wept and shrieked when they saw King
Arthur.   Now put me into the barge, said the king.   And so he
did softly; and there received him three queens with great
mourning; and so they set them down, and in one of their laps
King Arthur laid his head.   And then that queen said: Ah,
dear brother, why have ye tarried so long from me? alas, this
wound on your head hath caught over-much cold.   And so then
they rowed from the land, and Sir Bedivere beheld all those
ladies go from him.   Then Sir Bedivere cried: Ah my lord
Arthur, what shall become of me, now ye go from me and leave
me here alone among mine enemies?   Comfort thyself, said the
king, and do as well as thou mayest, for in me is no trust for to
trust in; for I will into the vale of Avilion to heal me of my
grievous wound: and if thou hear never more of me, pray for
my soul.   But ever the queens and ladies wept and shrieked,
that it was pity to hear.   And as soon as Sir Bedivere had lost
the sight of the barge, he wept and wailed, and so took the forest;

and so he went all that night, and in the morning he was ware
betwixt two holts hoar, of a chapel and an hermitage.

SIR THOMAS MALORY : *Le Morte d'Arthur.*

To be short, no day passed that he wrought not his full tale of
work, and the days wore, and his ship-wright's work throve.
Often the folk of that house, and from otherwhere round about,
came down to the strand to watch him working. Nowise did
they wilfully hinder him, but whiles when they could get no talk
from him, they would speak of him to each other, wondering
that he should so toil to sail upon the sea; for they loved the sea
but little, and it soon became clear to them that he was looking
to nought else; though it may not be said that they deemed he
would leave the land for ever. On the other hand, if they
hindered him not, neither did they help, saving when he prayed
them for somewhat which he needed, which they would then
give him blithely.

WILLIAM MORRIS : *The Story of the Glittering Plain.*

The special men-in-waiting who were to take the train went
down low and made as if to be lifting it from the floor with their
hands, and they went forward with their hands in the air. It
would not do to let it get about that they did not see anything.

Then the Ruler went on his way under the jewelled cover and
everybody in the streets and at the windows said, 'How bright
the Ruler's new garments are! What a train! And how well-
cut they are!' Nobody would let it seem that he was unable to
see anything, because then he was a foolish man or not good
enough for his position.

The Ruler's garments had not ever before made so great an
effect.

'But he has got nothing on,' said a little boy.

'What a thing for the baby to say,' said his father; and in a
low voice one person said to another what the boy had said.
'He has nothing on; a little boy says he has nothing on!'

'But he has nothing on!' came at last in a cry from everyone.

The Ruler was twisting his body about as if in pain, for it was
clear to him that it was true, but he said to himself, 'It all has to
go on now,' so he went forward stiffer than ever, and the men-in-
waiting kept up the train that was not there.

L. W. LOCKHART : *Hans Andersen in Basic English.*

Remember now thy Creator in the days of thy youth, while
the evil days come not, nor the years draw nigh, when thou shalt

say, I have no pleasure in them; while the sun, or the light, or
the moon, or the stars, be not darkened, nor the clouds return
after the rain: in the day when the keepers of the house shall
tremble, and the strong men shall bow themselves, and the
grinders cease because they are few, and those that look out of
the windows be darkened; and the doors shall be shut in the
streets, when the sound of the grinding is low, and he shall rise
up at the voice of the bird, and all the daughters of musick shall
be brought low. Also when they shall be afraid of that which
is high, and fears shall be in the way, and the almond tree shall
flourish, and the grasshopper shall be a burden, and desire shall
fail: because man goeth to his long home, and the mourners go
about the streets: or ever the silver cord be loosed, or the golden
bowl be broken, or the pitcher be broken at the fountain, or the
wheel broken at the cistern. Then shall the dust return to the
earth as it was: and the spirit shall return unto God who gave it.

Ecclesiastes xii, 1–7.

If it were not for the *Bible* and *Common Prayer Book* in the
Vulgar Tongue, we should hardly be able to understand anything that was written among us an hundred years ago; which
is certainly true: for those books, being perpetually read in
Churches, have proved a kind of standard for language, especially
to the common people. And I doubt whether the alterations
since introduced have added much to the beauty or strength of
the *English* Tongue, though they have taken off a great deal from
the *Simplicity* which is one of the greatest perfections of any
language. You, my Lord, who are so conversant in the sacred
writings, and so great a judge of them in their originals, will
agree, that no Translation our Country ever yet produced, has
come up to that of the *Old* and *New Testament*: And by the many
beautiful passages which I have often had the honour to hear
your Lordship cite from thence, I am persuaded that the Translators of the *Bible* were masters of an *English* style much fitter for
that work than any we see in our present writings; which I take
to be owing to the *Simplicity* that runs through the whole. Then,
as to the greatest part of our *Liturgy*, compiled long before the
Translation of the *Bible* now in use, and little altered since, there
seem to be in it as great strains of true sublime eloquence as
are anywhere to be found in our language; which every man of
good Taste will observe in the *Communion Service*, that of *Burial*,
and other parts.

SWIFT: *Dedicatory Letter to the Earl of Oxford.*

At last the gilded cross crowned the dwindling galaxies of
superimposed angels, the four continents in white marble stood

at the four corners of the base, and, seven years after its inception, in July 1872, the monument was thrown open to the public.

But four more years were to elapse before the central figure was ready to be placed under its starry canopy. It was designed by Mr. Foley, though in one particular the sculptor's freedom was restricted by Mr. Scott. 'I have chosen the sitting posture', Mr. Scott said, 'as best conveying the idea of dignity befitting a royal personage.' Mr. Foley ably carried out the conception of his principal. 'In the attitude and expression', he said, 'the aim has been, with the individuality of portraiture, to embody rank, character, and enlightenment, and to convey a sense of that responsive intelligence indicating an active, rather than a passive, interest in those pursuits of civilization illustrated in the surrounding figures, groups, and relievos. . . . To identify the figure with one of the most memorable undertakings of the public life of the Prince—the International Exhibition of 1851—a catalogue of the works collected in that first gathering of the industry of all nations is placed in the right hand.' The statue was of bronze gilt and weighed nearly ten tons. It was rightly supposed that the simple word 'Albert', cast on the base, would be a sufficient means of identification.

LYTTON STRACHEY : *Queen Victoria.*

This, by the way, is why children are never taught contemporary history. Their history books deal with periods of which the thinking has passed out of fashion, and the circumstances no longer apply to active life. For example, they are taught history about Washington, and told lies about Lenin. In Washington's time they were told lies (the same lies) about Washington, and taught history about Cromwell. In the fifteenth and sixteenth centuries they were told lies about Joan, and by this time might very well be told the truth about her. Unfortunately the lies did not cease when the political circumstances became obsolete. The Reformation, which Joan had unconsciously anticipated, kept the questions which arose in her case burning up to our own day (you can see plenty of the burnt houses still in Ireland), with the result that Joan has remained the subject of anti-Clerical lies, of specifically Protestant lies, and of Roman Catholic evasions of her unconscious Protestantism. The truth sticks in our throats with all the sauces it is served with : it will never go down until we take it without any sauce at all.

G. B. SHAW : *Preface to 'St. Joan'.*

Indeed, it is a question if the exclusive reign of this orthodox beauty is not approaching its last quarter. The new Vale of

Tempe may be a gaunt waste in Thule: human souls may find themselves in closer and closer harmony with external things wearing a sombreness distasteful to our race when it was young. The time seems near, if it has not actually arrived, when the chastened sublimity of a moor, a sea, or a mountain will be all of nature that is absolutely in keeping with the moods of the more thinking among mankind. And ultimately, to the commonest tourist, spots like Iceland may become what the vineyards and myrtle-gardens of South Europe are to him now: and Heidelberg and Baden be passed unheeded as he hastens from the Alps to the sand-dunes of Scheveningen.

The most thoroughgoing ascetic could feel that he had a natural right to wander on Egdon: he was keeping within the line of legitimate indulgence when he laid himself open to influences such as these. Colours and beauties so far subdued were, at least, the birthright of all. Only in summer days of highest feather did its mood touch the level of gaiety. Intensity was more usually reached by way of the solemn than by way of the brilliant, and such a sort of intensity was often arrived at during winter darkness, tempests, and mists. Then Egdon was aroused to reciprocity; for the storm was its lover, and the wind its friend. Then it became the home of strange phantoms; and it was found to be the hitherto unrecognized original of those wild regions of obscurity which are vaguely felt to be compassing us about in midnight dreams of flight and disaster, and are never thought of after the dream till revived by scenes like this.

It was at present a place perfectly accordant with man's nature—neither ghastly, hateful, nor ugly: neither commonplace, unmeaning, nor tame; but, like man, slighted and enduring; and withal singularly colossal and mysterious in its swarthy monotony. As with some persons who have long lived apart, solitude seemed to look out of its countenance. It had a lonely face, suggesting tragical possibilities.

THOMAS HARDY: *The Return of the Native.*

They are dark caves. Even when they open towards the sun, very little light penetrates down the entrance tunnel into the circular chamber. There is little to see, and no eye to see it, until the visitor arrives for his five minutes, and strikes a match. Immediately another flame arises in the depths of the rock and moves towards the surface like an imprisoned spirit: the walls of the circular chamber have been most marvellously polished. The two flames approach and strive to unite, but cannot, because one of them breathes air, the other stone. A mirror inlaid with lovely colours divides the lovers, delicate stars of pink and grey interpose, exquisite nebulae, shadings fainter than the tail of a comet or the midday moon, all the evanescent life of the granite, only here visible. Fists and fingers thrust above the advancing soil—here at last is their skin, finer than any covering acquired by the animals, smoother than windless water, more voluptuous than love. The radiance increases, the flames touch one another, kiss, expire. The cave is dark again, like all the caves.

E. M. FORSTER: *A Passage to India.*

The corn was orient and immortal wheat, which never should be reaped, nor was ever sown. I thought it had stood from everlasting to everlasting. The dust and stones of the street were as precious as gold: the gates were at first the end of the world. The green trees when I saw them first through one of the gates transported and ravished me, their sweetness and unusual beauty made my heart to leap, and almost mad with ecstasy, they were such strange and wonderful things. The Men! O what venerable and reverend creatures did the aged seem! Immortal Cherubims! And young men glittering and sparkling Angels, and maids strange seraphic pieces of life and beauty! Boys and girls tumbling in the street, and playing, were moving jewels. I knew not that they were born or should die; but all things abided eternally as they were in their proper places. Eternity was manifest in the light of the day, and something infinite behind everything appeared: which talked with my expectation and moved my desire. The city seemed to stand in Eden, or to be built in Heaven. The streets were mine, the temple was mine, the people were mine, their clothes and gold and silver were mine, as much as their sparkling eyes, fair skins, and ruddy faces. The skies were mine, and so were the sun and moon and stars, and all the World was mine; and I the only spectator and enjoyer of it.

THOMAS TRAHERNE: *Centuries of Meditations.*

David has very beautifully represented this steady reliance on God Almighty in his twenty-third Psalm, which is a kind of *Pastoral* Hymn, and filled with those allusions which are usual in that kind of writing. As the poetry is very exquisite, I shall present my reader with the following translation of it.

The Lord my pasture shall prepare,
And feed me with a shepherd's care:
His presence shall my wants supply,
And guard me with a watchful eye;
My noon-day walks he shall attend,
And all my mid-night hours defend.

When in the sultry glebe I faint,
Or on the thirsty mountain pant;
To fertile vales and dewy meads,
My weary wand'ring steps he leads;
Where peaceful rivers soft and slow
Amid the verdant landskip flow.

Tho' in the paths of death I tread,
With gloomy horrors over-spread;
My steadfast heart shall fear no ill,
For thou, O Lord, art with me still;
Thy friendly crook shall give me aid,
And guide me through the dreadful shade.

Tho' in a bare and rugged way,
Through devious lonely wilds I stray,
Thy bounty shall my pains beguile:
The barren wilderness shall smile
With sudden greens and herbage crown'd,
And streams shall murmur all around.

ADDISON: *The Spectator*, No. 441.

The Lord is my shepherd; I shall not want. He maketh me
to lie down in green pastures: he leadeth me beside the still
waters. He restoreth my soul: he leadeth me in the paths of
righteousness for his name's sake. Yea, though I walk through
the valley of the shadow of death, I will fear no evil: for thou
art with me; thy rod and thy staff they comfort me. Thou
preparest a table before me in the presence of mine enemies: thou
anointest my head with oil; my cup runneth over. Surely
goodness and mercy shall follow me all the days of my life: and
I will dwell in the house of the Lord for ever.

Psalm Twenty-three.

'Being now resolved to be a poet, I saw everything with a
new purpose; my sphere of attention was suddenly magnified;
no kind of knowledge was to be overlooked. I ranged mountains
and deserts for images and resemblances, and pictured upon my
mind every tree of the forest and flower of the valley. I observed
with equal care the crags of the rock and the pinnacles of the
palace. Sometimes I wandered along the mazes of the rivulet,
and sometimes watched the changes of the summer clouds. To
a poet nothing can be useless. Whatever is beautiful, and
whatever is dreadful, must be familiar to his imagination: he
must be conversant with all that is awfully vast or elegantly
little. The plants of the garden, the animals of the wood, the

minerals of the earth, and meteors of the sky, must all concur to store his mind with inexhaustible variety: for every idea is useful for the enforcement or decoration of moral or religious truth; and he who knows most will have most power of diversifying his scenes, and of gratifying his reader with remote allusions and unexpected instruction.

'All the appearances of nature I was therefore careful to study; and every country which I have surveyed has contributed something to my poetical powers.'

'In so wide a survey', said the prince, 'you must surely have left much unobserved. I have lived, till now, within the circuit of these mountains, and yet cannot walk abroad without the sight of something which I had never beheld before, or never heeded.'

'The business of a poet', said Imlac, 'is to examine, not the individual, but the species; to remark general properties and large appearances. He does not number the streaks of the tulip, or describe the different shades in the verdure of the forest: he is to exhibit in his portraits of nature such prominent and striking features, as recall the original to every mind; and must neglect the minuter discriminations, which one may have remarked, and another have neglected, for those characteristics which are alike obvious to vigilance and carelessness.'

JOHNSON: *Rasselas.*

Laodameia died; Helen died; Leda, the beloved of Jupiter, went before. It is better to repose in the earth betimes than to sit up late; better, than to cling pertinaciously to what we feel crumbling under us, and to protract an inevitable fall. We may enjoy the present, while we are insensible of infirmity and decay; but the present, like a note in music, is nothing but as it appertains to what is past and what is to come. There are no fields of amaranth on this side of the grave; there are no voices, O Rhodope, that are not soon mute, however tuneful; there is no name, with whatever emphasis of passionate love repeated, of which the echo is not faint at last.

LANDOR: *Aesop and Rhodope.*

The eldest of the three is called *Mater Lachrymarum*, Our Lady of Tears. She it is that night and day moans, calling for vanished faces. She stood in Rama, where a voice was heard of lamentation,—Rachel weeping for her children, and refusing to be comforted. She it was who stood in Bethlehem on the night when Herod's sword swept its nurseries of Innocents, and the little feet were stiffened for ever which, heard at times as they trotted along floors overhead, woke pulses of love in household hearts that were not unmarked in heaven. Her eyes are sweet and subtle, wild and sleepy, by turns; oftentimes rising to the clouds, oftentimes challenging the heavens. She wears a diadem round her head. And I knew by childish memories that she could go abroad upon the winds, when she heard the sobbing of litanies, or the thundering of organs, and when she beheld the mustering of summer clouds. This Sister, the elder, it is that carries keys more than papal at her girdle, which open every cottage and every palace. . . . By the power of the keys it is that Our Lady of Tears glides, a ghostly intruder, into the chambers of sleepless men, sleepless women, sleepless children, from Ganges to the Nile, from Nile to Mississippi. And her, because she is the firstborn of her house, and has the widest empire, let us honour with the title of 'Madonna'.

DE QUINCEY: *Suspiria de Profundis.*

The nights now are full of wind and destruction; the trees plunge and bend and their leaves fly helter skelter until the lawn is plastered with them and they lie packed in gutters and choke rain pipes and scatter damp paths. Also the sea tosses itself and breaks itself, and should any sleeper fancying that he might find on the beach an answer to his doubts, a sharer of his solitude, throw off his bedclothes and go down by himself to walk on the sand, no image with semblance of serving and divine promptitude comes readily to hand bringing the night to order and making the world reflect the compass of the soul. The hand dwindles in his hand; the voice bellows in his ear. Almost it would appear that it is useless in such confusion to ask the night those questions as to what, and why, and wherefore, which tempt the sleeper from his bed to seek an answer.

[Mr. Ramsay stumbling along a passage stretched his arms out one dark morning, but, Mrs. Ramsay having died rather suddenly the night before, he stretched his arms out. They remained empty.]

VIRGINIA WOOLF: *To the Lighthouse.*

Home! My people were not their sort out beyond there so far as I can. For all the bold and bad and bleary they are blamed, the seahags. No! Nor for all our wild dances in all their wild din. I can see meself among them, allaniuvia pulchrabelled. How she was handsome, the wild Amazia, when she would seize to my other breast! And what is she weird, haughty Niluna, that she will snatch from my ownest hair! For 'tis they are the stormies. Ho Hang! Hang Ho! And the clash of our cries till we spring to be free. Auravoles, they says, never heed of

your name! But I'm loothing them that's here and all I lothe.
Loonely in me loneness. For all their faults. I am passing out.
O bitter ending! I'll slip away before they're up. They'll
never see. Nor know. Nor miss me. And it's old and old it's
sad and old it's sad and weary I go back to you, my cold father, my
cold mad father, my cold mad feary father, till the near sight of
the mere size of him, the moyles and moyles of it, moananoaning,
makes me seasilt saltsick and I rush, my only, into your arms.
I see them rising! Save me from those therrble prongs! Two
more. One two moremens more. So. Avelaval. My leaves
have drifted from me. All. But one clings still. I'll bear it on
me. To remind me of. Lff! So soft this morning ours. Yes.
Carry me along, taddy, like you done through the toy fair. If
I seen him bearing down on me under white-spread wings like
he'd come from Arkangels, I sink I'd die down over his feet,
humbly dumbly, only to washup. Yes, tid. There's where.
First. We pass through grass behush the bush to. Whish! A
gull. Gulls. Far calls. Coming, far! End here. Us then.
Finn, again! Take. Bussoftlhee, mememormee! Till thous-
endsthee. Lps. The keys to. Given! A way a lone a last a
loved a long the

JAMES JOYCE: *Finnegans Wake.*

CHAPTER XII

VERSE

THERE is much confused thinking about Verse and Poetry which are often used as synonymous terms signifying a form of writing easily recognizable by its characteristic rhythm and rhyme. But rhyme is only one of many conventions, and by no means essential either to verse or to poetry; 'blank' verse indeed means verse 'unloaded' with rhyme; and if rhyming verse were the only poetry, then most of our hymns and nursery rhymes would have to be classed as poetry—some of them are—while the greater part of Shakespeare's and Milton's works would be excluded.

Whether verse, rhyming or blank, is at the same time poetry is another matter. For the moment it must be sufficient to say that most verse is not poetry, and to define poetry simply as 'great verse'.

By verse we mean writing that has a more or less regular rhythm which we call metre. Prose too, or at least good prose, has a rhythm, but it is a free and variable movement following no fixed pattern, as a dancer may perform the most intricate of figures without repeating his movements. But verse has a fixed pattern which it must follow, and though it may stray a little to one side or the other it must return to the pattern as its norm. It is simpler, however, to consider this regular rhythm or metre in its strictest form, without allowing for any deviation.

If we take the word 'again', it is obvious that the second syllable is stressed more strongly than the first, so that if we write the word four or five times we get a sequence of stressed and unstressed syllables, with the accent or stress falling on the even numbers, thus:

Agáin, agáin, agáin, agáin, agáin.

It will be seen that the pattern is the same in this line from Gray's *Elegy*:

The bréezy cáll of íncense-bréathing Mórn.

If therefore we denote an unstressed syllable by the sign ◡, and a stressed syllable by –, we can divide either line into five identical groups of two syllables:

$$|\cup-|\cup-|\cup-|\cup-|\cup-|$$

Each of these groups of two syllables is called a foot, and this particular foot is called an iamb. There are, therefore, five iambic feet in each of these lines.

In his last speech King Lear says of his dead daughter, Cordelia:

> Thou'llt come no more,
> Never, never, never, never, never.

Here in the second line the accent is reversed, so that in the repeated 'never' we have five feet in which the stress comes on the odd syllables:

$$|-\cup|-\cup|-\cup|-\cup|-\cup|$$

Longfellow in the *Song of Hiawatha* uses this type of foot:

> Fast and far they fled to northward,
> Fast and far through mist and sunshine,
> Fed among the moors and fenlands,
> Slept among the reeds and rushes.

This foot is called the trochee, and *Hiawatha* is written with four trochaic feet in the line.

Because some syllables are naturally stressed more strongly than others it is not possible to write verse in which every syllable is stressed or every syllable unstressed. There are, nevertheless, two-syllabled feet in which both are stressed or both unstressed. Consider the line—again from *Hiawatha*:

> Straightway to a brant they changed him.

The word 'straightway' is naturally pronounced with approximately the same stress on each syllable, so that the foot is really – –, that is a spondee. The next two syllables 'to a' are unstressed $\cup\cup$, a pyrrhic foot.

The analysis of a line of verse into its component feet is called scansion, so that the line in question might be scanned:

> | Strāightwāy | tŏ ă | brānt thěy | chānged hǐm. |

which would be more reasonable than:

> | Strāightwăy | tō ă | brānt thěy | chānged hǐm. |

M

Although therefore we cannot write verse—of any length—entirely in spondees or pyrrhics, it is possible to use them occasionally as substitutes for other feet. It will be seen later that this substitution of one foot for another is of paramount importance in the writing of verse.

So far we have considered feet of only two syllables, but there are three-syllabled feet, the commonest of which are the anapaest and dactyl. In the line:

> In a coign of the cliff between lowland and highland,

or,

> Where the weeds that grew green from the graves of its roses,

the main accent falls on every third syllable, so that we migh scan:

> | Ĭn ă cōign | ŏf thĕ clīff | bĕtweĕn lōw | lănd ănd hīgh | lănd

Here there are four anapaests followed by a redundant unstressed syllable; or the last four syllables might be treated as a pyrrhic followed by a trochee:

> | lănd ănd | hīghlănd. |

or even as a single four-syllabled foot called a paeon:

> | lănd ănd hīghlănd. |

But it is very rarely in English verse that we find a genuine foot of more than three syllables, so that nearly all our verse can be scanned as iambs, trochees, anapaests, or dactyls, with an occasional spondee or pyrrhic, a redundant syllable, or a syllable that must be considered equal to a foot.

The dactyl is not very common in English, and takes the form:

> | Tāke hĕr ŭp | tēndĕrlў, | līft hĕr wĭth | cāre,
> | Fāshiŏned sŏ | slēndĕrlў, | yōung ănd sŏ | fāir.

In English verse, therefore, the commonest feet are:

◡—	iamb.
—◡	trochee.
◡◡—	anapaest.
—◡◡	dactyl.

while occasionally we have:

——	spondee.
◡◡	pyrrhic.

The iambic foot, it should be noticed, is much the most common
in English verse because it is the nearest to our speech rhythm,
and for this reason is the normal foot in our verse plays. Blank
verse, if absolutely regular, has five iambic feet in a line—ten
syllables in all, with the accent on the even numbers—as in the
following extract from the earliest blank-verse tragedy, *Gorboduc*,
written about 1560 by Sackville and Norton.

> Your wonted true regard of faithful hearts
> Makes me, O king, the bolder to resume,
> To speak what I conceive within my breast:
> Although the same do not agree at all
> With that which other here my lords have said,
> Nor which yourself have seemed best to like.

It will be observed that these lines are as regular as it is possible
to make them; that the accent falls with precision and with
approximately the same emphasis on all the even-numbered
syllables; that the 'natural' rhythm of the words coincides with
the iambic pattern;—and that the whole passage is intolerably
wooden and monotonous. It rarely happens that the rhythm
is as inflexible and lifeless as this, where the value of all the
unstressed syllables is the same, and the weight of the stresses
equally heavy.

When we say that a syllable is stressed or unstressed we do not
thereby give it a fixed weight any more than we specify an exact
height when we say that a man is tall or short. We have a
concept of normal height, and a tall man may be one inch or
he may be six inches above this norm; in the same way a syllable
may be stressed beyond the norm, but it may be heavily or
comparatively lightly stressed. Although, therefore, verses may
be in regular iambics, in the sense that the stresses come on the
even numbers, if they are unequal in intensity and the unaccented
syllables similarly varied, variety and elasticity will be given to
the lines. Thus the opening lines of Shakespeare's sonnet—

> When fórty wínters shall besíege thy brów,
> And díg déep trénches in thy béauty's fíeld,
> Thy yóuth's próud lívery so gázed on nów,
> Will be a táttered wéed of smáll wórth héld.

—may without great violence be scanned as iambics, yet neither
odd nor even numbered syllables are equally light or heavy. The
principal stresses are marked; those on *shall*, *in*, *y* in *livery*, *be*
are much lighter; the stress on *deep*, if not as heavy as that on

dig or *trench*, is certainly stronger than that on *in*; and it would be absurd to give the same value to *of* and *worth*. Thus, although all the feet may be reckoned as iambic, variety is achieved by varying the stresses within the feet themselves.

All art is concerned with making a pattern, whether in space or time; but a pattern constructed of exactly similar parts, however beautiful in themselves, would be intolerably dull—as dull as the blank verse of *Gorboduc*—so the artist animates the pattern by varying the detail, sometimes boldly, sometimes so delicately that careful analysis is needed to detect the quickening quality. There must be variety within the pattern; variety as well as unity.

We have seen how one type of variety can be achieved by modifying the values of the stresses and 'slacks'. It may be remarked in passing that this is more difficult to accomplish in metres other than the iambic, possibly because they are more artificial in the sense that they are further removed from ordinary speech rhythm. The tendency in reading anapaests or trochees, for example, is to give much the same value to all the stressed syllables, and it is difficult to avoid falling into singsong.

But there are other ways of securing variety. Consider the beginning of Wyatt's sonnet—

> The lively sparks | that issue from those eyes, |
> Against the which | there vaileth no defence, |
> Have pierced my heart, | and done it none offence, |
> With quaking pleasure | more than once or twice. |
> Was never man | could anything devise, |
> Sunbeams to turn | with so great vehemence |
> To daze man's sight, | as by their bright presence |
> Dazéd am I. |

It is clear that the main pause in nearly every line comes after the fourth syllable, that is after the second foot. Not only this, but most of the lines are end-stopped; there is a natural pause at the end of the line, so that in effect the verse is a series of alternating groups of four and six syllables. The main pause in a line is called a caesura; there may be no caesura, or there may be a caesura and one or more subordinate pauses. Obviously the more these breaks are shifted and varied the more life will be given to the verse, and if skilfully done the more graceful will it be.

Compare Wyatt's sonnet with one by Wordsworth—

Milton ! | thou shouldst be living at this hour : |
England hath need of thee : | she is a fen
Of stagnant waters : | altar, sword, and pen,
Fireside, | the heroic wealth of hall and bower, |
Have forfeited their ancient English dower
Of inward happiness. |

The verse is fluid, for not only are the pauses varied within the line, but some of the lines run over into the following ones. The unit is the paragraph rather than the line, and the verse cannot be chopped into regular sections with the same number of syllables.

It is true that too great laxity in the construction of verse leads to chaos, as in Davenant :

Rhodolinda doth become her title
And her birth. Since deprived of popular
Homage she hath been queen over her great self.
In this captivity ne'er passionate
But when she hears me name the king, and then
Her passions not of anger taste but love :
Love of her conqueror : he that in fierce
Battle (when the cannon's sulphurous breath
Clouded the day) her noble father slew.

Finally, consider this passage from *Paradise Lost* in which Milton restores the balance between unity and variety :

All in a moment through the gloom were seen
Ten thousand banners rise into the air
With orient colours waving : with them rose
A forest of huge spears ; and thronging helms
Appeared, and serried shields in thick array
Of depth immeasurable. Anon they move
In perfect phalanx to the Dorian mood
Of flutes and soft recorders ; such as raised
To height of noblest temper heroes old
Arming to battle ; and, instead of rage,
Deliberate valour breathed, firm and unmoved
With dread of death to flight or foul retreat ;
Nor wanting power to mitigate and swage,
With solemn touches troubled thoughts, and chase
Anguish, and doubt, and fear, and sorrow, and pain,
From mortal or immortal minds.

The most important form of variety in the writing of verse remains to be considered. It is similar to counter-point in music, and has already been hinted at in discussing the spondee and pyrrhic, when it was seen that these feet might be substituted for others.

Here is the famous verse from Keats's *Ode to a Nightingale*:

> Thou wast not born for death, immortal Bird!
> No hungry generations tread thee down;
> The voice I hear this passing night was heard
> In ancient days by emperor and clown:
> Perhaps the self-same song hath found a path
> Through the sad heart of Ruth, when, sick for home,
> She stood in tears amid the alien corn;
> The same that oft-times hath
> Charmed magic casements, opening on the foam
> Of perilous seas, in faery lands forlorn.

This is obviously written in iambics, yet it would be monstrous to force the whole verse into the iambic mould—indeed it would be impossible to scan the eleven syllables of the last line as five iambic feet. We cannot read—

> Through thé sad héart of Rúth—

the accent must come on 'through', the first two syllables forming a trochee. Similarly in the last two lines—

> Charmed magic casements, opening on the foam
> Of perilous seas, in faery lands forlorn.

—although the first might be wrenched into iambics, it is really—

$$|-\ -|\cup-|\cup-|\cup\cup-|\cup-|$$

while the last line must be—

$$|\cup-|\cup\cup-|\cup-|\cup-|\cup-|$$

In these three lines, therefore, a trochee, a spondee, and two anapaests are substituted for iambs, yet there is no doubt that the basic rhythm is iambic. In addition to this new form of variety there are, of course, the effects already noticed: the shifting of the pauses, and the varied stresses on feet which might properly be classed as iambic; consider, for instance, the rhythm of—

> Thou wast not born for death,
> No hungry generations,
> emperor and clown.

There is, therefore, a second rhythm mounted on the primary or basic iambics, much as one sequence of shots is mounted on another in a film, or as one melody is woven into another in contrapuntal music. It is, in fact, contrapuntal rhythm, for the ear is conscious of both rhythms: the natural rhythm of the words, supported by the severe harmony of the basic foot. In diagrammatic form the line, 'Charmed magic casements, opening on the foam' might be rendered—

Charmed mag–ic case-ments op-en-ing on the foam.

This approximation of the particular to the ideal or standard rhythm, always approaching, sometimes coinciding, but continually slipping elusively away, is akin to the distortion in representational art, which is contrapuntal because it is not merely a facsimile, but a modified, simplified, and therefore distorted representation of the original. In a sculpture, for example, the original and the statue are conceived simultaneously by the spectator, as the two rhythms of verse are fused in the ear. If the two correspond exactly there is no art, only a cold and lifeless copy of the original.

Of course, verse in which the basic foot is too frequently replaced by other feet will be confusion. If, for example, in so-called iambic verse there are more trochees, dactyls, and anapaests than there are iambs, the contrapuntal effect will be lost, and it will disintegrate into doggerel.

The inexperienced reader can most easily appreciate verse with a well-defined swinging rhythm such as Kipling's:

> You couldn't pack a Broadwood half a mile—
> You mustn't leave a fiddle in the damp—
> You couldn't raft an organ up the Nile,
> And play it in an Equatorial swamp.

He can only just tell the difference between blank verse and prose, and is puzzled and angered by still freer metrical forms. The border-line between verse and prose is fluid, and there does come a time, it is true, when it is difficult to discover any metrical basis, as sometimes in Walt Whitman's verse:

Silent and amazed even when a little boy,
I remember I heard the preacher every Sunday put God in his
      statements,
As contending against some being or influence.

Compare this with a passage—a bad one—of Dickens's prose:

Go, teachers of content and honest pride, into the mine, the
mill, the forge, the squalid depths of deepest ignorance, and
uttermost abyss of man's neglect, and say can any helpful plant
spring up in air so foul that it extinguishes the soul's bright
torch as fast as it is kindled.

The Whitman extract is certainly less metrical than the Dickens,
which is blank verse with scarcely any irregularity. Verse
masquerading as prose is unpleasant, but is a common fault of
writers under the compulsion of some strong emotion, or when
they set out to produce a particularly purple passage.

The man who has, perhaps, most influenced modern poets in
their metrical forms is G. M. Hopkins. After commenting on
the contrapuntal nature of 'Common English Rhythm, called Running Rhythm', he goes on to explain his own 'Sprung Rhythm':

Sprung Rhythm is measured by feet of from one to four syllables,
regularly, and for particular effects any number of weak or slack
syllables may be used. It has one stress, which falls on the only
syllable, if there is only one, or, if there are more, then scanning
as above, on the first, and so gives rise to four sorts of feet, a
monosyllable and the so-called accentual Trochee, Dactyl, and
the First Paeon. And there will be four corresponding natural
rhythms; but nominally the feet are mixed and any one may
follow any other. And hence Sprung Rhythm differs from
Running Rhythm in having or being only one nominal rhythm,
a mixed or 'logaoedic' one, instead of three, but on the other
hand in having twice the flexibility of foot, so that any two
stresses may either follow one another running or be divided by
one, two, or three slack syllables. But strict Sprung Rhythm
cannot be counterpointed. In Sprung Rhythm, as in logaoedic
rhythm generally, the feet are assumed to be equally long or
strong and their seeming inequality is made up by pause or
stressing.

Remark also that it is natural in Sprung Rhythm for the lines
to be rove over, that is for the scanning of each line immediately
to take up that of the one before, so that if the first has one or
more syllables at its end the other must have so many the less
at its beginning; and in fact the scanning runs on without break

from the beginning, say, of a stanza to the end and all the stanza is one long strain, though written in lines asunder.

In the light of his explanation of sprung rhythm, consider Hopkins's magnificent sonnet *The Windhover*. It would be impossible to scan this poem in an orthodox way, but if it is realized that there are in each line five stresses followed by any number of slack syllables up to three, and that except for the stresses the metrical scheme is independent of the lines, it will be seen that there is a restraining rhythmical pattern very different from the free rhythm of prose.

I caught this morning morning's minion, king-
    dom of daylight's dauphin, dapple-dawn-drawn Falcon, in his
      riding
Of the rolling level underneath him steady air, and striding
High there, how he rung upon the rein of a wimpling wing
In his ecstasy! then off, off forth on swing,
    As a skate's heel sweeps smooth on a bow-bend: the hurl and
      gliding
Rebuffed the big wind. My heart in hiding
Stirred for a bird,—the achieve of, the mastery of the thing!

Brute beauty and valour and act, oh, air, pride, plume, here
    Buckle! And the fire that breaks from thee then, a billion
Times told lovelier, more dangerous, O my chevalier!

 No wonder of it: shéer plód makes plough down sillion
Shine, and blue-bleak embers, ah my dear,
    Fall, gall themselves, and gash gold-vermilion.

        Go, litel book, go litel myn tregedie,
        Ther god thy maker yet, er that he dye,
        So sende might to make in som comedie!
        But litel book, no making thou nenvye,
        But subgit be to alle poesye;
        And kis the steppes, wher-as thou seest pace
        Virgile, Ovyde, Omer, Lucan, and Stace.

        And for there is so greet diversitee
        In English and in wryting of our tonge,
        So preye I god that noon miswryte thee,
        Ne thee mismetre for defaute of tonge.
        And red wher-so thou be, or elles songe,
        That thou be understonde I god beseche!
               CHAUCER: *Troilus and Criseyde.*

Was this the face that launched a thousand ships,
And burnt the topless towers of Ilium?—
Sweet Helen, make me immortal with a kiss.—
Her lips suck forth my soul: see, where it flies!—
Come, Helen, come, give me my soul again.
Here will I dwell, for heaven is in these lips,
And all is dross that is not Helena.
I will be Paris, and for love of thee,
Instead of Troy, shall Wittenberg be sacked;
And I will combat with weak Menelaus,
And wear thy colours on my plumed crest;
Yea, I will wound Achilles in the heel,
And then return to Helen for a kiss.
O, thou art fairer than the evening air
Clad in the beauty of a thousand stars;
Brighter art thou than flaming Jupiter
When he appeared to hapless Semele;
More lovely than the monarch of the sky
In wanton Arethusa's azured arms;
And none but thou shalt be my paramour.

MARLOWE: *Dr. Faustus.*

What would it pleasure me to have my throat cut
With diamonds? or to be smothered
With cassia? or to be shot to death with pearls?
I know death hath ten thousand several doors
For men to take their exits; and 'tis found
They go on such strange geometrical hinges,
You may open them both ways; any way, for Heaven sake,
So I were out of your whispering. Tell my brothers
That I perceive death, now I am well awake,
Best gift is they can give or I can take.
I would fain put off my last woman's fault,
I'd not be tedious to you.

JOHN WEBSTER: *The Duchess of Malfi.*

Cromwell, I did not think to shed a tear
In all my miseries; but thou hast forced me,
Out of thy honest truth, to play the woman.
Let's dry our eyes: and thus far hear me, Cromwell;
And, when I am forgotten, as I shall be,
And sleep in dull cold marble, where no mention
Of me more must be heard of, say, I taught thee;
Say, Wolsey, that once trod the ways of glory,

And sounded all the depths and shoals of honour,
Found thee a way, out of his wreck, to rise in;
A sure and safe one, though thy master missed it.
Mark but my fall and that that ruined me.
Cromwell, I charge thee, fling away ambition:
By that sin fell the angels; how can man then,
The image of his Maker, hope to win by it?

SHAKESPEARE: *Henry VIII.*
(Or, more probably, JOHN FLETCHER.)

They dream of little Charles or William graced
With wig prolix, down flowing to his waist;
They see the attentive crowds his talents draw,
They hear him speak—the oracle of law.
The father, who designs his babe a priest,
Dreams him episcopally such at least;
And, while the playful jockey scours the room
Briskly, astride upon the parlour broom,
In fancy sees him more superbly ride
In coach with purple lined, and mitres on its side.
Events improbable and strange as these,
Which only a parental eye foresees,
A public school shall bring to pass with ease.

WILLIAM COWPER: *Tirocinium.*

Know then thyself, presume not God to scan;
The proper study of mankind is Man.
Placed on this isthmus of a middle state,
A being darkly wise, and rudely great:
With too much knowledge for the sceptic side,
With too much weakness for the Stoic's pride,
He hangs between; in doubt to act, or rest;
In doubt to deem himself a god, or beast;
In doubt his mind or body to prefer;
Born but to die, and reasoning but to err;
Alike in ignorance, his reason such,
Whether he thinks too little, or too much:
Chaos of thought and passion, all confused;
Still by himself abused, or disabused;
Created half to rise, and half to fall;
Great lord of all things, yet a prey to all;
Sole judge of truth, in endless error hurled:
The glory, jest and riddle of the world!

POPE: *Essay on Man.*

Thou shalt have one God only; who
Would be at the expense of two?
No graven images may be
Worshipped, except the currency:
Swear not at all; for, for thy curse
Thine enemy is none the worse:
At church on Sunday to attend
Will serve to keep the world thy friend:
Honour thy parents; that is, all
From whom advancement may befall:
Thou shalt not kill; but need'st not strive
Officiously to keep alive:
Do not adultery commit;
Advantage rarely comes of it:
Thou shalt not steal; an empty feat,
When it's so lucrative to cheat:
Bear not false witness; let the lie
Have time on its own wings to fly:
Thou shalt not covet, but tradition
Approves all forms of competition.

                    A. H. CLOUGH: *The Latest Decalogue.*

What of Rafael's sonnets, Dante's picture?
This: no artist lives and loves, that longs not
Once, and only once, and for one only,
(Ah, the prize!) to find his love a language
Fit and fair and simple and sufficient—
Using nature that's an art to others,
Not, this one time, art that's turned his nature.
Ay, of all the artists living, loving,
None but would forego his proper dowry,—
Does he paint? he fain would write a poem,—
Does he write? he fain would paint a picture,
Put to proof art alien to the artist's,
Once, and only once, and for one only,
So to be the man and leave the artist,
Gain the man's joy, miss the artist's sorrow.

                ROBERT BROWNING: *One Word More.*

Out of the golden remote wild west where the sea without shore is,
    Full of the sunset, and sad, if at all, with the fulness of joy,
As a wind sets in with the autumn that blows from the region of
        stories,
    Blows with a perfume of songs and of memories beloved from a
        boy,

Blows from the capes of the past oversea to the bays of the present,
   Filled as with shadow of sound with the pulse of invisible
     feet,
Far out to the shallows and straits of the future, by rough ways
   or pleasant,
   Is it thither the wind's wings beat?   Is it hither to me, O my
     sweet?
                    SWINBURNE: *Hesperia.*

     Cold eyelids that hide like a jewel
       Hard eyes that grow soft for an hour;
     The heavy white limbs, and the cruel
       Red mouth like a venomous flower;
     When these are gone by with their glories,
       What shall rest with thee then, what remain,
     O mystic and sombre Dolores,
       Our Lady of Pain?
                  SWINBURNE: *Dolores.*

      Spring and Fall (*to a young child*)
     Márgarét, are you grieving
     Over Goldengrove unleaving?
     Léaves, líke the things of man, you
     With your fresh thoughts care for, can you?
     Áh! ás the heart grows older
     It will come to such sights colder
     By and by, nor spare a sigh
     Though worlds of wanwood leafmeal lie;
     And yet you will weep and know why.
     Now no matter, child, the name:
     Sórrow's spríngs áre the same.
     Nor mouth had, no nor mind, expressed
     What heart heard of, ghost guessed:
     It ís the blight man was born for,
     It is Margaret you mourn for.
                  G. M. HOPKINS.

I do not know much about gods; but I think that the river
Is a strong brown god—sullen, untamed and intractable,
Patient to some degree, at first recognized as a frontier;
Useful, untrustworthy, as a conveyer of commerce;
Then only a problem confronting the builder of bridges.
The problem once solved, the brown god is almost forgotten
By the dwellers in cities—ever, however, implacable,
Keeping his seasons and rages, destroyer, reminder

Of what men choose to forget.   Unhonoured, unpropitiated
By worshippers of the machine, but waiting, watching and waiting.
His rhythm was present in the nursery bedroom,
In the rank ailanthus of the April dooryard,
In the smell of grapes on the autumn table,
And the evening circle in the winter gaslight.

T. S. ELIOT: *The Dry Salvages.*

The Hexameter is the great staple metre of Greek and Latin
Epic, in which the line consists of six feet, dactyls or spondees at
choice for the first four, but normally always a dactyl in the fifth
and always a spondee in the sixth—the latter foot being by special
licence sometimes allowed in the fifth also, but never a dactyl
in the sixth.

G. SAINTSBURY: *Manual of English Prosody.*

In the hexameter rises the fountain's silvery column;
In the pentameter aye falling in melody back.

S. T. COLERIDGE.

William, my teacher, my friend! dear William and dear
    Dorothea!
Smooth out the folds of my letter, and place it on desk or on
    table;
Place it on table or desk; and your right hands loosely half-
    closing,
Gently sustain them in air, and extending the digit didactic,
Rest it a moment on each of the forks of the five-forkéd left hand,
Twice on the breadth of the thumb, and once on the tip of each
    finger;
Read with a nod of the head in a humouring recitativo;
And, as I live, you will see my hexameters hopping before you.
This is a galloping measure; a hop, and a trot, and a gallop!

All my hexameters fly, like stags pursued by the stag-hounds,
Breathless and panting, and ready to drop, yet flying still onwards,
I would full fain pull in my hard-mouthed runaway hunter;
But our English Spondeans are clumsy yet impotent curb-reins;
And so to make him go slowly, no way left have I but to lame him.

S. T. COLERIDGE: *Hexameters.*

It was the afternoon; and the sports were now at the ending.
Long had the stone been put, tree cast, and thrown the hammer;
Up the perpendicular hill, Sir Hector so called it,
Eight stout gillies had run, with speed and agility wondrous:

Run too the course on the level had been; the leaping was over:
Last in the show of dress, a novelty recently added,
Noble ladies their prizes adjudged for costume that was perfect,
Turning the clansmen about, as they stood with upraised elbows;
Bowing their eye-glassed brows, and fingering kilt and sporran.
It was four of the clock, and the sports were come to the ending,
Therefore the Oxford party went off to adorn for the dinner.

ARTHUR HUGH CLOUGH: *The Bothie of Tober-na-vuolich.*

As to the metre used here, it should be said that neither the heroic couplet nor the English hexameter—the two metres most commonly used in translations of the Georgics—seemed to me adequate now for the rendering of the Latin hexameter. After much experiment, I decided to use a rhythm based on the hexameter, containing six beats in each line, but allowing much variation of pace and interspersed with occasional short lines of three stresses. This metre, I hoped, would be elastic enough to avoid the monotony of the English hexameter, and more consonant with the speech-rhythms of the present day.

For the rest, when the golden sun has driven winter to ground
And opened up all the leagues of the sky in summer light,
Over the glades and woodlands at once they love to wander
And suck the shining flowers and delicate sip the streams.
Sweet then is their strange delight
As they cherish their children, their nestlings: then with craftsmanship they
Hammer out the fresh wax and mould the tacky honey.
Then, as you watch the swarm bursting from hive and heavenward
Soaring, and floating there on the limpid air of summer—
A vague and wind-warped column of cloud to your wondering
eyes:—
Notice them, how they always make for fresh water and leafy
Shelter. Here you shall sprinkle fragrances to their taste—
Crushed balm, honeywort humble—
Make a tinkling noise round about and clash the Mother-god's
cymbals.
They will settle down of their own accord in the place you have
perfumed,
And crawl to the innermost room for rest, as their custom is.

C. DAY LEWIS: *The Georgics of Virgil.*

O you chorus of indolent reviewers,
Irresponsible, indolent reviewers,
Look, I come to the test, a tiny poem
All composed in the metre of Catullus,

All in quantity, careful of my motion,
Like the skater on ice that hardly bears him,
Lest I fall unawares before the people,
Waking laughter in indolent reviewers.
Should I flounder awhile without a tumble
Thro' this metrification of Catullus,
They should speak to me not without a welcome,
All that chorus of indolent reviewers.
Hard, hard, hard is it, only not to tumble,
So fantastical is the dainty metre.
Wherefore slight me not wholly, nor believe me
Too presumptuous, indolent reviewers.
O blatant Magazines, regard me rather—
Since I blush to belaud myself a moment—
As some rare little rose, a piece of inmost
Horticultural art, or half coquette-like
Maiden, not to be greeted unbenignly.

TENNYSON : *Hendecasyllabics.*

Friend of Humanity:
'Needy Knife-grinder! whither are you going?
Rough is the road, your wheel is out of order—
Bleak blows the blast; your hat has got a hole in't,
          So have your breeches!

'Weary Knife-grinder! little think the proud ones,
Who in their coaches roll along the turnpike—
road, what hard work 'tis crying all day "Knives and
          Scissors to grind O!"

'Tell me, Knife-grinder, how you came to grind knives?
Did some rich man tyrannically use you?
Was it the squire, or parson of the parish?
          Or the attorney?

'Was it the squire, for killing of his game? or
Covetous parson, for his tithes distraining?
Or roguish lawyer, made you lose your little
          All in a lawsuit?

'(Have you not read the *Rights of Man*, by Tom Paine?)
Drops of compassion tremble on my eyelids,
Ready to fall, as soon as you have told your
          Pitiful story.'

Knife-grinder:

'Story! God bless you! I have none to tell, sir,
Only last night a-drinking at the Chequers,
This poor old hat and breeches, as you see, were
        Torn in a scuffle.

'Constables came up for to take me into
Custody; they took me before the justice;
Justice Oldmixon put me in the parish
        Stocks for a vagrant.

'I should be glad to drink your Honour's health in
A pot of beer, if you will give me sixpence;
But for my part, I never love to meddle
        With politics, sir.'

Friend of Humanity:

'I give thee sixpence! I will see thee damn'd first—
Wretch! whom no sense of wrongs can rouse to vengeance;
Sordid, unfeeling, reprobate, degraded,
        Spiritless outcast!'

(Kicks the Knife-grinder, overturns his wheel, and exit in a
transport of Republican enthusiasm and universal philanthropy.)

             GEORGE CANNING and J. H. FRERE.

N

CHAPTER XIII

RHYME

RHYME has nothing to do with the definition of verse or of poetry; it is an accidental, not an essential attribute—if not, 'blank verse' would be a contradiction in terms—merely one of the many conventions of metrical composition. Greek and Latin verse do not rhyme, and early English writers, such as Langland in the fourteenth century, used the convention of alliteration instead of rhyme:

> In a somer seson . when soft was the sonne,
> I shope me in shroudes . as I a shepe were,
> In habite as an heremite . unholy of workes,
> Went wide in this world . wondres to here.
> Ac on a May mornynge . on Malverne hulles,
> Me byfel a ferly . of fairy, me thoughte;
> I was wery forwandered . and went me to reste
> Under a brode banke . bi a bornes side,
> And as I lay and lened . and looked in the wateres,
> I slombered in a slepyng . it sweyved so merye.

In the thirteenth century experiments were made with rhyme, but it was Chaucer who finally established rhyme as a more successful convention than alliteration.

Rhyme is the arrangement of word-endings so that the final vowel at least, and the succeeding consonant or consonants, if any, are identical in sound. It is therefore a form of assonance, the repetition of a vowel sound, generally combined with alliteration, the repetition of a consonant. Though rhyme generally occurs at the end of a line it may be internal, that is within the line.

The most usual form is the single rhyme, though double rhyme is fairly common:

> Music when soft voices die
> Vibrates in the memory;
> Odours when sweet violets sicken
> Live within the sense they quicken.
> Rose leaves when the rose is dead
> Are heaped for the beloved's bed;

And so thy thoughts when thou art gone,
Love itself shall slumber on.

Triple rhyme generally has a humorous effect, though Hood uses it in one of his most serious poems:

Touch her not scornfully;
Think of her mournfully,
Gently and humanly;
Not of the stains of her,
All that remains of her
Now is pure womanly.

Sometimes words or syllables are spelled in the same way but are pronounced differently:

And I could tell
What made your eyes a growing gloom of love
As a warm south wind sombres a March grove.

'Love' and 'grove' do not rhyme when spoken, but they are an eye-rhyme, a kind of consonantal rhyme.

A Cockney rhyme is the result of ignoring the pronunciation of the letter 'r':

I shall again see Phoebus in the morning,
Or flushed Aurora in the roseate dawning.

No Scot would confuse 'morn' with 'dawn'.
Other bad rhymes such as,

Though the niggard pasturage
Bears not on its shaven ledge
Aught but leaves,

though not strictly Cockney rhymes share the common defect of slovenly pronunciation. Elizabeth Barrett Browning and D. G. Rossetti are notoriously careless with their rhymes.

It should be noted that words that were once perfect rhymes may no longer be so owing to changes in pronunciation:

Here thou, great Anna! whom three realms obey
Dost sometimes counsel take—and sometimes tea.

Alliteration was the forerunner of rhyme, but there was an intermediate stage when assonance was used as a simplified form of rhyme. Thus in primitive verse such as nursery rhymes and ballads there is often a similarity of vowel sounds only:

> Oranges and lemons,
> Say the bells of St. Clement's.
> You owe me five farthings,
> Say the bells of St. Martin's.
> When will you pay me?
> Say the bells of Old Bailey?

And

> Half ower, half ower to Aberdour,
> It's fifty fathom deep;
> And there lies guid Sir Patrick Spens,
> Wi' the Scots lords at his feet.

Wilfred Owen developed another form of half-rhyme often adopted by modern poets; an alliterative or consonantal rhyme where the vowels vary, but the consonants, generally those immediately before as well as those after the vowel, are repeated. This has the advantage of greater freedom, and instead of the metallic clash of the epigrammatic couplet or the over-sweet rhyming of some verse it suggests an atmosphere of mystery and echoes.

Consider the effect of Owen's poem, *Miners*:

> There was a whispering in my hearth,
>   A sigh of the coal,
> Grown wistful of a former earth
>   It might recall.
>
> I listened for a tale of leaves
>   And smothered ferns;
> Frond-forests; and the low, sly lives
>   Before the fawns.
>
> My fire might show steam-phantoms simmer
>   From Time's old cauldron,
> Before the birds made nests in summer,
>   Or men had children.
>
> But the coals were murmuring of their mine,
>   And moans down there
> Of boys that slept wry sleep, and men
>   Writhing for air.
>
> And I saw white bones in the cinder-shard.
>   Bones without number;
> For many hearts with coal are charred
>   And few remember.

I thought of some who worked dark pits
    Of war, and died
Digging the rock where Death reputes
    Peace lies indeed.

Comforted years will sit soft-chaired
    In rooms of amber;
The years will stretch their hands, well-cheered
    By our lives' ember.

The centuries will burn rich loads
    With which we groaned,
Whose warmth shall lull their dreaming lids
    While songs are crooned.
But they will not dream of us poor lads
    Lost in the ground.

As rhymes may occur inside the lines as well as at the end, and as they may be assonantal or consonantal as well as perfect, rhyme-schemes may be exceedingly intricate. For analysis a rhyme is indicated by a letter of the alphabet; the first rhyme being called 'a', the second 'b', and so on. The combination of these letters represents the rhyme-scheme; thus, the rhyme-scheme of the last verse of *Miners* is: ababab; of the Spenserian stanza it is: ababbcbcc, thus:

A gentle Knight was pricking on the plain,	a
Yclad in mighty arms and silver shield,	b
Wherein old dints of deep wounds did remain,	a
The cruel marks of many a bloody field;	b
Yet arms till that time did he never wield:	b
His angry steed did chide his foaming bit,	c
As much disdaining to the curb to yield:	b
Full jolly knight he seemed, and fair did sit	c
As one for knightly jousts and fierce encounters fit.	c

If poetry lies in the way a thing is said, the rhyme—or lack of rhyme—should be an important factor in the total effect, so that in trying to analyse the appeal of a poem we should consider how far the rhyme is an essential part of the expression. The Spenserian stanza would not be a suitable vehicle for Pope's *Dunciad*, nor would blank verse do for Byron's *Vision of Judgment*; and though we would not have Shakespeare's *King Lear* in rhyming couplets, rhyme is of the essence of his Sonnets.

This brutish poetry, though it had not the beginning in this country, yet so hath it been affected here, that the affection thereof would never—nor, I think, ever will—be rooted up again:—I mean this tinkerly verse which we call rhyme. Master Ascham saith, that it first began to be followed and maintained among the Huns and Gothians, and other barbarous nations, who, with the decay of all good learning, brought it into Italy. From thence it came into France, and so to Germany, at last conveyed into England by men, indeed of great wisdom and learning, but not considerate nor circumspect in that behalf.

E. WEBBE: Discourse (1586).

The measure is English heroic verse without rhyme, as that of Homer in Greek, and of Virgil in Latin; rhyme being no necessary adjunct or true ornament of poem or good verse, in longer works especially, but the invention of a barbarous age, to set off wretched matter and lame metre; graced, indeed, since by the use of some famous modern poets, carried away by custom, but much to their own vexation, hindrance, and constraint to express many things otherwise, and for the most part worse, than else they would have expressed them. Not without cause, therefore, some both Italian and Spanish poets of prime note have rejected rhyme both in longer and shorter works, as have also long since our best English tragedies, as a thing of itself, to all judicious ears, trivial, and of no true musical delight; which consists only in apt numbers, fit quantity of syllables, and the sense variously drawn out from one verse into another, not in the jingling sound of like endings, a fault avoided by the learned ancients both in poetry and all good oratory. This neglect, then, of rhyme so little is to be taken for a defect, though it may seem so perhaps to vulgar readers, that it is rather to be esteemed an example set, the first in English, of ancient liberty recovered to heroic poem, from the troublesome and modern bondage of rhyming.

MILTON: Preface to Paradise Lost (1667).

On His Blindness

When I consider how my light is spent
  Ere half my days, in this dark world and wide,
  And that one talent which is death to hide,
  Lodged with me useless, though my soul more bent
To serve therewith my Maker, and present
  My true account, lest He, returning, chide;
  'Doth God exact day-labour, light denied?'
  I fondly ask: but Patience, to prevent

That murmur, soon replies, 'God doth not need
  Either man's work, or his own gifts; who best
  Bear his mild yoke, they serve Him best; his state
Is kingly; thousands at his bidding speed,
  And post o'er land and ocean without rest;
  They also serve who only stand and wait.

MILTON.

                        Thus with the year
Seasons return, but not to me returns
Day, or the sweet approach of ev'n or morn,
Or sight of vernal bloom, or summer's rose,
Or flocks, or herds, or human face divine;
But cloud instead, and ever-during dark
Surrounds me, from the cheerful ways of men
Cut off, and for the Book of Knowledge fair
Presented with a universal blank
Of Nature's works to me expunged and rased,
And wisdom at one entrance quite shut out.

MILTON: Paradise Lost.

If blank verse be not tumid and gorgeous it is crippled prose....
Blank verse will, I fear, be too often found in description
exuberant, in argument loquacious, and in narrative tiresome.

SAMUEL JOHNSON.

The advantages which rhyme has over blank verse are so
many that it were lost time to name them. Sir Philip Sidney, in
his *Defence of Poesy*, gives us one, which, in my opinion, is not the
least considerable; I mean the help it brings to memory, which
rhyme so knits up, by the affinity of sounds, that, by remembering
the last word in one line, we often call to mind both the verses.
Then, in the quickness of repartees (which in discoursive scenes
fall very often), it has so particular a grace, and is so aptly suited
to them, that the sudden smartness of the answer, and the sweetness of the rhyme, set off the beauty of each other. But that
benefit which I consider most in it, because I have not seldom
found it, is, that it bounds and circumscribes the fancy. For
imagination in a poet is a faculty so wild and lawless that, like
an high-ranging spaniel, it must have clogs tied to it, lest it outrun
the judgment. The great easiness of blank verse renders the
poet too luxuriant; he is tempted to say many things which
might better be omitted, or at least shut up in fewer words; but
when the difficulty of artful rhyming is interposed, where the
poet commonly confines his sense to his couplet, and must con-
trive that sense into such words that the rhyme shall naturally

follow them, not they the rhyme; the fancy then gives leisure
to the judgment to come in, which, seeing so heavy a tax imposed,
is ready to cut off all unnecessary expenses.   This last consideration has already answered an objection which some have made,
that rhyme is only an embroidery of sense, to make that which is
ordinary in itself pass for excellent with less examination.   But
certainly, that which most regulates the fancy, and gives the
judgment its busiest employment, is like to bring forth the richest
and clearest thoughts.   The poet examines that most which he
produceth with the greatest leisure, and which he knows must
pass the severest test of the audience, because they are aptest to
have it ever in their memory; as the stomach makes the best
concoction when it strictly embraces the nourishment, and takes
account of every little particle as it passes through.

> DRYDEN : *Epistle Dedicatory of ' The Rival Ladies* ' (1694).

Romeo.   If I profane with my unworthiest hand
          This holy shrine, the gentle fine is this,
          My lips, two blushing pilgrims, ready stand
          To smooth that rough touch with a tender kiss.
Juliet.   Good pilgrim, you do wrong your hand too much,
           Which mannerly devotion shows in this;
           For saints have hands that pilgrims' hands do touch,
           And palm to palm is holy palmers' kiss.
Romeo.   Have not saints lips, and holy palmers too?
Juliet.   Ay, pilgrim, lips that they must use in prayer.
Romeo.   O, then, dear saint, let lips do what hands do;
           They pray, grant thou, lest faith turn to despair.
Juliet.   Saints do not move, though grant for prayers' sake.
Romeo.   Then move not, while my prayer's effect I take.
           Thus from my lips by thine my sin is purged.
Juliet.   Then have my lips the sin that they have took.
Romeo.   Sin from my lips?   O trespass sweetly urged!
           Give me my sin again.
Juliet.   You kiss by the book.

> SHAKESPEARE.

Everyman.   Alas, I am so faint I may not stand,
             My limbs under me do fold.
             Friends, let us not turn again to this land,
             Not for all the world's gold;
             For into this cave must I creep
             And turn to the earth, and there to sleep.
Beauty.   What! into this grave? alas!
Everyman.   Yes, there shall you consume, more and less.

Beauty.	And what! should I smother here?
Everyman.	Yea, by my faith, and never more appear.
	In this world live no more we shall,
	But in heaven before the highest Lord of All.
Beauty.	I cross out all this! adieu by Saint John!
	I take my cap in my lap and am gone.
Everyman.	What, Beauty, whither will ye?
Beauty.	Peace, I am deaf; I look not behind me,
	Not if thou would give me all the gold in thy chest!
Everyman.	Alas, whereto may I trust?
	Beauty goeth fast away from me;
	She promised with me to live and die.

Everyman (c. 1500).

Tempter.	My Lord, a nod is as good as a wink.
	A man will often love what he spurns.
	For the good times past that are come again
	I am your man.
Thomas.	Not in this train.
	Look to your behaviour. You were safer
	Think of penitence and follow your master.
Tempter.	Not at this gait!
	If you go so fast, others may go faster.
	Your Lordship is too proud!
	The safest beast is not the one that roars most loud.
	This was not the way of the King our master!
	You were not used to be so hard upon sinners
	When they were your friends. Be easy, man!
	The easy man lives to eat the best dinners.
	Take a friend's advice. Leave well alone,
	Or your goose may be cooked and eaten to the bone.
Thomas.	You come twenty years too late.
Tempter.	Then I leave you to your fate.
	I leave you to the pleasure of your higher vices,
	Which will have to be paid for at higher prices.
	Farewell, my Lord, I do not wait upon ceremony,
	I leave as I came, forgetting all acrimony,
	Hoping that your present gravity
	Will find excuse for my humble levity.
	If you will remember me, my Lord, at your prayers,
	I'll remember you at kissing time below the stairs.

T. S. ELIOT: Murder in the Cathedral.

Our author, by experience, finds it true,
'Tis much more hard to please himself than you;

And out of no feigned modesty, this day
Damns his laborious trifle of a play;
Not that it's worse than what before he writ,
But he has now another taste of wit;
And, to confess a truth, though out of time,
Grows weary of his long-loved mistress, Rhyme.
Passion's too fierce to be in fetters bound,
And nature flies him like enchanted ground:
What verse can do, he has performed in this,
Which he presumes the most correct of his;
But spite of all his pride, á secret shame
Invades his breast at Shakespeare's sacred name:
Awed when he hears his godlike Romans rage,
He, in a just despair, would quit the stage;
And to an age less polished, more unskilled,
Does, with disdain, the foremost honours yield.

DRYDEN: *Prologue to Aurengzebe* (1676).

Aurengzebe. When I consider life, 'tis all a cheat;
              Yet, fooled with hope, men favour the deceit;
              Trust on, and think to-morrow will repay:
              To-morrow's falser than the former day;
              Lies worse, and, while it says, we shall be blest
              With some new joys, cuts off what we possest.
              Strange cozenage! None would live past years again,
              Yet all hope pleasure in what yet remain;
              And, from the dregs of life, think to receive,
              What the first sprightly running could not give.
              I'm tired with waiting for this chemic gold,
              Which fools us young, and beggars us when old.
Nourmahal. 'Tis not for nothing that we life pursue;
              It pays our hopes with something still that's new:
              Each day's a mistress, unenjoyed before;
              Like travellers, we're pleased with seeing more.
              Did you but know what joys your way attend,
              You would not hurry to your journey's end.
Aurengzebe. I need not haste the end of life to meet;
              The precipice is just beneath my feet.

DRYDEN: *Aurengzebe.*

In my style, I have professed to imitate the divine Shakespeare;
which that I might perform more freely, I have disencumbered
myself from rhyme. Not that I condemn my former way, but
that this is more proper to my present purpose.

DRYDEN. (Preface to *All for Love*, his version of
SHAKESPEARE's *Antony and Cleopatra*.)

The barge she sat in, like a burnished throne,
Burned on the water: the poop was beaten gold;
Purple the sails, and so perfumed that
The winds were love-sick with them; the oars were silver,
Which to the tune of flutes kept stroke and made
The water which they beat to follow faster,
As amorous of their strokes. For her own person,
It beggared all description: she did lie
In her pavilion, cloth-of-gold of tissue,
O'er-picturing that Venus where we see
The fancy outwork nature: on each side her
Stood pretty dimpled boys, like smiling Cupids,
With divers-coloured fans, whose wind did seem
To glow the delicate cheeks which they did cool,
And what they undid did. . . .
Her gentlewomen, like the Nereides,
So many mermaids, tended her i' the eyes,
And made their bends adornings: at the helm
A seeming mermaid steers: the silken tackle
Swell with the touches of those flower-soft hands,
That yarely frame the office. From the barge
A strange invisible perfume hits the sense
Of the adjacent wharfs. The city cast
Her people out upon her; and Antony,
Enthroned i' the market place, did sit alone,
Whistling to the air; which, but for vacancy,
Had gone to gaze on Cleopatra too,
And made a gap in nature.

> SHAKESPEARE: *Antony and Cleopatra.*

Her galley down the silver Sydnos rowed,
The tackling silk, the streamers waved with gold;
The gentle winds were lodged in purple sail:
Her nymphs, like nereids, round her couch were placed;
Where she, another sea-born Venus, lay. . . .
She lay, and leaned her cheek upon her hand,
And cast a look so languishingly sweet,
As if, secure of all beholders' hearts,   .
Negle.ting she could take them! boys like cupids
Stood fanning with their painted wings, the winds
That played about her face: but if she smiled,
A darting glory seemed to blaze abroad:
That men's desiring eyes were never wearied,
But hung upon the object! To soft flutes
The silver oars kept time; and while they played
The hearing gave new pleasure to the sight,

And both to thought. 'Twas Heaven, or something more!
For she so charmed all hearts, that gazing crowds
Stood panting on the shore, and wanted breath
To give their welcome voice.   DRYDEN: *All for Love.*

Chaucer, I confess, is a rough diamond, and must first be
polished ere he shines. I deny not likewise, that, living in our
early days of poetry, he writes not always of a piece; but sometimes mingles trivial things with those of greater moment. . . .
Having observed this redundancy in Chaucer (as it is an easy
matter for a man of ordinary parts to find a fault in one of greater),
I have not tied myself to a literal translation; but have often
omitted what I judged unnecessary, or not of dignity enough to
appear in the company of better thoughts. I have presumed
further, in some places, and added somewhat of my own where I
thought my author was deficient, and had not given his thoughts
their true lustre, for want of words in the beginning of our
language.   DRYDEN: *On Translating the Poets.*

Ther saugh I first the derke imagining
Of felonye, and al the compassing;
The cruel ire, reed as any glede;
The pykepurs, and eke the pale drede;
The smyler with the knyf under the cloke;
The shepne brenning with the blake smoke;
The treson of the mordring in the bedde;
The open werre, with woundes al bi-bledde;
Contek, with blody knyf and sharp manace;
Al ful of chirking was that sory place.
The sleere of him-self yet saugh I ther,
His herte-blood hath bathed al his heer;
The nayl y-driven in the shode a-night;
The colde deeth, with mouth gaping up-right.
    CHAUCER: *The Knight's Tale.*

There saw I how the secret felon wrought,
And treason labouring in the traitor's thought;
And midwife Time the ripened plot to murder brought.
There the red Anger dared the pallid Fear;
Next stood Hypocrisy, with holy leer,
Soft smiling, and demurely looking down,
But hid the dagger underneath the gown:
The assassinating wife, the household fiend;
And far the blackest there, the traitor-friend.
On the other side, there stood Destruction bare;
Unpunished Rapine, and a waste of War.

Contest, with sharpened knives, in cloisters drawn,
And all with blood bespread the holy lawn.
Loud menaces were heard, and foul disgrace,
And bawling infamy, in language base;
Till sense was lost in sound, and silence fled the place.
The slayer of himself yet saw I there,
The gore congealed was clotted in his hair;
With eyes half closed, and gaping mouth he lay,
And grim, as when he breathed his sullen soul away.

DRYDEN : Tales from Chaucer.

Standing aloof in giant ignorance,
   Of thee I hear and of the Cyclades,
As one who sits ashore and longs perchance
   To visit dolphin-coral in deep seas.
So thou wast blind;—but then the veil was rent,
   For Jove uncurtained Heaven to let thee live,
And Neptune made for thee a spermy tent,
   And Pan made sing for thee his forest-hive;
Aye on the shores of darkness there is light,
   And precipices show untrodden green,
There is a budding morrow in midnight,
   There is a triple sight in blindness keen;
Such seeing hadst thou, as it once befell
To Dian, Queen of Earth, and Heaven, and Hell.

KEATS : Homer.

I have been endeavouring to discover a better Sonnet Stanza
than we have. The legitimate does not suit the language over
well from the pouncing rhymes—the other kind appears too
elegiac—and the couplet at the end of it has seldom a pleasing
effect—I do not pretend to have succeeded—it will explain itself.

If by dull rhymes our English must be chained,
And, like Andromeda, the Sonnet sweet
Fettered, in spite of pained loveliness;
Let us find out, if we must be constrained,
Sandals more interwoven and complete
To fit the naked foot of Poesy;
Let us inspect the Lyre, and weigh the stress
Of every chord, and see what may be gained
By ear industrious, and attention meet;
Misers of sound and syllable, no less
Than Midas of his coinage, let us be
Jealous of dead leaves in the bay wreath crown,
So, if we may not let the Muse be free,
She will be bound with garlands of her own.

KEATS : Letters.

And more to lull him in his slumber soft,
A trickling stream from high rock tumbling down,
And ever drizzling rain upon the loft,
Mixed with a murmuring wind, much like the sowne
Of swarming bees, did cast him in a swowne.
No other noise, nor people's troublous cries,
As still are wont to annoy the walled town,
Might there be heard; but careless Quiet lies
Wrapt in eternal silence far from enemies.

SPENSER: *The Fairie Queene.*

Such names at present cut a convict figure,
  The very Botany Bay in moral geography;
Their loyal treason, renegado rigour,
  Are good manure for their more bare biography.
Wordsworth's last quarto, by the way, is bigger
  Than any since the birthday of typography;
A drowsy frowsy poem, called the 'Excursion',
Writ in a manner which is my aversion.

BYRON: *Don Juan.*

Of these, the false Achitophel was first;
A name to all succeeding ages cursed:
For close designs, and crooked counsels fit;
Sagacious, bold, and turbulent of wit;
Restless, unfixed in principles and place;
In power unpleased, impatient of disgrace:
A fiery soul, which, working out its way,
Fretted the pigmy body to decay,
And o'er-informed the tenement of clay.
A daring pilot in extremity;
Pleased with the danger when the waves went high,
He sought the storms; but for a calm unfit,
Would steer too nigh the sands, to boast his wit.
Great wits are sure to madness near allied,
And thin partitions do their bounds divide;
Else why should he with wealth and honour blest,
Refuse his age the needful hours of rest.

DRYDEN: *Absalom and Achitophel.*

But most by numbers judge a poet's song;
And smooth or rough, with them, is right or wrong:
In the bright Muse, though thousand charms conspire,
Her voice is all these tuneful fools admire;
Who haunt Parnassus but to please their ear,
Not mend their minds; as some to church repair,

Not for the doctrine, but the music there.
These equal syllables alone require,
Though oft the ear the open vowels tire;
While expletives their feeble aid do join,
And ten low words oft creep in one dull line:
While they ring round the same unvaried chimes,
With sure returns of still expected rhymes;
Where'er you find 'the cooling western breeze',
In the next line, it 'whispers through the trees':
If crystal streams 'with pleasing murmurs creep',
The reader's threatened (not in vain) with 'sleep'.
Then, at the last and only couplet fraught
With some unmeaning thing they call a thought,
A needless Alexandrine ends the song
That, like a wounded snake, drags its slow length along.

POPE: *Essay on Criticism.*

Row us out from Desenzano, to your Sirmione row!
So they row'd, and there we landed—'O venusta Sirmio!'
There to me thro' all the groves of olive in the summer glow,
There beneath the Roman ruin where the purple flowers grow
Came that 'Ave atque Vale' of the Poet's hopeless woe,
Tenderest of Roman poets nineteen-hundred years ago,
'Frater Ave atque Vale'—as we wander'd to and fro
Gazing at the Lydian laughter of the Garda Lake below
Sweet Catullus's all-but-island, olive-silvery Sirmio.

TENNYSON.

Epitaph on an Army of Mercenaries
These, in the day when heaven was falling,
    The hour when earth's foundation fled,
Followed their mercenary calling
    And took their wages and are dead.

Their shoulders held the sky suspended;
    They stood, and earth's foundations stay;
What God abandoned, these defended,
    And saved the sum of things for pay.

A. E. HOUSMAN: *Last Poems.*

Love is enough: though the World be a-waning,
And the woods have no voice but the voice of complaining,
    Though the sky be too dark for dim eyes to discover
The gold-cups and daisies fair blooming thereunder,
Though the hills be held shadows, and the sea a dark wonder,

And this day draw a veil over all deeds pass'd over,
Yet their hands shall not tremble, their feet shall not falter;
The void shall not weary, the fear shall not alter
These lips and these eyes of the loved and the lover.

WILLIAM MORRIS.

Ye Goat-herd Gods, that love the grassy mountains,
Ye Nymphs, that haunt the springs in pleasant valleys;
Ye Satyrs, joyed with free and quiet forests,
Vouchsafe your silent ears to plaining music,
Which to my woes gives still an early morning,
And draws the dolour on till weary evening.

O Mercury, foregoer to the evening,
O heavenly huntress of the savage mountains,
O lovely star, entitled of the morning,
While that my voice doth fill these woeful valleys,
Vouchsafe your silent ears to plaining music,
Which oft hath Echo tired in secret forests.

I that was once free burgess of the forests:
Where shade from sun, and sports I sought at evening.
I that was once esteemed for pleasant music,
Am banished now among the monstrous mountains
Of huge despair, and foul affliction's valleys,
Am grown a scritch-owl to myself each morning.

I that was once delighted every morning,
Hunting the wild inhabiters of forests:
I that was once the music of these valleys,
So darkened am, that all my day is evening,
Heart broken so, that mole-hills seem high mountains:
And fill the vales with cries instead of music.

Long since, alas, my deadly swannish music
Hath made itself a cryer of the morning:
And hath with wailing strength climbed highest mountains:
Long since my thoughts more desert be than forests:
Long since I see my joys come to their evening,
And state thrown down to over-trodden valleys.

Long since the happy dwellers of these valleys,
Have prayed me leave my strange exclaiming music,
Which troubles their day's work, and joys of evening:
Long since I hate the night, more hate the morning:
Long since my thoughts chase me like beasts in forests,
And make me wish myself laid under mountains.

These mountains witness shall, so shall these valleys,
These forests eke, made wretched by our music.
Our morning hymn is this, and song at evening.

SIR PHILIP SIDNEY: Arcadia.

Tears, idle tears, I know not what they mean,
Tears from the depth of some divine despair
Rise in the heart, and gather to the eyes,
In looking on the happy Autumn-fields,
And thinking of the days that are no mere.

Fresh as the first beam glittering on a sail,
That brings our friends up from the underworld,
Sad as the last which reddens over one
That sinks with all we love below the verge;
So sad, so fresh, the days that are no more.

Ah, sad and strange as in dark summer dawns
The earliest pipe of half-awaken'd birds
To dying ears, when unto dying eyes
The casement slowly grows a glimmering square;
So sad, so strange, the days that are no more.

Dear as remembered kisses after death,
And sweet as those by hopeless fancy feigned
On lips that are for others; deep as love,
Deep as first love, and wild with all regret;
O Death in Life, the days that are no more.

TENNYSON.

Lark, skylark, spilling your rubbed and round
Pebbles of sound in air's still lake,
Whose widening circles fill the noon; yet none
Is known so small beside the sun:

Be strong your fervent soaring, your skyward air!
Tremble there, a nerve of song!
Float up there where voice and wing are one,
A singing star, a note of light!

Buoyed, embayed in heaven's noon-wide reaches—
For soon light's tide will turn—Oh stay!
Cease not till day streams to the west, then down
That estuary drop down to peace.

C. DAY LEWIS: A Time to Dance.

o

Nay, here shall my whistling and singing
Set all his street's echoes a-ringing
Long after the last of your number
Has ceased my front-court to encumber
While, treading down rose and ranunculus,
You Tommy-make-room-for-your-Uncle us!
Troop, all of you—man or homunculus,
Quick march! for Xanthippe, my house maid,
If once on your pates she a souse made
With what, pan or pot, bowl or skoramis
First comes to her hand—things were more amiss!
I would not for worlds be your place in—
Recipient of slops from the basin!
You, Jack-in-the-Green, leaf-and-twiggishness
Won't save a dry thread on your priggishness!
While as for Quilp-Hop-o'-my-thumb there—
Banjo-Byron that twangs the strum-strum there—
He'll think, as the pickle he curses,
I've discharged on his pate his own verses!

> R. BROWNING: *Pacchiarotto.*

Perishing gloomily,
Spurr'd by contumely,
Cold inhumanity,
Burning insanity,
    Into her rest.—
Cross her hands humbly
As if praying dumbly,
    Over her breast!

> T. HOOD: *The Bridge of Sighs.*

Thou didst hear when God said to Adam:—
        (Sing Eden Bower!)
'Of all this wealth I have made thee warden;
Thou'rt free to eat of the trees of the garden:

Only of one tree eat not in Eden;
        (Alas the hour!)
All save one I give to thy freewill,—
The Tree of the Knowledge of Good and Evil.'

> D. G. ROSSETTI: *Eden Bower.*

If I were a cassowary
    On the plains of Timbuctoo,
I would eat a missionary,
    Coat, and hat, and hymn-book too.

> SYDNEY SMITH.

CHAPTER XIV

POETRY

'Tout ce qui n'est point prose est vers, et tout ce qui n'est point vers est prose.' Prose is the non-metrical language of everyday life; verse is simply metrical language. Rhyme, it should once again be noted, has nothing to do with any definition of verse; the presence or absence of metre is all that differentiates verse from prose. Nor has rhyme anything to do with the definition of poetry, for there must be far more unrhyming than rhyming poetry in the world.

It is easy enough to define verse, and with this definition in mind to say with some confidence that a certain piece of writing is verse or prose; but we cannot say positively that it is poetry, any more than we can affirm, with the certainty that everyone will agree with us, that a man is good, a taste pleasant, or a story amusing. When there is a scientific or objective definition, as of length or temperature, it is easy to decide without fear of contradiction whether a particular thing possesses this quality and in what degree; but when the standard is emotional and subjective we can only say that for us a man is good, a taste pleasant, and a story amusing, knowing that many people will disagree with our opinion.

In the narrowest sense poetry is confined to writing in verse form, though we may remark here such phrases as the 'poetry of motion', or the 'poetry of dress', which indeed give a clue to the meaning of poetry, for if we talk of the poetry of motion presumably we mean grace or beauty of movement, so that poetry in its limited and literary sense should be a beautiful mode of expression in verse form. One definition of poetry then is great or beautiful verse, verse that contains this indefinable and elusive quality of beauty, verse that moved Sir Philip Sidney's heart more than with a trumpet, or pierced Housman like a spear. But though to one man a passage of verse may seem all that is lovely in language, to another it may be only a rhapsody of words, for again these is no objective standard of beauty, and each man must decide for himself when a difference of quantity makes a difference of quality, when verse accumulates so much beauty that it becomes something more than verse and assumes the powers of poetry.

Even when we know that for us certain lines of verse are consummate poetry, we cannot say why they are so, but only that we feel them to be so. To me this is poetry:

> O lang, lang may their ladies sit,
> Wi' their fans into their hand.

And this:

> Daffodils,
> That come before the swallow dares, and take
> The winds of March with beauty.

And this:

> That dolphin-torn, that gong-tormented sea.

If asked why this is poetry I can only say that for me it is language raised to the highest pitch of loveliness, and recognizable as poetry by certain physical sensations similar to those described by A. E. Housman.

'Poetry indeed', he writes, 'seems to me more physical than intellectual. A year or two ago, in common with others, I received from America a request that I would define poetry. I replied that I could no more define poetry than a terrier can define a rat, but that I thought we both recognized the object by the symptoms which it provoked in us. One of these symptoms was described in connexion with another subject by Eliphaz the Temanite: "A spirit passed before my face: the hair of my flesh stood up." Experience has taught me, when I am shaving of a morning, to keep watch over my thoughts, because, if a line of poetry strays into my memory, my skin bristles so that the razor ceases to act. This particular symptom is accompanied by a shiver down the spine; there is another which consists in a constriction of the throat and a precipitation of water to the eyes; and there is a third which I can only describe by borrowing a phrase from one of Keats's last letters, where he says, speaking of Fanny Brawne, "everything that reminds me of her goes through me like a spear". The seat of this sensation is the pit of the stomach.' *

It will be noticed that there is nothing profound, or even remarkable, in the thought expressed in the passages of verse

---

* *The Name and Nature of Poetry.*

quoted above : 'the ladies will never again see Sir Patrick Spens', or 'daffodils bloom in March' are commonplace remarks, yet as expressed by the anonymous ballad-writer and by Shakespeare they are strange enough to hale souls out of men's bodies.   There is more manifest content in the following lines—

> This above all : to thine own self be true,
> And it must follow, as the night the day,
> Thou canst not then be false to any man.

—but they mean no more than they say ; there is no latent content, no significance beyond that of their literal meaning to quicken the dead thoughts into a new birth.   Many people seem to think that poetry varies directly with its didactic content, and mistake the body of thought for the spirit of poetry ; for them poetry is the daily aphorism on the calendar, and Polonius's advice to Laertes greater poetry than Hamlet's 'this fell sergeant, death, is strict in his arrest'.   This is to fall into much the same error as to value a picture for its representational qualities, and to confuse the pleasure derived from these with an aesthetic experience.   Great thinking is obviously one of the most important functions of life, and a clever imitation may be a delightful thing ; but visual art is not dependent on representation, and though great thinking may make great literature it has little to do with poetry.

This does not mean that poetry should be devoid of sense, or that there is only one kind of enjoyment legitimately to be derived from it ; it simply means that the poetry is not to be confused with the literal meaning of the words, which may be as trivial as—

> Come unto these yellow sands
> And then take hands.

—or as profound as—

> Our birth is but a sleep and a forgetting.

It means, in the words of Housman, that 'poetry is not the thing said, but a way of saying it' ; words 'that can draw tears to the eyes', because 'they find their way to something in man which is obscure and latent, something older than the present organization of his nature'.

If poetry is a spirit infused into the literal meaning of words and adding a new and higher significance, it may be asked why poetry should be confined to verse and not extended to prose. This is a question which must be decided by every reader for himself: if poetry is great verse, may it not also be great prose? Certainly there are passages of prose, notably by the writers of the seventeenth century, such as Shakespeare, Donne, Milton, Sir Thomas Browne, Traherne, and the translators of the Bible, that have much the same effect as great verse.

'It comes equally to us all, and makes us all equal when it comes. The ashes of an Oak in the Chimney are no Epitaph of that Oak to tell me how high or how large that was; it tells me not what flocks it sheltered while it stood, nor what men it hurt when it fell. The dust of great persons' graves is speechless too, it says nothing, it distinguishes nothing: as soon the dust of a wretch whom thou wouldest not, as of a Prince thou couldest not look upon, will trouble thine eyes, if the wind blow it thither; and when a whirlwind hath blown the dust of the Churchyard into the Church, and the man sweeps out the dust of the Church into the Churchyard, who will undertake to sift those dusts again, and to pronounce, This is the Patrician, this is the noble flower, and this the yeomanly, this the Plebeian bran. So is the death of Jesabel (Jesabel was a Queen) expressed; "They shall not say, this is Jesabel"; not only not wonder that it is, nor pity that it should be, but they shall not say, they shall not know, This is Jesabel.'

The word poetry may be used to include prose such as this of Donne, though it might be maintained that there is sufficient difference to distinguish great verse from great prose, and that to call them both poetry is to make for confusion. The difference is, of course, between the free rhythm of prose and the restraint which metre imposes on verse. There are certain things that can be said in verse that cannot possibly be said in prose:

> Where the bee sucks, there suck I:
> In a cowslip's bell I lie;
> There I couch when owls do cry.

This may be because prose demands a greater thought content than verse, while the convention of metre removes verse sufficiently far from reality to allow the most intimate revelation of feeling without embarrassment.

Nevertheless it is true that great prose, like great verse, expresses far more than its literal meaning, that it too has something of this indefinable quality that raises verse to the plane of poetry, and that in this sense it is poetry in prose form.

And that in this sense great music, painting, and all great art share the quality of poetry is suggested by the fact that the physical sensations aroused by poetry are not effects peculiar to great verse. Cecil Day Lewis, for example, experiences the same sensation—'one of suffocation, followed by a sense of physical lightening, at the entrance of the celestial motif in Beethoven's A minor quartet', as well as 'on approaching a passage of poetry where that strong enchantment lies in wait'. There is much the same distinction between painting and great painting as between verse and poetry: the Victorian Academy show-piece means no more than it says, while the significance of a Rembrandt or a Cézanne may be inexhaustible. Similarly the 'light-classical' music so dear to the restaurant merely flutters the emotions, while a Beethoven symphony contains within its finite score an infinity of meaning. The element of poetry is common to all the arts; it is the expression, the way of saying it, the form, that adds the little more, and how much it is, to verse, architecture, sculpture, painting, music, and all the other arts, and invests them with an emotional significance more profound than their literal meaning, appealing directly to the irrational mind rather than to the intellect, so that they have the power of moving us, as we say, by their beauty.

On the other hand W. H. Auden maintains that verse may be poetry because it is intellectually exciting. 'Of the many definitions of poetry', he writes, 'the simplest is still the best: "memorable speech". That is to say, it must move our emotions, or excite our intellect, for only that which is moving or exciting is memorable.' * 'Memorable', of course, means 'that which is worthy of being remembered', not all that is in fact remembered; 'speech worthy of being remembered because it moves the emotions or excites the intellect'.

In a sense, of course, all poetry is dependent on the intellectual perception of its meaning; gibberish will not do, but it need not be profound, and much of the greatest poetry is very simple. Without a meaning there could be no poetry, but the poetry is not the literal meaning, indeed it need not be fully understood— 'Poetry gives most pleasure when only generally and not perfectly understood.' The poet is not a prophet uttering oracles in verse —Tennyson, Lord Tennyson, might not have agreed with that. Prose is the proper vehicle for profound thinking, poetry for platitude.

> True wit is Nature to advantage dressed,
> What oft was thought, but ne'er so well expressed.

* *The Poet's Tongue.*

However lofty the thought it cannot be made into poetry merely by putting it into verse form, nor will it by virtue of its profundity make better poetry than the nonsense of a Shakespearean lyric. The didactic is not intellectually exciting.

But there is a limited sense in which the intellect may be involved, and through the intellect, the emotions. The solution of a problem is intellectually exciting: the resolution of a duality, the perception of harmony in apparent discord, the discovery of unity within diversity. These may be intellectual processes, but they will have emotional consequences, though once again their intensity will depend on the expression. Much poetry, particularly metaphysical poetry—and also mere simile and metaphor—does excite the intellect in this way, and produce secondary emotional effects; but it should be noted that conceit, metaphor, and simile are all inessential to poetry; they may provide poetry, but poetry is not dependent on them. Thus in the following lines there is aesthetic pleasure—though how much of this is the result of the felicitous expression it is impossible to say—following the intellectual resolution of comets and glow-worms as omens of disaster:

> Ye Country Comets, that portend
> No War, nor Prince's funeral,
> Shining unto no higher end
> Than to presage the Grasses fall.

This super-imposition of ideas is another example of the contrapuntal principle in art, and when spontaneous is classed by Coleridge and Wordsworth as Imagination, an emotional fusion in the mind of the author; when merely ingenious, as Fancy, an intellectual union for the occasion. It is the distinction between metaphor and conceit; between—

> Beauty's ensign yet
> Is crimson in thy lips and in thy cheeks,
> And death's pale flag is not advanced there.

and (to take an extreme example).—

> Mark but this flea, and mark in this
> How little that which thou deny'st me is;
> It sucked me first, and now sucks thee,
> And in this flea our two bloods mingled be.

Shakespeare's metaphor it is true excites the intellect, but there is an immediate emotional appeal because the image is clearly an imaginative fusion of ideas; Donne's conceit also is intellectually exciting, but its emotional effect is indirect—by way of the intellect—and slight, partly because it is so artificial, partly because the expression itself lacks poetry.

Addison distinguishes between 'true' wit, which 'generally consists in the resemblance and congruity of ideas', and 'false' wit, 'which chiefly consists in the resemblance and congruity, sometimes of single letters, as in anagrams and acrostics: sometimes of syllables, as in echoes and doggerel rhymes: sometimes of words, as in puns and quibbles; and sometimes of whole sentences or poems'. Finally he analyses 'mixed wit, which consists partly in the resemblance of ideas, and partly in the resemblance of words', and gives as an example: 'Cowley observing the cold regard of his mistress's eyes, and at the same time their power of producing love in him, considers them as burning-glasses made of ice; and finding himself able to live in the greatest extremities of love, concludes the Torrid Zone to be habitable.'

True wit, because it is a spontaneous product of the imagination, will both excite the intellect and move the emotions. Mixed wit, a more rational process, is intellectually stimulating and may have indirect emotional effects, so that it is often a welcome element in poetry; but that neither true nor mixed wit is essential to poetry can be proved by quoting passages where the intellectual content is negligible:

> Since golden October declined into sombre November
> And the apples were gathered and stored.

or:

> When I do count the clock that tells the time,
> And see the brave day sunk in hideous night,
> When I behold the violet past prime,
> And sable curls all silvered o'er with white.

or:

> Anon they move
> In perfect phalanx to the Dorian mood
> Of flutes and soft recorders.

But how far is the poetry in the following verse the result of the wit, that is of the imaginative fusion of ideas, and how far of the expression as a whole?

On russet floors, by waters idle,
   The pine lets fall its cone;
The cuckoo shouts all day at nothing
   In leafy dells alone;
And traveller's joy beguiles in autumn
   Hearts that have lost their own.

False wit—

If the man who turnips cries,
Cry not when his father dies,
'Tis a proof that he had rather
Have a turnip than his father.

—would seem to have little to do with poetry, but that it may be pleasing and worth rememberéing most people will agree.

It would be fatal to confine our reading of verse to what Matthew Arnold calls the Grand Style, and to noble subjects, for 'everything that we remember no matter how trivial . . . is equally the subject of poetry'. Yet it is interesting to note how those who have either little knowledge or little love of poetry are the first to resent such a catholic interpretation of the subject-matter of poetry. Poetry is after all an interpretation of life, and if the artist is to confine his interpretation to a highly arbitrary selection of experiences expressed in some language peculiar to verse the result will be something divorced from ordinary life, and read only by the Mr. Bonses of this world. Still, many people persist in an idealized conception of the artist and his work. 'This is the kind of criticism', writes Stephen Spender, 'which goes far to explain why so many people detest poetry. It speaks of poets as though they were superior beings incapable of experiencing the feelings of ordinary people; it translates simple and direct poetry, which easily explains itself, into high-flown and indirect language. In trying to elevate poetry, it puts it on the shelf.'

Art is an aspect of life, and life does not stand still. We are not living in the seventeenth or even in the nineteenth century, and our way of life is very different from that of our ancestors— we have for instance the revolutionary effect of the internal combustion engine and wireless, and now atomic energy. The ordinary man rarely reads Victorian novels, still less seventeenth-century prose, for he likes his reading to be up-to-date both in matter and manner. Why then should he expect poetry, or any other art, to confine itself to the subject-matter of a former age —what age exactly he might be hard pressed to identify—and an archaic form of expression, to the neglect of this age's monstrous problems and peculiar idiom?

It is true that it takes some time for people to assimilate new additions to their environment—steam-engines and telephones for instance—and if the artist forces the pace too hard he may find himself running alone, a poet without an audience, a painter without a public, at best the prophet of an esoteric cult. Still less should art deliberately go out of its way to be eccentric; there are certain problems that are always fundamentally the same and always a subject for poetry—birth and death for example; but even then the approach will vary with the age as will, or should, the expression; and what sense could there be in describing an aeroplane flight in the phraseology of the eighteenth century? It was against the tyranny of poetic conventions that Wordsworth revolted, against such verse as this—

> In vain to me the smiling mornings shine,
> And reddening Phoebus lifts his golden fire:
> The birds in vain their amorous descant join,
> Or cheerful fields resume their green attire.

—and choosing to write in 'a selection of language really used by men' he wrote poetry such as this:

> Never did sun more beautifully steep
> In his first splendour, valley, rock, or hill;
> Ne'er saw I, never felt, a calm so deep!
> The river glideth at his own sweet will:
> Dear God! the very houses seem asleep;
> And all that mighty heart is lying still!

Art is a living thing, and if it is not to perish like the dinosaur through failure to adapt itself to a changing environment it must assimilate the inventions and idiom of another age; it must experiment with new forms, and though some of these may be freaks, their production is after all a sign of vitality. There is no formula or standard to which poetry must conform. If it is aesthetically moving, then for us it is poetry; if we can say with Emily Dickinson that 'it makes my whole body so cold no fire can ever warm me', then again for us it is poetry.

Boswell. Then, Sir, what is poetry?
Johnson. Why, Sir, it is much easier to say what it is not. We all *know* what light is; but it is not easy to *tell* what it is.
BOSWELL: Life of Johnson.

If I were obliged, not to define poetry, but to name the class of things to which it belongs, I should call it a secretion; whether a natural secretion, like turpentine in the fir, or a morbid secretion, like the pearl in the oyster.

A. E. HOUSMAN: *The Name and Nature of Poetry.*

No form of words has ever been discovered capable of pinning down the nature of poetry. . . . So it is that, in despair of ever grasping this capricious and untamed flyer, we are driven to define the nature of poetry by its effects upon us.

C. DAY LEWIS: *A Hope for Poetry.*

We learn what poetry is—if we ever learn—by reading it.

T. S. ELIOT: *The Sacred Wood.*

Poetry is not the proper antithesis to prose, but to science. Poetry is opposed to science, and prose to metre. The proper and immediate object of science is the acquirement, or communication, of truth; the proper and immediate object of poetry is the communication of immediate pleasure. This definition is useful; but as it would include novels and other works of fiction, which yet we do not call poems, there must be some additional character by which poetry is not only divided from opposites, but likewise distinguished from disparate, though similar modes of composition. . . . What is this? It is that pleasurable emotion, that peculiar state and degree of excitement, which arises in the poet himself in the act of composition.

COLERIDGE: *Essay on Shakespeare.*

I wish our clever young poets would remember my homely definitions of prose and poetry; that is, prose = words in their best order;—poetry = the *best* words in the best order.

COLERIDGE: *Table Talk.*

Poetry is the spontaneous overflow of powerful feelings: it takes its origin from emotion recollected in tranquillity.

WORDSWORTH: *Preface to Lyrical Ballads.*

Poetry is the record of the best and happiest moments of the happiest and best minds. . . .
Poets are the hierophants of an unapprehended inspiration; the mirrors of the gigantic shadows which futurity casts upon the present; the words which express what they understand not; the trumpets which sing to battle, and feel not what they inspire;

the influence which is moved not, but moves. Poets are the unacknowledged legislators of the world.

SHELLEY: *Defence of Poetry.*

The lunatic, the lover and the poet
Are of imagination all compact:
One sees more devils than vast hell can hold,
That is, the madman: the lover, all as frantic,
Sees Helen's beauty in a brow of Egypt:
The poet's eye, in a fine frenzy rolling,
Doth glance from heaven to earth, from earth to heaven;
And as imagination bodies forth
The forms of things unknown, the poet's pen
Turns them to shapes, and gives to airy nothing
A local habitation and a name.

SHAKESPEARE: *A Midsummer Night's Dream.*

On a poet's lips I slept
Dreaming like a love adept
In the sound his breathing kept;
Nor seeks nor finds he mortal blisses,
But feeds on the aerial kisses
Of shapes that haunt thought's wildernesses.
He will watch from dawn to gloom
The lake-reflected sun illume
The yellow bees in the ivy bloom,
Nor heed nor see what things they be;
But from these create he can
Forms more real than living man,
Nurslings of immortality!

SHELLEY: *Prometheus Unbound.*

Hotspur. I had rather be a kitten and cry mew
Than one of these same metre ballad-mongers;
I had rather hear a brazen canstick turned,
Or a dry wheel grate on the axle-tree;
And that would set my teeth nothing on edge,
Nothing so much as mincing poetry:
'Tis like the forced gait of a shuffling nag.

SHAKESPEARE: *Henry IV, Part I.*

I think poetry should surprise by a fine excess, and not by singularity; it should strike the reader as a wording of his own highest thoughts, and appear almost a remembrance.

Its touches of beauty should never be half-way, thereby making the reader breathless, instead of content.

KEATS: *Letters.*

No poetry which when mastered is not better heard than read
is good poetry.

W. H. AUDEN : *The Poet's Tongue.*

This book is not about heroes.   English Poetry is not yet fit to
speak of them.

Nor is it about deeds, or lands, nor anything about glory,
honour, might, majesty, dominion, or power, except War.

Above all I am not concerned with Poetry.

My subject is War, and the pity of War.

The Poetry is in the pity.

Yet these elegies are to this generation in no sense consolatory.
They may be to the next.   All a poet can do to-day is warn.
That is why the true Poets must be truthful.

WILFRED OWEN : *Préface to Poems.*

If now, as we have seen, in the plastic arts, and in an art which
appears to us so pure as music, the Greeks perceived and valued,
along with the immediate pleasure of beauty, a definite ethical
character and bent, much more was this the case with poetry,
whose material is conceptions and ideas.   The works of the poets,
and especially of Homer, were in fact to the Greeks all that
moral treatises are to us; or rather, instead of learning their
lessons in abstract terms, they learnt them out of the concrete
representation of life.   Poetry was the basis of their education,
the guide and commentary of their practice, the inspiration of
their speculative thought. . . .

From this conception of poetry as a storehouse of practical
wisdom the transition is easy to a purely ethical judgment of its
value; and that transition, as has been already noted, was actually
made by Plato, who even goes so far as to prescribe to poets the
direct inculcation of such morals as are proper to a tract, as that
the good and just man is happy even though he be poor, and the
bad and unjust man miserable even though he be rich.   This
didacticism, no doubt, is a parody; but it is a parody of the
normal Greek view, that the excellence of a poem is closely
bound up with the compass and depth of its whole ethical content,
and is not to be measured, as many moderns maintain, merely
by the aesthetic beauty of its form.   When Strabo says, 'it is
impossible to be a good poet unless you are first a good man',
he is expressing the common opinion of the Greeks that the poet
is to be judged not merely as an artist but as an interpreter of
life; and the same presupposition underlies the remark of
Aristotle that poets may be classified according as the characters
they represent are as good as, better, or worse than the average
man.   G. LOWES DICKINSON : *The Greek View of Life.*

This being the case, the peevish temper furnishes an infinite variety of materials for imitation; whereas the temper, which is wise and calm, is so constantly uniform and unchanging, that it is not easily imitated; and when imitated, it is not easily understood, especially by a general gathering of all sorts of persons, collected in a theatre. For these people witness the imitation of a state which, if I am not mistaken, is far from being their own.

It is unquestionably.

Hence it is clear, that the imitative poet has, in the nature of things, nothing to do with this calm temper of soul, and that his wisdom is not set on pleasing it, if he is intended to gain a reputation in the world; but his business is with the peevish and changeful temper, because it is easily imitated.

That is clear.

Then we shall be justified now in laying hands on him, and placing him on a level with the painter. For he resembles the painter in producing things that are worthless when tried by the standard of truth; and he resembles him also in this, that he holds intercourse with a part of the soul which is like himself, and not with the best part. And, this being the case, we shall henceforth be justified in refusing to admit him into a state that would fain enjoy a good constitution, because he excites and feeds and strengthens this worthless part of the soul, and thus destroys the rational part; like a person who should strengthen the hands of the dissolute members of a state and raise them to supreme power, and at the same time bring the educated class to destruction. Precisely in the same way we shall assert that the imitative poet likewise implants an evil constitution in the soul of each individual, by gratifying that senseless part which, instead of distinguishing the greater from the less, regards the same things now as great, and now as small, and manufactures phantastic phantoms that are very widely removed from truth. . . .

With the single exception of hymns to the gods and panegyrics on the good, no poetry ought to be admitted into a state. For if you determine to admit the highly-seasoned muse of lyric or epic poetry, pleasure and pain will have sovereign power in your state, instead of law and those principles which, by the general consent of all time, are most conformable to reason.

PLATO: *The Republic.* (Trans. J. L. DAVIES and D. J. VAUGHAN.)

For indeed the greatest part of poets have apparelled their poetical inventions in that numberous kind of writing which is called verse. Indeed but apparelled, verse being but an ornament and no cause to poetry, sith there have been many most excellent poets that never versified, and now swarm many versifiers that need never answer to the name of poets. . . . It is not rhyming and versing that maketh a poet (no more than a long gown maketh an advocate, who, though he pleaded in armour, should be an advocate and no soldier,) but it is that feigning notable images of virtues, vices, or what else, with that delightful teaching, which must be the right describing note to know a poet by. . . .

Now therein of all sciences, (I speak still of human, and according to the human conceit,) is our poet the monarch. For he doth not only show the way, but giveth so sweet a prospect into the way as will entice any man to enter into it. Nay, he doth, as if your journey should lie through a fair vineyard, at the very first give you a cluster of grapes, that full of that taste you may long to pass further. He beginneth not with obscure definitions, which must blur the margin with interpretations, and load the memory with doubtfulness. But he cometh to you with words set in delightful proportion, either accompanied with, or prepared for, the well-enchanting skill of music; and with a tale, forsooth, he cometh unto you, with a tale which holdeth children from play, and old men from the chimney-corner; and pretending no more, doth intend the winning of the mind from wickedness to virtue; even as the child is often brought to take most wholesome things, by hiding them in such other as have a pleasant taste.

SIR PHILIP SIDNEY : *Defence of Poesy.*

The writer may certainly learn of the ancients, better than anywhere else, three things which it is vitally important for him to know:—the all importance of the choice of a subject; the necessity of accurate construction; and the subordinate character of the expression.

MATTHEW ARNOLD : *Preface to Poems.*

Meaning is of the intellect, poetry is not. If it were the eighteenth century would have been able to write it better.

A. E. HOUSMAN : *The Name and Nature of Poetry.*

The metaphysical poets were men of learning, and to show their learning was their whole endeavour; but, unluckily resolving to show it in rhyme, instead of writing poetry, they only wrote verses, and very often such verses as stood the trial of the finger better than of the ear; for the modulation was so imperfect, that they were only found to be verse by counting the syllables.

If the father of criticism has rightly denominated poetry τέχνη μιμητικὴ, *an imitative art*, these writers will, without great wrong, lose their right to the name of poets; for they cannot be said to have imitated anything; they neither copied nature nor life; neither painted the forms of matter, nor represented the operations of intellect.

Those however who deny them to be poets, allow them to be wits. Dryden confesses of himself and his contemporaries, that they fall below Donne in wit, but maintains that they surpass him in poetry.

If Wit be well described by Pope, as being, 'that which has been often thought, but was never before so well expressed', they certainly never attained, nor ever sought it; for they endeavoured to be singular in their thoughts, and were careless of their diction. But Pope's account of wit is undoubtedly erroneous: he depresses it below its natural dignity, and reduces it from strength of thought to happiness of language.

If by a more noble and more adequate conception that be considered as Wit, which is at once natural and new, that which, though not obvious is, upon its first production, acknowledged to be just; if it be that, which he that never found it, wonders how he missed; to wit of this kind the metaphysical poets have seldom risen. Their thoughts are often new, but seldom natural; they are not obvious, but neither are they just; and the reader, far from wondering that he missed them, wonders more frequently by what perverseness of industry they were ever found.

But Wit, abstracted from its effects upon the hearer, may be more rigorously and philosophically considered as a kind of *discordia concors*; a combination of dissimilar images, or discovery of occult resemblances in things apparently unlike. Of wit, thus defined, they have more than enough. The most heterogeneous ideas are yoked by violence together; nature and art are ransacked for illustrations, comparisons, and allusions; their learning instructs, and their subtilty surprises; but the reader commonly thinks his improvement dearly bought, and, though he sometimes admires, is seldom pleased. . . .

What they wanted however of the sublime, they endeavoured to supply by hyperbole; their amplification had no limits; they left not only reason but fancy behind them; and produced combinations of confused magnificence, that not only could not be credited, but could not be imagined.

Yet great labour, directed by great abilities, is never wholly lost: if they frequently threw away their wit upon false conceits, they likewise sometimes struck out unexpected truths: if their conceits were far-fetched, they were often worth the carriage. To write on their plan, it was at least necessary to read and think. No man could be born a metaphysical poet, nor assume the dignity of a writer, by descriptions copied from descriptions, by imitations borrowed from imitations, by traditional imagery,

P

and hereditary similes, by readiness of rhyme, and volubility of syllables.

JOHNSON: *Life of Cowley.*

There was a whole age of English in which the place of poetry was usurped by something very different which possessed the proper and specific name of wit: wit not in its modern sense, but as defined by Johnson, 'a combination of dissimilar images, or discovery of occult resemblances in things apparently unlike'. Such discoveries are no more poetical than anagrams; such pleasure as they give is purely intellectual and is intellectually frivolous; but this was the pleasure principally sought and found in poems by the intelligentsia of fifty years and more of the seventeenth century. Some of the writers who purveyed it to their contemporaries were, by accident, considerable poets; and though their verse was generally inharmonious, and apparently cut into lengths and tied into faggots by deaf mathematicians, some little of their poetry was beautiful and even superb. Simile and metaphor, things inessential to poetry, were their great engrossing preoccupation, and were prized the more in proportion as they were further fetched. They did not mean these accessories to be helpful, to make their sense clearer or their conceptions more vivid; they hardly even meant them for ornament, or cared whether an image had any independent power to please: their object was to startle by novelty and amuse by ingenuity a public whose one wish was to be so startled and amused. The pleasure, however luxurious, of hearing St. Mary Magdalene's eyes described as

> Two walking baths, two weeping motions,
> Portable and compendious oceans,

was not a poetic pleasure; and poetry, as a label for this particular commodity, is not appropriate.

A. E. HOUSMAN: *The Name and Nature of Poetry.*

Johnson, who employed the term 'metaphysical poets', apparently having Donne, Cleveland, and Cowley chiefly in mind, remarks of them that 'the most heterogeneous ideas are yoked by violence together'. The force of this impeachment lies in the failure of the conjunction, the fact that the ideas are yoked but not united; and if we are to judge of styles of poetry by their abuse, enough examples may be found in Cleveland to justify Johnson's condemnation. But a degree of heterogeneity of material compelled into unity by the operation of the poet's mind is omnipresent in poetry. We need not select for illustration such a line as:

Notre âme est un fois trois-mâts cherchant son Icarie;

we may find it in some of the best lines of Johnson himself (*The Vanity of Human Wishes*):

> His fate was destined to a barren strand,
> A petty fortress, and a dubious hand;
> He left a name at which the world grew pale,
> To point a moral, or adorn a tale.

where the effect is due to a contrast of ideas, different in degree but the same in principle, as that which Johnson mildly reprehended. And in one of the finest poems of the age (a poem which could not have been written in any other age), the *Exequy* of Bishop King, the extended comparison is used with perfect success: the idea and the simile become one, in the passage in which the Bishop illustrated his impatience to see his dead wife, under the figure of a journey:

> Stay for me there; I will not faile
> To meet thee in that hollow Vale.
> And think not much of my delay;
> I am already on the way,
> And follow thee with all the speed
> Desire can make, or sorrows breed.
> Each minute is a short degree,
> And ev'ry houre a step towards thee.
> At night when I betake to rest,
> Next morn I rise nearer my West
> Of life, almost by eight houres sail,
> Than when sleep breathed his drowsy gale. . . .
> But heark! My Pulse, like a soft Drum
> Beats my approach, tells Thee I come;
> And slow howere my marches be,
> I shall at last sit down by Thee.

(In the last few lines there is that effect of terror which is several times attained by one of Bishop King's admirers, Edgar Poe.) . . .

It is to be observed that the language of these poets is as a rule simple and pure; in the verse of George Herbert this simplicity is carried as far as it can go—a simplicity emulated without success by numerous modern poets. The *structure* of the sentences, on the other hand, is sometimes far from simple, but this is not a vice; it is a fidelity to thought and feeling. The effect, at its best, is far less artificial than that of an ode by Gray. And as this fidelity induces variety of thought and feeling, so it induces variety of music.

T. S. ELIOT: Selected Essays.

A Valediction: forbidding mourning

As virtuous men passe mildly away,
   And whisper to their soules, to goe,
Whilst some of their sad friends doe say,
   The breath goes now, and some say, no;

So let us melt, and make no noise,
   No teare-floods, nor high tempests move,
'Twere prophanation of our joyes
   To tell the layetie our love.

Moving of th'earth brings harmes and feares,
   Men reckon what it did and meant,
But trepidation of the spheares,
   Though greater farre, is innocent.

Dull sublunary lovers' love
   (Whose soule is sense) cannot admit
Absence, because it doth remove
   Those things which elemented it.

But we by a love, so much refin'd,
   That our selves know not what it is,
Inter-assured of the mind,
   Care lesse, eyes, lips, and hands to misse.

Our two soules therefore, which are one,
   Though I must goe, endure not yet
A breach, but an expansion,
   Like gold to ayery thinnesse beate.

If they be two, they are two so
   As stiffe twin compasses are two,
Thy soule the fixt foot, makes no show
   To move, but doth, if the other doe.

And though it in the center sit,
   Yet when the other far doth rome,
It leanes, and hearkens after it,
   And growes erect, as that comes home.

Such wilt thou be to mee, who must
   Like th'other foot, obliquely runne;
Thy firmness makes my circle just,
   And makes me end, where I begunne.

JOHN DONNE.

The Romantic movement in England destroyed the convention
of a specialized poetic diction. It is possible that Eliot and the
post-war poets will be chiefly recognized by posterity as the

inaugurators of a movement which finally destroyed the convention of a specialized poetic vocabulary. The field of sense-data has been very considerably enlarged in the last 150 years, and it is generally admitted now that there are no sense-data necessarily ineligible for poetic metaphor: it is no longer accepted by the poet that a factory has not the qualifications for poetic treatment possessed by a flower. It will be objected that the modern poet is not inaugurating anything here: both Shakespeare and the metaphysical school took their material, not only from the preserve of traditionally 'poetical' objects, but from the whole field of the senses and the intellect.   C. DAY LEWIS: *A Hope for Poetry.*

For those who had the power,
Unhesitating whether to kill or cure:
Those who were not afraid
To dam the estuary or start the forest fire:
Whose hearts were filled
With enthusiasm as with a constant wind
That, lifting the fog, the pall of vision, unveiled
Their own memorial, the stars:
There need be neither obituary nor wreath,
Accomplices of death.
These disappeared into the darkness ahead:
Followers shall find
Them walking larger than legends in that virgin land,
Their spirit shall be blowing out of the sunrise,
Their veins our rivers, their bones our bread.

Others, too, will die hard.
Spenders of life, they dealt freely with danger:
These could not learn to hoard,
To count the cost or to examine the change.
A hungry soul
Urged them to try new air-routes, and their skill
Raftered the sky with steel:
They took the field with laughter, they attacked the bowling.
In the machine's heart, regularly breathing,
We hear their hearts still beat,
Inherit their strength and swiftness through the turbine:
Pausing between shifts or in the pub at evening
We feel their generous heat;
We remember them as the glowing fruit remembers
Sap-flow and sunshine.   C. DAY LEWIS: *A Time to Dance.*

Degas. 'Quel métier, j'ai perdu toute ma journée avec un sacré sonnet sans advancer d'un pas. . . . Et cependant ce ne sont pas les idées qui me manquent. . . . J'en suis plein. . . . J'en ai trop.'

Mallarmé. 'Ce n'est pas avec les idées qu'on fait les sonnets, Degas; c'est avec les mots.'

CHAPTER XV

CLASSICAL AND ROMANTIC

THOUGH it is a dangerous practice to label and pigeonhole works of art, it is possible to assign most of them, with some confidence, to one or other of the two great schools, Classical and Romantic. The terms themselves are ambiguous, as they have acquired ill-defined and popular meanings; but used critically, Classical is not synonymous with highbrow, nor is Romantic necessarily the same thing as picturesque. The distinction is fundamentally one between Reason and Emotion.

The actions of a scientist when making an experiment are the result of logical thought; but if he sings and dances round his laboratory when he has made an important discovery his action is obviously unpremeditated: the triumphant expression of emotion, and not a deliberate and rational process. Another kind of emotional reaction is described by A. E. Housman: 'In these six simple words of Milton—

Nymphs and shepherds, dance no more—

what is it that can draw tears, as I know it can, to the eyes of more readers than one? What in the world is there to cry about? Why have the mere words the physical effect of pathos when the sense of the passage is blithe and gay? I can only say, because they are poetry, and find their way to something in man which is obscure and latent, something older than the present organization of his nature, like the patches of fen which still linger here and there in the drained lands of Cambridgeshire.'

It is important to recognize the distinction between actions that are logically impelled by the conscious mind, and those that spring involuntarily from the 'obscure and latent something in man', the remote regions of the unconscious mind. Man is the only creature capable of sustained conscious thought, and it is this faculty of logical reasoning which has raised him above the other animals, most of which are actuated mainly by unconscious impulses. But man still retains his primitive animal mind which is the source of his emotional life, and his actions are rarely or never quite free from its control.

It is true that our unconscious minds are more highly developed than those of other animals, for though the instinct of self-preservation and the primary emotion of fear are at the core of our being, man has a finer and more delicate emotional life, and far more channels for discharging the energy of the life-force. One of these channels is artistic creation, for the compulsion to produce materially useless works of art can scarcely be explained as a function of the rational and conscious mind. It too has its source in the mysterious territory of the unconscious.

But the unconscious mind will, of itself, rarely bring forth a finished work of art; rather it produces the raw material, like the manifest content—the images we remember—of a dream: vital, but sprawling and ineffective because its parts are distorted and unarticulated. There follows, therefore, the more or less conscious process of selection and co-ordination, necessary to give it form and concentrate its strength. Thus, though the initial impulse and the material of any work of art are irrational in origin, bursting from the unconscious mind, and though the expression itself may be largely irrational, almost certainly the conscious mind will take a hand in fashioning it into its final form.

> And as imagination bodies forth
> The form of things unknown, the poet's pen
> Turns them to shapes, and gives to airy nothing
> A local habitation and a name.

Obviously the relative influence of conscious and unconscious mind may be infinitely varied: the conscious control, for example, may be comparatively slight, as in Romantic art, or it may be absent, as in the final Romanticism of the Surrealists. At the other extreme is the product of man's mind that is entirely rational —in so far as any of our activities can be entirely rational; this is scientific exposition.

This may be arranged schematically, if we remember that both impulse and expression may be partly rational and partly irrational, that is emotional. For instance, a completely ration-alized expression will neutralize any emotional content, while completely uncontrolled emotion will produce Surrealism.* In Classical art more emphasis is laid on rational control, in Romantic art the conscious element is less.

---

* It should, in fairness, be noted that the Surrealists do not altogether exclude conscious control in art. 'Verbal and graphic automatism', writes André Breton, 'only represents a *limit* towards which the poet or artist should tend.'

Thus:

> Rational impulse and rational expression is Science.
> Rational impulse and emotional expression is Pseudo-art.
> Emotional impulse and rational expression is Classical art.
> Emotional impulse and emotional expression is Romantic art.

If it is admitted that a work of art must have an emotional impulse, only the last two can come within the catalogue of art. Most people will agree with Mr. Herbert Read when he asserts 'the absolute impossibility of producing a work of art by the conscious exercise of talents. The notion that a work of art can be created by observing a set of rules is only to be compared with the notion that a human being can be produced in a test-tube', but when he says, 'Classicism . . . has always represented the forces of repression', and talks of its 'complete irrelevance, its *anaesthetic* effect, its contradiction of the creative impulse', he seems merely to define Classicism by implication as the antithesis of Surrealism, 'verbal and graphic rationalism', which it is not, any more than Romanticism is necessarily Surrealistic.

The second is the class of those uninspired productions when the artist, or would-be artist, without a vital creative impulse, imitates the expression of art that is impelled by a genuine emotion. Much so-called art is hack work of this type, where a false emotional expression is substituted for a real emotional content, as when a poet, such as Wordsworth or Swinburne, imitates his own inspired mannerisms; or, more commonly, when somebody without real aesthetic sensibility copies a landscape in paint, or writes verse with some of the popularly recognized conventions of poetry. In any event, the result will be some form of insincerity: probably the insincerity of sentimentalism, or possibly that of pedantry. Great art is always sincere in this sense, and if emotional expression is not in fact the expression of emotion there is bound to be insincerity.

If it has been sufficiently established that the fundamental distinction between Classical and Romantic art is that of reason and emotion, that the Classical artist subjects his emotions to a stricter control than the Romantic, certain characteristics of the two schools will follow.

Matthew Arnold may be taken as the ablest modern apologist of the Classical tradition. 'Greek literature', Arnold writes, 'can help to cure us of what is, it seems to me, the great vice of our intellect, manifesting itself in our incredible vagaries in literature, in art, in religion, in morals; namely, that it is *fantastic* and wants *sanity*. Sanity—that is the great virtue of ancient literature: the want of that is the great defect of the modern, in spite of all its variety and power.' The Classical artist, then, exercises more restraint than the Romantic, who may give rein to his imagination in pursuit of the bizarre and violent. This restraint is shown first of all in choice of subject: 'all depends upon the subject; choose a fitting action, penetrate yourself with the feeling of its situation; this done, everything else will follow'. Without a noble subject, art, according to Arnold, can never be great art. This is a far cry from W. H. Auden's, 'Everything that we remember no matter how trivial: the mark on the wall, the joke at luncheon, word games, these, like the dance of a stoat or the raven's gamble, are equally the subject of poetry'; or Roger Fry's, 'There is no excuse for a china pot being ugly, there is every reason why Rembrandt's and Degas' pictures should be, from the purely sensual point of view, supremely and magnificiently ugly.'

Again Arnold writes that 'with the Greeks the action predominated over the expression of it; with us the expression predominates over the action. . . . But their expression is so excellent because it is so admirably kept in its right degree of prominence; because it is so simple and so well subordinated; because it draws its force directly from the pregnancy of the matter which it conveys'. Compare this with Housman's dictum that 'Poetry is not the thing said, but a way of saying it.'

The restraint and order imposed on the imagination by the conscious mind naturally makes the Classical artist insist more on design and on the whole. 'The radical difference between Greek poetical theory and ours consists, as it appears to me, in this; that with them, the poetical character of the action in itself, and the conduct of it, was the first consideration; with us attention is fixed mainly on the value of the separate thoughts and images which occur in the treatment of an action. They regarded the whole; we regard the parts. . . . We have poems which seem to exist merely for the sake of single lines and passages; not for the sake of producing any total impression.' The same idea is expressed by Pope in his *Essay on Criticism*:

> In wit, as nature, what affects our hearts
> Is not th'exactness of peculiar parts;
> 'Tis not a lip, or eye, we beauty call,
> But the joint force and full result of all.

> Thus when we view some well-proportion'd dome,
> (The world's just wonder, and ev'n thine, O Rome!)
> No single parts unequally surprise,
> All comes united to th'admiring eyes;
> No monstrous height, or breadth, or length appear;
> The Whole at once is bold and regular.

'Poetry should surprise by a fine excess', wrote Keats, the Romantic. '"A rose-red city half as old as time"—a single line surviving from the complete works of a poet, and surviving precisely by virtue of its irrationality', adds Herbert Read, the defender of the extreme Romantic position.

The Greeks avoided an unresolved dualism where two parts of equal importance claim the attention of the reader or spectator, as in Shakespeare's *Henry IV* where the comic Falstaffian interludes compete with the serious historical scenes. It was to avoid this distraction that Aristotle insisted on unity of action in drama, and the same ideal of subordinating detail and expression to the whole is well illustrated in the construction of the Parthenon. In this building there is no feature so dominating that it can distract attention from the whole, as for instance the spire of Salisbury Cathedral might lead one to forget the church below. But the perfection of the whole is the result of the deliberate distortion of the parts. The long horizontal lines of the stylobate and entablature would appear to sag if they were not slightly curved. In the same way the shafts of the columns swell towards the middle to prevent their contours appearing concave; and the angle columns seen against the sky are thicker and more closely set than those against the darker background of the walls. To prevent the appearance of splaying outwards the axes of the columns are set back, so that if produced they would meet at a point a mile above the centre of the building.

Because the Romantic believes that inspired expression is more important than conscious design, the typical Romantic work of art is likely to be structurally weak, and remarkable rather for the beauty and vigour of its parts than for the grandeur of the whole. The Classical method is highly selective, and anything that does not contribute to the structural integrity of the work is rejected. This makes for simplicity and severity—its opponents would say for formality and sterility—and it is true that carried to extremes the emotional content is buried under a frigid structure of pure form. The balance and lucidity of conscious thought distinguish Classical art from the emotional exuberance of the Romantics; the one suggests stability and repose, the other restlessness and action. The simple horizontal lines of a Greek temple, and the complex vertical lines of a Gothic cathedral are symbolic. The Parthenon is Classical, Chartres Cathedral is Romantic; Bach, Piero della Francesca, and Milton are Classical; Brahms, van Gogh, and Shakespeare are Romantic.

One other characteristic of Romantic art remains to be noticed: the exploitation of the medium; the exhaustion of the emotional significance of the material itself. Thus the late Gothic builders extracted—sometimes, it must be confessed, by third-degree methods—the final consequence of stone; the Romantic painter exploits the emotional properties of colour, and the musician those of rhythm and melody—consider modern dance music and the music of Schubert. Finally the Romantic writer, by using words with a semi-mysterious connotation, wrings from his work an emotional significance beyond that of its literal meaning.

In his *Decline and Fall of the Romantic Ideal* Mr. F. L. Lucas writes:

Romantic. . . . It is worth trying first what sort of examples the word spontaneously calls to memory. A little free association will help.

> The Lady of the Lake
> Sole-sitting by the shores of old Romance.

'Forlorn'—the very word is like a bell.

> The foam
> Of perilous seas in faery lands forlorn.

Antres vast and deserts idle.

> And airy tongues that syllable men's names
> On Sands and Shoars and desert Wildernesses.

'On dirait des silences qui succèdent à des silences.'

'The owl for all his feathers was a-cold.' 'The sedge is withered from the lake.'

> La Belle Dame sans Merci
> Hath thee in thrall.

> A casement open to the night
> To let the warm love in.

'Où sont les neiges d'antan?' 'Sunt apud infernos tot milia formosarum.' The ghost of Elsinore. 'Or woman wailing for her demon lover.'

> The day doth daw, the cock doth craw,
>   The channerin' worm doth chide.

'Es war ein König in Thule.' 'Les violons vibrant derrière les collines.'

>   Le vent qui vient à travers la montagne
>   Me rendra fou.

>   'Is there anybody there?' said the Traveller,
>   Knocking on the moonlit door.

It is clear that the effect of these passages depends largely on the mysterious remoteness of the words and their associations: *Romance, forlorn, faery, deserts, wildernesses, silences, a-cold, withered, in thrall, casement, neiges d'antan, apud infernos, ghost, demon, Thule, derrière les collines, à travers la montagne, moonlit.*

The difference between the Romantic and Classical treatment of words will be appreciated by comparing these passages with one from Milton's *Samson Agonistes*, where the separate words are clear-cut and precise as words can be, the effect being the steady mounting one of the passage as a whole, not an irregular succession of brilliant and violent shocks:

> This utter'd, straining all his nerves he bow'd;
> As with the force of winds and waters pent,
> When mountains tremble, those two massy pillars
> With horrible convulsion to and fro
> He tugg'd, he shook, till down they came, and drew
> The whole roof after them, with burst of thunder
> Upon the heads of all who sat beneath,
> Lords, ladies, captains, counsellors, or priests,
> Their choice nobility and flower, not only
> Of this but each Philistian city round,
> Met from all parts to solemnize this feast.
> Samson, with these immix'd, inevitably
> Pull'd down the same destruction on himself;
> The vulgar only 'scaped who stood without.

The impetuosity, the generous expense of spirit, and the vigorous action of the Romantics naturally appeal more to most people than the restrained and disciplined style of the Classical school with its greater intellectual demands; Romantic art is the product of the fierce furnace of the emotions, and inevitably appears more inspired than the colder lapidary style of Classical art.

It seems probable that the greatest art is that which has a

profound emotional inspiration, sifted, selected and ordered by a process, partly unconscious partly conscious, so that the finished product is a structural whole instead of a rhaspody of words or colours. Great art does not vary far from this norm, where emotional content is balanced by conscious control; if it errs too far on the side of emotion it becomes a neurotic symptom rather than art, while on the side of reason it is in danger of becoming formal, uninspired, didactic, and finally not art but science. Where the emotions are trivial and uncontrolled we have the sentiment of a degraded popular art; where trivial and highly rationalized we are in the realms of the pedant.

The charm, therefore, of what is classical, in art or literature, is that of the well-known tale, to which we can, nevertheless, listen over and over again, because it is told so well. To the absolute beauty of its artistic form is added the accidental, tranquil charm of familiarity. There are times, indeed, at which these charms fail to work on our spirits at all, because they fail to excite us. '*Romanticism*', says Stendhal, 'is the art of presenting to people the literary works which, in the actual state of their habits and beliefs, are capable of giving them the greatest possible pleasure; *classicism*, on the contrary, of presenting them with that which gave the greatest possible pleasure to their grandfathers.' . . . And in the classical literature of Greece and Rome, as in the classics of the last century, the essentially classical element is that quality of order in beauty, which they possess, indeed, in a pre-eminent degree, and which impresses some minds to the exclusion of everything else in them.

It is the addition of strangeness to beauty, that constitutes the romantic character in art; and the desire of beauty being a fixed element in every artistic organization, it is the addition of curiosity to this desire of beauty, that constitutes the romantic temper. Curiosity and the desire of beauty, have each their place in art, as in all true criticism. When one's curiosity is deficient, when one is not eager enough for new impressions, and new pleasures, one is liable to value mere academical properties too highly, to be satisfied with worn-out or conventional types, with the insipid ornament of Racine, or the prettiness of that later Greek sculpture, which passed so long for true Hellenic work. . . .

If there is a great overbalance of curiosity, then, we have the grotesque in art: if the union of strangeness and beauty, under very difficult and complex conditions, be a successful one, if the union be entire, then the resultant beauty is very exquisite, very attractive.   PATER: *Appreciations*.

Classical and romantic—these are the systole and diastole of the human heart in history. They represent on the one hand our need of order, of synthesis, of a comprehensive yet definite, therefore *exclusive* as well as inclusive, ordering of thought and feeling and action; and on the other hand the inevitable finiteness of every human synthesis, the inevitable discovery that, in Carlyle's metaphor, our clothes no longer fit us, that the classical has become the conventional, that our spiritual aspirations are being starved, or that our secular impulses are 'cribb'd, cabin'd, and confined'.

SIR HERBERT GRIERSON: *The Background of English Literature.*

There is a taint of insincerity about romantic criticism, from which not even the great romantics are free. They are never in danger from the pitfalls that waylay the plodding critic; but they are always falling upward, as it were, into vacuity. They love to lose themselves in an *O altitudo*. From the most worthless material they will fashion a new hasty altar to the unknown God. When they are inspired by their divinity they say wonderful things; when the inspiration fails them their language is maintained at the same height, and they say more than they feel. You can never be sure of them.

SIR WALTER RALEIGH: *Six Essays on Johnson.*

The world into which Cézanne tumbled was a world still agitated by the quarrels of Romantics and Realists. The quarrel between Romance and Realism is the quarrel of people who cannot agree as to whether the history of Spain or the number of pips is the more important thing about an orange. The Romantics and Realists were deaf men coming to blows about the squeak of a bat. The instinct of a Romantic invited to say what he felt about anything was to recall its associations. A rose, for instance, made him think of old gardens and young ladies and Edmund Waller and sundials, and a thousand quaint and gracious things that, at one time or another, had befallen him or someone else. A rose touched life at a hundred pretty points. A rose was interesting because it had a past. 'Bosh,' said the Realist, 'I will tell you what a rose is; that is to say, I will give you a detailed account of the properties of *Rosa setigera*, not forgetting to mention the urn-shaped calyx-tube, the five imbricated lobes, or the open corolla of five obovate petals.' To a Cézanne one account would appear as irrelevant as the other, since both omit the thing that matters—what philosophers used to call 'the thing in itself', what now, I imagine, they call 'the essential reality'.

CLIVE BELL: *Art.*

These principles being established, let us now discuss the proper structure of the Plot, since this is the first and most important thing in Tragedy.

Now, according to our definition, Tragedy is an imitation of an action that is complete, and whole, and of a certain magnitude. A whole is that which has a beginning, a middle, and an end. A beginning is that which does not itself follow anything by causal necessity, but after which something naturally is or comes to be. An end, on the contrary, is that which itself naturally follows some other thing, either by necessity, or as a rule, but has nothing following it. A middle is that which follows something as some other thing follows it. A well-constructed plot, therefore, must neither begin nor end at haphazard, but conform to these principles.

Again, a beautiful object, whether it be a living organism or any whole composed of parts, must not only have an orderly arrangement of parts, but must also be of a certain magnitude; for beauty depends on magnitude and order. Hence a very small animal organism cannot be beautiful; for the view of it is confused, the object being seen in an almost imperceptible moment of time. Nor, again, can one of vast size be beautiful; for as the eye cannot take it all in at once, the unity and sense of the whole is lost for the spectator; as for instance if there were one a thousand miles long. As, therefore, in the case of animate bodies and organisms a certain magnitude is necessary, and a magnitude which may be easily embraced in one view; so in the plot, a certain length is necessary, and a length which can be easily embraced by the memory. . . . And to define the matter roughly, we may say that the proper magnitude is comprised within such limits, that the sequence of events, according to the law of probability or necessity, will admit of a change from bad fortune to good, or from good fortune to bad. . . .

As therefore, in the other imitative arts, the imitation is one when the object imitated is one, so the plot, being the imitation of an action, must imitate one action and that a whole, the structural unity of the parts being such that, if any one of them is displaced or removed, the whole will be disjointed and disturbed. For a thing whose presence or absence makes no visible difference, is not an organic part of the whole.

ARISTOTLE: *Poetics*. (Trans. BUTCHER.)

But it is evident that, in tragedy and in comedy, the plot contains one action only, or two that by their interdependence can be considered one . . . not because the fable itself is unsuited to contain more actions than one, but because the space of time, of twelve hours at most, in which the action is represented, and in the strait limits of the place in which it is represented likewise, do not permit a multitude of actions.

CASTELVETRO: Poetica d'Aristotele (1570).

Our Tragedies, and Comedies (not without cause cried out against), observing rules neither of honest civility nor of skilful Poetry, excepting *Gorboduc* (again, I say, of those that I have seen), which notwithstanding, as it is full of stately speeches and well sounding Phrases, climbing to the height of *Seneca* his style, and as full of notable morality, which it doth most delightfully teach, and so obtain the very end of Poesy; yet in truth it is very defectious in the circumstances: which grieveth me, because it might not remain as an exact model of all Tragedies. For it is faulty both in Place and Time, the two necessary companions of all corporal actions. For where the stage should always represent but one place, and the uttermost time presupposed in it should be, both by *Aristotle's* precept and common reason, but one day: there is both many days and many places, inartificially imagined. But if it be so in *Gorboduc*, how much more in all the rest? where you shall have *Asia* of the one side, and *Afric* of the other, and so many other under-kingdoms, that the Player, when he cometh in, must ever begin with telling where he is; or else, the tale will not be conceived. Now ye shall have three Ladies walk to gather flowers, and then we must believe the stage to be a Garden. By and by, we hear news of shipwreck in the same place, and then we are to blame, if we accept it not for a Rock. Upon the back of that, comes out a hideous Monster, with fire and smoke, and then the miserable beholders are bound to take it for a Cave. While in the meantime, two Armies fly in, represented with four swords and bucklers, and then what hard heart will not receive it for a pitched field?

Now, of time they are much more liberal. For ordinary it is that two young Princes fall in love: after many traverses, she is got with child, delivered of a fair boy; he is lost, groweth a man, falls in love, and is ready to get another child, and all this in two hours' space: which how absurd it is in sense, even sense may imagine, and Art hath taught, and all ancient examples justified: and at this day, the ordinary Players in Italy will not err in. . . .

Certainly I must confess my own barbarousness, I never heard the old song of *Percy* and *Douglas*, that I found not my heart moved more than with a trumpet.

SIR PHILIP SIDNEY: Defence of Poesy.

For the whole, as it consisteth of parts, so without all the parts it is not the whole; and to make it absolute is required not only the parts, but such parts as are true. For a part of the whole was true, which, if you take away, you either change the whole or it is not the whole. For if it be such a part, as, being present or absent, nothing concerns the whole, it cannot be called a part of the whole.

BEN JONSON : *Discoveries.*

By their (the French) servile observations of the unities of time and place, and the integrity of scenes, they have brought on themselves that dearth of plot, and narrowness of imagination, which may be observed in all their plays. How many beautiful accidents might naturally happen in two or three days, which cannot arrive within any probability in the compass of twenty-four hours?

DRYDEN : *Essay on Dramatic Poesy.*

It is not enough that Aristotle has said so, for Aristotle drew his models of tragedy from Sophocles and Euripides : and, if he had seen ours, might have changed his mind.

DRYDEN.

> First follow Nature, * and your judgment frame
> By her just standard, which is still the same :
> Unerring NATURE, still divinely bright,
> One clear, unchang'd, and universal light,
> Life, force, and beauty, must to all impart,
> At once the source, and end, and test of Art. . . .
>
> 'Tis more to guide, than spur the Muse's steed ;
> Restrain his fury, than provoke his speed ;
> The winged courser, like a gen'rous horse,
> Shows most true mettle when you check his course.
>   Those RULES of old discovered, not devis'd,
> Are Nature still, but Nature methodiz'd ;
> Nature, like liberty, is but restrain'd
> By the same laws which first herself ordained. . . .
>
> Learn hence for ancient rules a just esteem ;
> To copy nature is to copy them.

POPE : *Essay on Criticism.*

All that regards design, form, fable, which is the soul of poetry ; all that concerns exactness, or consent of parts, which is the body, will probably be wanting. Only pretty conceptions, fine

---

* It must be remembered that by *Nature* Pope and his contemporaries meant *Reason*, or that which is reasonable or natural, as opposed to that which is unnatural or highly imaginative.

Q

metaphors, glittering expressions, and something of a neat cast of verse, which are properly the dress, gems, or loose ornaments of poetry, may be found in these verses (of Crashaw).

POPE: *Letters.*

'The business of a poet', said Imlac, 'is to examine, not the individual but the species; to remark general properties and large appearances. He does not number the streaks of the tulip, or describe the different shades in the verdure of the forest; he is to exhibit in his portraits of nature, such prominent and striking features, as recall the original to every mind; and must neglect the minuter discriminations, which one may have remarked, and another have neglected, for those characteristics which are alike obvious to vigilance and to carelessness.'

JOHNSON: *Rasselas.*

The principal object, then, proposed in these Poems was to choose incidents and situations from common life, and to relate or describe them, throughout, as far as was possible in a selection of language really used by men, and, at the same time, to throw over them a certain colouring of imagination, whereby ordinary things should be presented to the mind in an unusual aspect; and further, and above all, to make these incidents and situations interesting by tracing in them, truly though not ostentatiously, the primary laws of our nature: chiefly, as far as regards the manner in which we associate ideas in a state of excitement.

WORDSWORTH: *Preface to Lyrical Ballads.*

In this idea originated the plan of the *Lyrical Ballads*; in which it was agreed that my endeavours should be directed to persons and characters supernatural, or at least romantic; yet so as to transfer from our inward nature a human interest and a semblance of truth sufficient to procure for these shadows of imagination that willing suspension of disbelief for the moment, which constitutes poetic faith. Mr. Wordsworth, on the other hand, was to propose to himself, as his object, to give the charm of novelty to things of every day, and to excite a feeling analogous to the supernatural, by awakening the mind's attention from the lethargy of custom, and directing it to the loveliness and the wonders of the world before us; an inexhaustible treasure, but for which in consequence of the film of familiarity and selfish solicitude, we have eyes, yet see not, ears that hear not, and hearts that neither feel nor understand.

COLERIDGE: *Biographia Literaria.*

Beauty was awake!
Why were ye not awake? But ye were dead
To things ye knew not of,—were closely wed
To musty laws lined out with wretched rule
And compass vile: so that ye taught a school
Of dolts to smooth, inlay, and clip, and fit,
Till, like the certain wands of Jacob's wit,
Their verses tallied. Easy was the task:
A thousand handicraftsmen wore the mask
Of Poesy. Ill-famed impious race!
That blasphemed the bright Lyrist to his face,
And did not know it,—no, they went about,
Holding a poor decrepid standard out
Marked with most flimsy mottoes, and in large
The name of one Boileau!

KEATS: Sleep and Poetry.

The poem of *Isabella*, then, is a perfect treasure-house of graceful and felicitous words and images: almost in every stanza there occurs one of those vivid and picturesque turns of expression, by which the object is made to flash upon the eye of the mind, and which thrill the reader with a sudden delight. This one short poem contains, perhaps, a greater number of happy single expressions which one could quote than all the extant tragedies of Sophocles. But the action, the story? The action in itself is an excellent one; but so feebly is it conceived by the Poet, so loosely constructed, that the effect produced by it, in and for itself, is absolutely null. Let the reader, after he has finished the poem of Keats, turn to the same story in the *Decameron*: he will then feel how pregnant and interesting the same action has become in the hands of a great artist, who above all things delineates his object; who subordinates expression to that which it is designed to express.

MATTHEW ARNOLD: Preface to Poems (1853–1854).

In the summer of the year 1797, the Author, then in ill health, had retired to a lonely farm-house between Porlock and Linton, on the Exmoor confines of Somerset and Devonshire. In consequence of a slight indisposition, an anodyne had been prescribed, from the effects of which he fell asleep in his chair at the moment that he was reading the following sentence, or words of the same substance, in *Purchas's Pilgrimage*; 'Here the Khan Kubla commanded a palace to be built, and a stately garden thereunto. And thus ten miles of fertile ground were inclosed with a wall.' The Author continued for about three hours in a profound sleep, at least of the external senses, during which

Q*

time he has the most vivid confidence, that he could not have composed less than from two to three hundred lines; if that indeed can be called composition in which all the images rose up before him as *things*, with a parallel production of the correspondent expressions, without any sensation or consciousness of effort. On awaking he appeared to himself to have a distinct recollection of the whole, and taking his pen, ink, and paper, instantly and eagerly wrote down the lines that are here preserved. At this moment he was unfortunately called out by a person on business from Porlock, and detained by him above an hour, and on his return to his room, found, to his no small surprise and mortification, that though he still retained some vague and dim recollection of the general purport of the vision, yet, with the exception of some eight or ten scattered lines and images, all the rest had passed away like the images on the surface of a stream into which a stone has been cast, but, alas! without the restoration of the latter!

> In Xanadu did Kubla Khan
> A stately pleasure-dome decree:
> Where Alph, the sacred river, ran
> Through caverns measureless to man
>   Down to a sunless sea.
> So twice five miles of fertile ground
> With walls and towers were girdled round:
> And there were gardens bright with sinuous rills,
> Where blossomed many an incense-bearing tree;
> And here were forests ancient as the hills,
> Enfolding sunny spots of greenery.
>
> But oh! that deep romantic chasm which slanted
> Down the green hill athwart a cedarn cover!
> A savage place! as holy and enchanted
> As e'er beneath a waning moon was haunted
> By woman wailing for her demon-lover!
> And from this chasm, with ceaseless turmoil seething,
> As if this earth in fast thick pants were breathing,
> A mighty fountain momently was forced:
> Amid whose swift half-intermitted burst
> Huge fragments vaulted like rebounding hail,
> Or chaffy grain beneath the thresher's flail:
> And 'mid these dancing rocks at once and ever
> It flung up momently the sacred river.
> Five miles meandering with a mazy motion
> Through wood and dale the sacred river ran,
> Then reached the caverns measureless to man,

And sank in tumult to a lifeless ocean:
And 'mid this tumult Kubla heard from far
Ancestral voices prophesying war!
   The shadow of the dome of pleasure
   Floated midway on the waves;
   Where was heard the mingled measure
   From the fountain and the caves.
It was a miracle of rare device,
A sunny pleasure-dome with caves of ice!

   A damsel with a dulcimer
   In a vision once I saw:
   It was an Abyssinian maid,
   And on her dulcimer she played,
   Singing of Mount Abora.
   Could I revive within me
   Her symphony and song,
To such a deep delight 'twould win me,
That with music loud and long,
I would build that dome in air,
That sunny dome! those caves of ice!
And all who heard should see them there,
And all should cry, Beware! Beware!
His flashing eyes, his floating hair!
Weave a circle round him thrice,
And close your eyes with holy dread,
For he on honey-dew hath fed,
And drunk the milk of Paradise.

                    COLERIDGE.

I happen to remember distinctly the genesis of the piece which
stands last in my first volume.   Two of the stanzas, I do not say
which, came into my head, just as they were printed, while I
was crossing the corner of Hampstead Heath between the
Spaniard's Inn and the footpath to Temple Fortune.   A third
stanza came with a little coaxing after tea.   One more was
needed, but it did not come: I had to turn to and compose it
myself, and that was a laborious business.   I wrote it thirteen
times, and it was more than a twelvemonth before I got it right.

    A. E. HOUSMAN: *The Name and Nature of Poetry.*

    I hoed and trenched and weeded,
      And took the flowers to fair:
    I brought them home unheeded;
      The hue was not the wear.

So up and down I sow them
    For lads like me to find,
When I shall lie below them,
    A dead man out of mind.

Some seeds the birds devour,
    And some the season mars,
But here and there will flower
    The solitary stars,

And fields will yearly bear them
    As light-leaved spring comes on,
And luckless lads will wear them
    When I am dead and gone.

A. E. HOUSMAN.   (The last poem in *A Shropshire Lad.*)

To trace the parallel between dream-formation and poem-formation it is necessary to analyse a particular poem, and of necessity such a poem must be one of my own (or otherwise I should have to conduct a long and searching analysis of another poet). The poem I shall take is actually based on a dream. On December 31, 1935, I was present at a family gathering in Yorkshire, and at midnight we celebrated the passing of the Old Year and the birth of the New Year by drinking a rum-punch (I am, it will be seen, about to confirm Housman's diagnosis). I retired to bed and dreamt a vivid dream. It was still vivid to me when next day I travelled by train back to London, and since, like several poets of my acquaintance, I have always found the rhythm of a train journey conducive to poetic composition, I began to transfer to paper the haunting images of my dream. The following poem was the result—I will explain the significance of the italics presently:

The narrow labyrinth has light
which casts our shadows on the wall
as in extremity of flight
I follow one whose face I have not seen.

The walls are white
and turn at intervals to make a screen
on which our racing shadows rise and fall
like waves against the bleached cliff.

Anxious to make my mentor turn
I lift my hands and make a pass
which casts upon the facing wall
a silhouette hovering like a baffled bird.

But on he leads unmoved
and fatally I follow till at last
we leave the labyrinth and I find myself
alone, upon a plinth.

The houses in the square below
stand newly built, brick-rough, bright
bathed in some *Castilian* light.
In the unpaved area a few children play.

This must be a foreign land, I say,
and gaze about with eager eyes.
Then suddenly know that it is *Heaven*
to which *Death* has led me in disguise.

What I described in this poem was, of course, the *manifest*
content of my dream; the *latent* content could only be elicited
by analysis, and is of no immediate interest. But our poetic
analysis of the poem should begin by asking to what extent I
succeeded in conveying the manifest content. Is the poem
efficient merely as the narrative of an experience? As far as the
events of the poem are concerned, I think it is only towards the
end that I myself am conscious of any failure. I fancy that in
the dream the identity of the unknown figure was revealed to
me, and that immediately I awoke—in the process of awaking—
this identity slipped from me and I was left with a sense of being
baffled. The notion of suddenly finding myself in a Heaven was
present in the dream, but identifying the figure with Death was
a subsequent rationalization; it did not, if I can trust my
memory, occur to me until I began to write the poem.

Let us now examine the images in the poem. In the dream
the labyrinth was real; an intricate maze always turning at
right angles and full of an evenly diffused white light; the
figure, clad rather like a harlequin in close-fitting tights, never
turned. I made the pass by lifting my hands above my head
and making a shadow on the wall in the manner of the shadow
game played by children; the image of the baffled bird—the
fluttering shadow like a bird beating against a window-pane—
occurred to me in my dream. In this it differs from the wave-image
I have used to describe the shadows of our bodies on the walls of
the labyrinth, which is a conscious image produced in the process
of writing the poem; I would on that account call it a metaphor
rather than an image. In a similar way the word 'Castilian',
used to describe the peculiar light which was diffused over the
square, is an epithet derived from my conscious experience;
the nearest equivalent in my memory being certain effects of

sunlight in Spain. I have not conveyed exactly enough the vivid impression I have of the effect of this dream-light on the houses; I have a distinct sensuous image of the porous quality of the brick into which the light seemed to soak, as if absorbed. The children in the square (it was a new square, not yet paved or laid out in any way, rough and uneven) seemed to be self-centred, detached, in a different perspective to the rest of the scene; an effect which Salvador Dali often conveys in his paintings.

HERBERT READ: *Surrealism.*

That son of Italy who tried to blow,
Ere Dante came, the trump of sacred song,
In his light youth amid a festal throng
Sate with his bride to see a public show.

Fair was the bride, and on her front did glow
Youth like a star; and what to youth belong,
Gay raiment, sparkling gauds, elation strong.
A prop gave way: crash fell a platform! lo,

Mid struggling sufferers, hurt to death, she lay!
Shuddering they drew her garments off—and found
A robe of sackcloth next the smooth, white skin.

Such, poets, is your bride, the Muse! young, gay,
Radiant, adorn'd outside; a hidden ground
Of thought and of austerity within.

MATTHEW ARNOLD.

CONCLUSION

IN the preceding chapters it has been maintained that the subject-matter of a work of art, whatever the medium, is at most an irrelevant necessity, and that the work of art must be judged on its own merits as the artist's creation with an independent existence, and not as a product that derives its value from some original—an attitude that savours strongly of snobbery in the library as well as in the drawing-room.

At the one extreme is sheer reproduction: in painting and sculpture the accurate imitation of some model, in literature the literal statement of fact or opinion; at the other extreme is sheer abstraction: two- or three-dimensional form that defies positive identification, or a rhapsody of words without rational significance. Now, admittedly, the accurate imitation of a beautiful object will normally be beautiful—though a life-like model of a man or woman, however beautiful, will be merely disturbing—and the accurate reproduction of an ugly object will be ugly. Here the beauty of the reproduction and of the original are immediately related, the one varying directly with the other. Such a reproduction may be very pleasing, but it is not a work of art: its beauty is derived from and dependent on that of the original: the craftsman has created nothing.

Similarly in literature, the greater the thought expressed the greater will its moral value be, but it by no means follows that the words make poetry or great prose. For example, the thought is more profound in,

> Joys are like oil; if thrown upon the tide
> Of flowing life, they mix not, nor subside:
> Griefs are like waters on the river thrown,
> They mix entirely, and become its own.

than in,

> So, we'll go no more a-roving
>   So late into the night,
> Though the heart be still as loving
>   And the moon be still as bright.

Yet the first means no more than is said, while the second means infinitely more; it is, in fact, poetry. The one has some profundity of subject-matter, the other profundity of expression.

It may be objected that given two passages of equal beauty of expression the one with the nobler thought content will be the greater poetry, that,

> Our birth is but a sleep and a forgetting:
> The Soul that rises with us, our life's Star,
> Hath had elsewhere its setting,
>   And cometh from afar:
> Not in entire forgetfulness
> And not in utter nakedness
> But trailing clouds of glory do we come
> From God, who is our home.

is greater poetry than,

> The cataracts blow their trumpets from the steep;
> No more shall grief of mine the season wrong;
> I hear the echoes through the mountains throng,
> The winds come to me from the fields of sleep,
>   And all the earth is gay.

The moral content of the one is greater than that of the other, and for that reason may be more moving; it may be greater literature, but it is scarcely greater *poetry*. Neither beauty of subject nor loftiness of thought is an essential ingredient in a work of art, though of course the artist is more likely to be inspired by a great subject rather than by a mean one, and the subject-matter of most works of art is not ignoble. The point is that nobility of subject must not be confused with nobility of expression.

Are we therefore driven to the other extreme and forced to defend the absolute, abstract position? That if the subject is unimportant, and the essential element in a work of art is the expression—not the thing said, but the way of saying it—then painting, sculpture, and poetry may dispense with a subject and be produced without any element of representation, and simply by the pleasing arrangement of forms or words?

It should first be noted that much admittedly great art is abstract: Chinese porcelain, Chippendale chairs, and Persian carpets, for instance. Then again, few so-called abstract paintings and sculptures are entirely devoid of representation: the illusion of the third dimension in painting, for example, is an elementary form of representation, and a sculpture may represent, or suggest, a quality instead of a person, Strength instead of Hercules. It is in fact doubtful whether pure abstraction, that is expression devoid of any rational interpretation, is possible: even the most abstract of the fine arts, music and architecture, have some elements of representation: music suggests some emotion or other, and a building may be referred either to its function or to the natural forms of mountain masses. Finally, there are abstract qualities in essentially representational art: not only in Cézanne, Gauguin and other Post-Impressionists, but in Masaccio, Piero della Francesca, and the painters of the Italian Renaissance.

Yet this is by no means a complete and satisfactory answer, for the fact remains that the greatest painting, sculpture, and poetry is frankly representational, and some recognizable subject does seem to be desirable in these arts.

> Sweetly that away so lips
> O forsworn were take those take,

though not unattractive, can scarcely be compared with

> Take, O take those lips away
> That so sweetly were forsworn.

If then, neither the reproduction of a subject on the one hand, nor abstract form on the other, is sufficient in itself to account for the beauty of a work of art, what is it that gives it the dazzling power of haling souls out of men's bodies? Once again, the expression, the way of saying it, the artist's creation, is the all-important thing, it is indeed the work of art itself; it is also the variable factor. Given a theme, be it an emotion, a landscape, or a thought, the artist will create his own peculiar expression, and no two paintings or poems on the same subject will be identical: Constable and van Gogh, Pope and Browning, to take extreme examples, would produce very different versions of the same theme, yet all might be, almost certainly would be, real works of art, and all would be variations on the same common factor, the given subject. Is it possible then that the aesthetic reaction to a work of art is the product of the relation between a fixed and unimportant subject, and a variable and all-important expression: between the original and the work of art itself?

Perhaps art is akin to wit: the spontaneous perception of similarity in dis-similarity, the imaginative fusing of subject and expression; or, to change the metaphor, it seems possible that there is a certain significant relationship between subject and

expression, a tension which when it reaches a certain critical
intensity generates the spark and the miracle happens, the
aesthetic ecstasy.

Certainly there is this relation in some of the components that
go to make up a work of art. Metaphor, for example, is a
species of wit, the identification for the time being of one thing
with another:

> Shall I believe
> That unsubstantial death is amorous,
> And that the lean abhorred monster keeps
> Thee here in dark to be his paramour?

Then again, verse and music are partly dependent for their effect
on the variation of the particular rhythm about an ideal and
rigid norm; if the two coincide for long the effect is deadly, and
in good verse and music the rhythm only approximates towards
the perfect pattern. Yet the reader or listener apprehends both
rhythms, the regular and the irregular, and his enjoyment is
derived partly from his appreciation of the tension that exists
between the two. Consider the dual or contrapuntal rhythm
in:

> Be not afeard; the isle is full of noises,
> Sounds and sweet airs, that give delight, and hurt not.
> Sometimes a thousand twangling instruments
> Will hum about mine ears; and sometimes voices,
> That, if I then had waked after long sleep,
> Will make me sleep again.

If it is true that our appreciation of some of the elements that
constitute a work of art is dependent on this faculty of apprehend-
ing unity in apparent diversity, of realizing imaginatively the
significant relation between things not obviously related, may it
not also be true of the work of art as a whole? That, for instance,
the aesthetic pleasure derived from the contemplation of the
statue of John the Baptist at Chartres is the result, at least in
part, of the imaginative fusion of subject and expression, the
simultaneous perception of a man and the artist's representation
of a man?

If this be so it will explain why abstract art is less satisfying
than that which has some element of representation, why poetry
must have some intelligible meaning, however trivial. But it
should be noted that the expression, the work of art, does not
derive its importance from the subject; on the contrary, the

subject is important only in its relation to the expression, the variable and dynamic quantity, which by its appearance or sound can assume that significant relationship towards the subject by virtue of which it becomes a work of art.

However this may be, there is always the danger that in those arts which lend themselves to representation, in painting, sculpture, and poetry, the subject may overwhelm the expression, the object represented being confused with the work of art itself; and this is why these arts are so easy to understand for the wrong, or at any rate aesthetically unimportant reasons, and so difficult to appreciate for the right ones; and why there is so much prejudice against, and ill-informed criticism of modern art; and incidentally, why innovations in music, where representation is negligible, are so much more easily assimilated and accepted.

Let it at once be admitted that there is much bad and bogus modern art, though probably not more than in any other age, for there has always been more bad than good art; time has sifted and rejected the rubbish of former centuries, that is all. On the other hand, there is undoubtedly a great body of good and even great modern art, and possibly never has the artist taken his work more seriously; for one thing he realizes, which the greater part of his public does not, that the primary object of so-called representational art is not to represent, but to create a work of art; that the subject is important only in relation to the expression.

Unfortunately this often leads by another route back to the position which the artist wishes to avoid—the over-emphasis of the subject, at least in the mind of the ordinary man. For just as a 'beautiful' subject is likely to dominate a painting, and to make mere sentiment or even pornography of it, or as a great subject—religious painting and poetry, for example—may easily be mistaken for great art, so may an odd or unusual subject obscure the art by the violence of its intrusion. If the subject is superficially ugly or positively unpleasant it may be difficult so to modify its insistence that we may see through it to the work of art on the other side. Similarly, obscurity of meaning even if unintentional may be so irritating, if perverse so infuriating, that the attention is diverted from the significance of the expression, if any, as in so many tedious surrealist variations of the Victorian problem picture.

The trouble is that the artist in his excitement at his emancipation from the tyranny of subject may abuse his liberty and, ignoring the fact that art is a communication as well as a record, plunge into extremes of abstraction and obscurity. If he does, he cannot justly blame an uninitiated public for failing to keep up with him. Like any other progressive thinker the artist must show the way, but if he goes too fast to begin with his progress may ultimately be slower, for he will inevitably alienate the sympathies of many potential disciples by expecting them to assimilate what to him seem platitudes, but to them may well appear strange and incomprehensible ideas. The artist may be right, and he must push ever forward, but if he is too impatient and neglects to educate his public he risks not only his own reputation but also that of his art.

Most artists to-day, whatever the medium they work in, agree that anything—love, death, heroism, religion, politics, pylons, chairs, and gentlemen's second-hand suits—is potentially subject-matter for their art. Those who attach a narrow ethical function to art might not agree, but they would appear to be wrong: in looking for an elevating subject they may well miss the ecstasy of the art itself. Art is neither moral nor immoral in the narrow meaning of the word: it is amoral; though it may well be maintained that it has a splendid spiritual significance of its own. And there is no need for alarm; obscenity, for the reasons given above, is unlikely to be great art, the subject-matter will be too insistent; and noble, or at any rate innocuous, subjects will continue to inspire the great body of art. But we must beware; the subject is only an excuse for the artist's creative work and important only in relation to that; it must never be confused with the work of art itself.

The artist does not, or should not, set out primarily to teach, or preach, or persuade, or to represent; he may of course do any or all of these things, but in so far as he lets any of them interfere with his real work, the creation of a work of art and its communication to others, the less artist he. That is why the beautiful subject, the startling, the obscure, and the unpleasant are dangerous material; and that is why the subject-matter of so much great art is commonplace and unobtrusive.

INDEX OF AUTHORS

Quoted at the Ends of Chapters

INDEX